SO-ALK-061

MEDALS AWARDED TO THE MEN IN THIS BOOK

FRONT COVER—CLOCKWISE FROM TOP LEFT
Silver Star—Distinguished Flying Cross—Purple Heart—Bronze Star
Defense Meritorious Service Medal—Army Good Conduct Medal
Meritorious Service Medal—Prisoner of War Medal Army Commendation
Medal—Air Medal

BACK COVER—LEFT TO RIGHT
Top Row—Asiatic Pacific Campaign Medal—WWII Victory Medal—Navy
and Marine Corp Commendation Medal
Center—Philippines Defense Medal
Bottom Row—American Campaign Medal—Marine Corps Good Conduct
Medal—Marine Corps Expeditionary Medal

MEDALS AWARDED BUT NOT SHOWN
Army of Occupation WWII—Gold Life Saving Medal—Navy Good
Conduct Medal—Navy and Marine Corps Medal—US Antarctica
Expeditions Medal

1

ACKNOWLEDGMENTS

I wish to thank my wife, Lepta Terrell for her help in researching this book. I also want to extend my sincere and profound gratitude to Charles Jackson, one of my classmates, Tom Axelrod and Bill Bisard, members of the 70th Division, 274 Battalion, "K" Company. These men encouraged me, helped keep my spirits high, and contributed many suggestions and details to this book. Their guidance, assistance and encouragement have been infinitely invaluable in allowing me to tell these stories.

My kudos and heart felt thanks to my son, Gary, who helped me resolve the many problems I encountered while committing these chapters into computer language. His knowledge and computer skills were invaluable to me while writing this book and to my sister-in-law, Anita Jump, for suggesting Heroes Among Us as the title for this book. I also want to thank Mr. Marc Drzewwiecki for the excellent effort he made in editing my book.

I especially want to thank my daughter, Terry Webber, for sharing her excellent writing skills with me. Without the help and guidance from this group of people, my book could not have been written.

Hal Terrell

COMMENTS

"A reader is fortunate when he hooks into a book that is so good he doesn't want it to end. A newspaper reporter is even luckier when he talks to a subject who has so many stories the reporter doesn't want the interview to end. That is how it turned out when I interviewed Hal Terrell about a book he's writing on local World War II veterans."
The Glenwood Post Independent

"Wow! This is going to be some book! Hal has been hiding under this editorial blanket all these years. He has the touch. All the stats, the trip to Europe, his letter writing, the footwork, the years in the making looks to be paying off. From what I've seen and read it appears to be one of those best sellers."
Tom Axelrod, 70ᵗʰ Division, 274 Battalion, Company K

"You have summarized the feelings and thoughts of most Americans, my generation included. The war should, and will not ever be forgotten, and your generation will be remembered not only as the greatest but also the one that **could** and **did**. You have said far more in a few words than many of the historians have in volumes. THE OLD NATIVE WAY! This book should be required reading by all our leaders in government, all teachers who teach history, at all levels of learning."
Larry Schmueser & Associates

"I found tears rolling down my cheek while reading about Alex and Raymond. Two such different lives, but both heroes just the same. The stories you tell are very touching and should be identifiable to people from all generations and backgrounds, just like your heroes are. It is hard to imagine the fear of being in the tail of that B-17, or having to live with the challenges of Raymond. But, your story has brought me as close as I will ever know of what it was like. I only hope that if I had been dealt the same hand as they were I would have been man enough to play it as well as they did."
Hal Capron

"I just finished reading one of the most moving and compelling manuscripts I have ever read. Your first chapter sent chills up my spine and brought tears to my eyes. Your descriptions of the battlefields, the walk through the cemetery at Omaha Beach, and the letter from the military doctor in San Antonio all put into perspective how insignificant and fortunate we really are. The fact that you have put all of this on paper is a tribute to you and your character. I, for one, thank you for opening my eyes."
Fox 23 Clear Channel Television

"Great reading! You are both tough and tender, and the combination makes for a unique and inspiring narrative. When the book is actually published, I look forward to being one of your first customer. I know my Dad would enjoy this book."
Steve Beattie, Attorney at Law

"If you hadn't written this book, I would have gone to my grave having no idea about the true greatness of the individuals in GCHS (Garfield County High School) class of 1944. We were/are a pretty impressive bunch of people, and before the book, I didn't have a clue."
Charles Jackson

"Just wanted to tell you how deeply touched John and I were while reading your book chapters. You have a rare gift of not only poetry, charisma—we all know that about you—but even more importantly of sharing your heart and your vision. Good luck with the rest. We can't wait."
Resa and John Wing, Wing International

"I read the first chapter of your book to Gene as he is almost blind now. It was great! We were both quite impressed and we both had tears in our eyes. I got choked up, especially when reading the poem at the end of this chapter. Gene is eighty years old now and your book has brought back a lot of his WWII memories. Thanks."
Norma and Gene Stromberg

"Heroes Among Us" by Hal Terrell is obviously a labor of love. So many of us, who are alive today remember little or nothing of the enormous conflict of WWII. As Hal points out in his epilogue, WWII was indeed a world war, a war of almost unbelievable scope. It involved sixty-eight countries and resulted in the deaths of many millions of people, both military and civilian. Through his research, his persistence and his words, Hal has presented slices from the personal and military lives of twenty-one men. These men joined the armed services, shipped out for places of terrible danger, fought, and in some cases died for their country. Most of them were yet to reach voting age.

"The Great Depression, the enormous death toll of WWII, the terrible injuries of many of the survivors are all things that slip all too easily into the mists of time. Thanks to Hal Terrell, at least some of the battles, some of the horror, some of the men will not be so easily forgotten".
Jim Nelson, published author of many books

ABOUT THE AUTHOR

Mr. Terrell grew up in a small town in Western Colorado during the Great Depression that began with the stock market crash in 1929. The economy did not recover until the start of World War Two. He enlisted in the US Army Air Corps on July7, 1943 and served as a crewmember on a medium bomber during the war. After the war he returned home from Europe and married his high school sweetheart on September 20, 1946. He operated his own business until 1952, at which time he accepted a position with the Caterpillar Dealer in Colorado.

From 1952 until his retirement in 1984 Mr. Terrell held management positions with various Caterpillar Dealers throughout the Pacific area, Europe and the Middle East. He became a modern Gulliver, having lived in thirteen foreign countries over the following thirty-two years. Since his retirement he has remained active as a consultant in the construction industry as well as in the housing development industry. He also spent over three years researching and writing his book, HEROES AMONG US.

Email: **proft@rof.net**   Web: **www.realheroesamongus.com**

HEROES AMONG US

By Hal Terrell

This book tells the story of twenty-two boys who grew up in a small western Colorado town during The Great Depression and how they dealt with their circumstances. It also delves into each individual's WWII experiences and what each one did after WWII to help build America into what it is today.

Each chapter is loaded with emotions and humor. How many other young men from other small towns across America have shared similar experiences? This book will appeal to all veterans as well as our young people and the public in general.

PROLOGUE

This book was inspired by Tom Brokaw's book, **The Greatest Generation,** and Stephen Ambrose's book, **Citizen Soldiers**. These two books tell of the selfless way individual men and women of that generation who were "in-the-trenches" served their country during WWII. People of that generation overcame the handicap of growing up during the great depression and went on to perform many heroic acts during the war. After the war they then helped build modern America into what it is today. That generation was united, not only by a common purpose, but also by common values including duty, honor, service, courage, love of family and country, and, above all, responsibility for oneself.

I was a part of **The Greatest Generation**, and I was **A Citizen Soldier,** having graduated from Garfield County High School (now Glenwood Springs High School) in Glenwood Springs, Colorado in 1944. There were twenty-one boys in the class of '44 and nineteen of them served in the military. Most enlisted before graduation and many of those who served distinguished themselves with heroic acts during WWII. Their stories are told in the following chapters in this book.

After deciding to write this book I initiated an in-depth research and discussions with many of my classmates about their careers. I had to dig hard for their stories because they were, at first, reluctant to talk about their military careers. This was partly because they didn't want to remember unpleasant experiences, and partly because it was characteristic of people of my generation to feel they had simply done what "anyone else in their situation would have done." They were also too modest to reveal any information about their post-war careers, but I was persistent. The end result was a large volume of data that shows, even though our class was small in numbers, it was huge in contributions to the freedom and greatness of our country.

After learning the stories of the individuals in my grade school and high school classes, I am proud that these "**Citizen Soldiers**" were a significant part of "**The Greatest Generation.**" Consequently, I couldn't rest until one small part of **The Greatest Generation** was written to document our accomplishments and tell our stories.

In Tom Brokaw's book he points out that WWII veterans are dying at the rate of 1,500 each day. Many of my school classmates and WWII buddies are already gone and those of us who are still alive realize that we don't have many Christmases left to spend with our families and loved ones.

SHOULD YOU GO FIRST
Author Unknown

Should you go first and I remain
To walk the road alone,
I'll live in memory's garden, dear,
With happy days we have known.
In spring I'll wait for the roses red,
When fades the lilac blue,
In early Fall when brown leaves fall,
I'll catch a glimpse of you.

Should you go first and I remain
To finish with the scroll,
No lengthening shadows shall creep in
To make this life seem droll.
We've known so much happiness,
We've known our cup of joy,
And memory is one gift of God
That death cannot destroy.

Should you go first and I remain
For battles to be fought,
Each thing you have touched along the way
Will be a hallowed spot.
I'll hear your voice,
I'll see your smile,
Though blindly I may grope,
The memory of your helping hand
Will buoy me on with hope.

Should you go first and I remain,
One thing I'd have you do:
Walk slowly down the path of death,
For one day I'll follow you.
I'll want to know each step you take,
That I may walk the same,
For some day down that lonely road,
You'll hear me call your name.

Table of Contents

CHAPTER ONE
Normandy

It was a sunny day but a bit chilly as I stood among thousands of white marble crosses. My wife and I came to this place to honor the memory of all the young men who fought and died here on D-Day and the following few days after June 6, 1944. United States and Allied Forces landed on the beaches of Normandy, France, on D-Day to liberate Europe from German occupation, one of the most significant and important events in the annals of military history. We also wanted to honor all of America's young men who fought and died on every other far flung shore or foreign country during WWII. It had been almost sixty years since that morning of June 6, 1944 when American forces stormed ashore at Omaha and Utah beaches. Time has inevitably relegated their heroic deeds and suffering to a storage room of dusty archives and all that remains are the fading memories of those who lived through those terrible days. Time is gradually defeating all WWII veterans. That is something Imperial Japan and Nazi Germany could not do.

The Normandy American Cemetery at Coleville, France overlooks Omaha Beach and the English Channel. Its 172.5 acres is only one of fourteen permanent American Cemeteries located on foreign soil. There are two American Cemeteries in Normandy. The Coleville Cemetery (Omaha Beach) has 9,386 American War Dead and the American Cemetery at Montjoie-Saint-Martin with 4,410 graves. At Omaha Beach there are 307 crosses marking the graves of "Unknowns" and another 1,557 names of the missing engraved on stone tablets in the Garden of the Missing. The remains of approximately 14,000 others originally buried in this region were returned home at the request of their next of kin. In addition to the two American Cemeteries there are sixteen British Cemeteries where 29,946 of their young men are interred, three Canadian Cemeteries with 5,007 graves, one Polish Cemetery with 650 graves and five German Cemeteries with a total of 58,172 graves. In total, more than 109,071 young American, British, Canadian, Polish and German soldiers are buried in Normandy. Among those 9,386 American service men and women who are buried at Omaha Beach, there are three Congressional Medal of Honor recipients, four women, a father and son and thirty-three pairs of brothers. Carved on the inner face of the colonnade's lintel at the Reflecting Pool is the inscription: THIS EMBATTLED SHORE, PORTAL OF FREEDOM, IS FOREVER HALLOWED BY THE IDEALS, THE VALOR AND THE SACRIFICE OF OUR FELLOW COUNTRYMEN.

Carved into the limestone of the chapel is the inscription: THINK NOT ONLY UPON THEIR PASSING – REMEMBER THE GLORY OF THEIR SPIRIT. The memorial area consists of a semicircular colonnade with large maps and a loggia at each end. At the center is the bronze statue, "Spirit of American Youth." This is where I, along with two other WWII veterans, were given the honor and the privilege of placing the memorial wreath at the feet of the "Spirit of American Youth" statue during the D-Day ceremony on June 6, 2001.

At the conclusion of the wreath-laying ceremony I found myself strolling slowly among the white marble crosses. All I could hear was the soft whisper of a sea breeze caressing my face, the sound of the surf against the sandy beach below, and the twittering of the birds in the surrounding trees. As I looked around, I realized I was standing in a place where every blade of grass appeared to have its own private caretaker. Yet I felt no joy or particular appreciation for the aesthetic value of this place. I was completely overwhelmed with a somber and desperate feeling of sadness and grief that surrounded me. My emotions were almost uncontrollable as I struggled to get

13

my breath. I felt the hot tears streaming down my cheeks. I felt a burning lump in my throat and my body began to involuntarily shake. Suddenly the silence was broken by a soft, low moaning or sobbing sound. I looked around to see who was in distress but no one was near me. I suddenly realized the sobs and moans were coming from my own chest and throat. I felt no shame nor experienced not the slightest bit of embarrassment whatsoever. I never before in my entire life experienced such emotions. My mind was going crazy trying to make some reasonable sense out of what had happened here so many years ago. I have concluded that even though a visitor to this place may never have been in the military service, or lost a family member or friend in battle, they would without a doubt experience the same emotions I was experiencing. I think it would be impossible not to experience the overwhelming emotions and sadness of this place.

Perhaps President Reagan best expressed my feeling in his speech at Omaha Beach on June 6, 1984. He said, "It is, in a way, an odd thing to honor those who died in defense of our country, in defense of us, in wars far away. The imagination plays a trick. We see these soldiers in our mind as old and wise. We see them as something like the Founding Fathers, grave and gray haired. But most of them were boys when they died, and they gave up two lives—the one they were living and the one they would have lived. When they died, they gave up their chance to be revered old men. They gave up everything for our country, for us. And all we can do is remember." Those who did not come home are the real heroes.

For a long time I have felt a compelling urgency to write this book before I join other WWII veterans who have already departed this life. When my turn comes to answer the call, will there be anyone left to write these stories about the young boys I grew up with? Each chapter in this book tells the story of my classmates from grade school, high school, the war years, and what each of us accomplished after the war. I desperately want to share these stories with my own children, my classmates and all of my friends and associates. I believe the following will afford them the opportunity to get to know us and understand the reasons why WWII veterans are like we are.

It is almost time for my classmates and WWII veterans to say our "goodbyes" so if you listen closely, you can hear us whisper our farewells. I want to be alert and in full command of all of my faculties when my time comes. I want to be able to look out the window and see the storm clouds and enjoy the smell of fresh rain. I want my children to really know me because my generation is truly unique. I want them to know I tried my very best to live a good and upstanding life. I want them to know what brought everyone of my generation to this moment in time.

It isn't enough to say, "It was a hard road we traveled to get where we are." They must explore that road if they are to truly understand us. No generation has ever given its children a sturdier or more reliable start in life than has my generation. I sincerely hope all of the generations who follow will begin to really understand the forces that molded our personalities.

As the years have overtaken me, I have found it increasingly difficult to communicate with our young people. Perhaps the fault lies with me and other veterans who shared a common experience so many years ago. It seems to me that all of us from my generation speak a different language than the youth of today. Sometimes I feel closer to the "enemy" whom we fought and defeated than I do to our own young people. At least we shared a common bond with our enemies that somehow bound us together. We each, in our own way, fought for what we perceived to be an honorable cause, which is the common thread that binds all WWII veterans together. However, of late, I have observed that our youth are far more perceptive than I had imagined. I have recognized a new resurgence of loyalty in America

15

and a new interest in my generation. I have observed the youth of today expressing this loyalty in so many ways. I cried when I read the following letter that was written by a young military doctor who works in a trauma center in San Antonio, Texas. This fine young man certainly doesn't need anyone to teach him about love for his fellowman, loyalty to his country or respect for WWII veterans---he already has these attributes!

"I am a doctor specializing in Emergency Medicine in the Emergency Departments of the only two military Level One trauma centers. They are both in San Antonio, Texas and they care for civilian emergencies as well as military personnel.

"San Antonio has the largest military retiree population in the world living here, because of the location of these two large military medical centers. As a military doctor in training for my specialty, I work long hours and the pay is less than glamorous. One tends to become jaded by the long hours, lack of sleep, tasteless food, lack of family contact and the endless parade of human suffering passing before you. The arrival of another ambulance does not mean more pay, only more work.

"Most often, it is a victim from a motor vehicle crash. Often it is a person of dubious character who has been shot or stabbed. With our large military retiree population, it is often a nursing home patient. Even with my enlisted service and minimal combat experience in Panama, prior to medical school, I have caught myself groaning when the ambulance brought in yet another sick, elderly person from one of the local retirement centers that cater to military retirees. I had not stopped to think of what citizens of this age group represented.

"I saw 'Saving Private Ryan. I was touched deeply. Not so much by the carnage in the first 30 minutes, but by the sacrifices of so many. I was touched mostly by the scene of the elderly survivor at the graveside, asking his wife if he'd been a good man. I realized that I had seen these same men and women coming through my Emergency Department and had not realized what magnificent sacrifices they had made. The things they did for me and everyone else that has lived on this planet since the end of that conflict are priceless.

"Situation permitting, I now try to ask my patients about their experiences. They would never bring up the subject without the inquiry. I have been privileged to an amazing array of experiences, recounted in the brief minutes allowed in an Emergency Department encounter. These experiences have revealed the incredible individuals I have had the honor of serving in a medical capacity, many on their last admission to the hospital.

"There was a frail, elderly woman who reassured my young enlisted medic, trying to start an IV line in her arm. She remained calm and poised, despite her illness and the multiple needle-sticks into her fragile veins. She was what we call a 'hard-stick'. As the medic made another attempt, I noticed a number tattooed across her forearm. I touched it with one finger and looked into her eyes. She simply said, 'Auschwitz.' Many of later generations would have loudly and openly berated the young medic in his many attempts. How different was the response from this person who's seen unspeakable suffering.

"Also, there was this long retired Colonel, who as a young officer had parachuted from his burning plane over a Pacific Island held by the Japanese. Now an octogenarian, his head cut in a fall at home where he lived alone. His CT scan and suturing had been delayed until after midnight by the usual parade of high priority ambulance patients. Still spry for his age, he asked to use the phone to call a taxi, to take him home. Then he realized the ambulance had brought him here without his wallet. He asked again if he could use the phone to make a long distance call to his daughter who lived several miles away. With great pride we told him that he could not, as he'd done enough for his country and the least we could do was get him a taxi home, even if we had to pay for it ourselves. My only regret was that my shift wouldn't end for several more hours, so I could drive him home myself.

"I was there the night MSgt Roy Benavidez came through the Emergency Department for the last time. He was very sick. I was not the doctor taking care of him but I walked to his bedside and took his hand. I said nothing. He was so sick he didn't know I was there. I'd read his Congressional Medal of Honor citation and wanted to shake his hand. He died a few days later.

"The gentleman who served with Merrill's Marauders, the survivor of the Baatan Death March, the survivor of Omaha Beach, the 101 year old World War 1 veteran, the former POW held in frozen North Korea, the former Special Forces medic – now with non-operable liver cancer, the former Viet Nam Corps Commander, I remember these citizens. I may still groan when yet another ambulance comes in, but now I am much more aware of what an honor it is to serve these particular men and women. I am angered at the cut backs, implemented and proposed, that will continue to decay their meager retirement benefits.

"I see the President and Congress who would turn their backs on these individuals, who've sacrificed so much to protect our liberty. I see generations that seem to be totally engrossed in abusing these same liberties, won with such sacrifice. It has become my personal endeavor, to make the nurses and young enlisted medics aware of these amazing individuals when I encounter them in our Emergency Department. Their response to these particular citizens has made me think that perhaps all is not lost in the next generation. My experiences have solidified my belief that we are losing an incredible generation, and this nation knows not what it is losing. Our uncaring government and ungrateful civilian populace should all take note.

We should all remember that we must Earn This." Captain Stephen R. Ellison, M.D.

I have met the female version of Dr. Stephen R. Ellison at the Veterans Hospital in Grand Junction, Colorado. Her name is Dr. Kelly King, a lovely and caring young lady doctor to whom I was assigned as one of her patients. After the third visit to her office she said to me, "It is such a pleasure for me to care for you WWII Veterans. You never complain or ask for special attention. Somehow all of you have a way of making my life more pleasant and enjoyable." As I got up to leave her office that day she gave me a big hug. I shall never forget that moment as it made me realize I was an important person to her and that she really cared about me. One cannot buy such powerful medicine over the counter or from a pharmacy. These two young doctors are very special human beings and deserve all the thanks we can give them. Their concern for our welfare does not go unnoticed by WWII veterans!

President Reagan best expressed the Nation's deep-felt gratitude to all the young Americans who rest so far away from home on foreign soil, yet so close to the place where they spent their final hours. "In all of the far flung operations of our armed forces the toughest job has been performed by the average, easy-going, hard-fighting young American who carries the weight of the battle on his own young shoulders. It is to him that we, and all future generations must pay grateful tribute." President Truman said, "In deep and everlasting appreciation of the heroic efforts of those who, in keeping their country free, made the supreme sacrifice in World War II. The entire nation has been dedicated to disposing of the mortal remains of those honored dead in a manner consistent with the wish of their next of kin."

The young men who rest in the Coleville American Cemetery at Omaha Beach came from all 50 states of the Union, the District of Columbia and US possessions. We should remember the glory of their spirit for to these we owe the high resolve that the cause for which they died shall live. So today, in our hearts, let us honor all young Americans who died in wars. Let us celebrate the triumph of democracy as we reaffirm the unity of all democratic people who fought in wars and then joined with the vanquished in a firm resolve to keep the peace. Let us teach our children's children a truth so easily forgotten. It is this: The office of a soldier is an honorable estate, for it is upon the willingness of the soldier sustained by the fellowship and discipline of the troops, to enter into mortal danger. It is upon his readiness to risk his very life that order and peace itself ultimately depends.

Every evening at sunset the haunting notes of "Taps" are played at the American Cemetery in Normandy, France. Its mournful and haunting sound always gives me chills and brings tears to my eyes. This was especially true when my wife and I visited the Coleville Cemetery at Omaha Beach. It was impossible for me to hold back the tears that ran down my cheeks. But how many of us know the story behind "Taps"? Reputedly, it began during the Civil War. Union Captain Robert Ellicombe and his men were near Harrison's Landing in Virginia, separated from the Confederate Army by a narrow strip of land. One night Captain Ellicombe heard the moans of a soldier who had been seriously wounded and left to die on the battlefield. Not knowing if the wounded soldier was one of his own men or an enemy soldier, Captain Ellicombe crawled on his stomach through gunfire to try to save the stricken soldier. He began pulling the wounded man toward his encampment and when he finally reached his own lines, he was shocked to discover it was a Confederate soldier, but the soldier was dead. Captain Ellicombe lit a lantern, caught his breath and almost went into shock. In the dim light of the lantern he recognized the face of the Confederate soldier. It was his only son!

His son had been studying music in the South when the war broke out. He had joined the Confederate Army without ever telling his father. The next morning, Captain Ellicombe requested permission from his superior officer to give his son a full military burial despite his enemy status, but his request was denied. However, out of respect for Captain Ellicombe, he was allowed one musician to take part in the burial ceremony. Captain Ellicombe chose a bugler. He asked the bugler to play a series of notes he had found scribbled on a piece of paper found in his son's pocket. The haunting melody we now know as "Taps" was born and is now used at all military funerals.

If it could be said something good came out of all the death and suffering by so many people during WWII it would have to be the enactment of "The GI Bill." Michael D. Haydock summed it up well when he wrote, "The United States was richer by 450,000 engineers, 238,000 teachers, 91,000 scientists, 67,000 doctors, 22,000 dentists, and more than one million other college-trained men and women. The loss of so many of their comrades during the war turned uncertainty into opportunity for thousands of war veterans. We owe them everything!"

Today's Normandy is a serene, peaceful place. Visiting this area where the Allies landed sixty-two years ago gives the impression that little has changed. Even though war was an interruption, life has returned to its pre-war state. Small villages grace the area and stopping in any of them assures a gracious meal of Normandy specialties. The many narrow and winding roads lead one through stretches of farmland where the grazing cattle barely look up as one passes by in a car. It is hard to imagine that sixty-two years ago, this area was torn apart by war. Tanks ripped through the landscape and villagers went into hiding. Today the tanks are on display in the many

21

museums and the villagers go out of their way to show their appreciation to Americans.

After our return home from Normandy, my wife and I began the task of locating my classmates as I was more determined than ever to write this book. The following chapters are the results from our efforts to find and interview these men.

YOUNG FELLOW MY LAD
Written by Robert W. Service

"Where are you going, Young Fellow My Lad, on this glittering morn in May?"
"I'm going to join the Colors. Dad; They're looking for men they say."
"But you're only a boy, Young Fellow My Lad; You aren't obliged to go."
"I'm seventeen and a quarter, Dad, and ever so strong, you know"

"So you're off to France, Young Fellow My Lad, and you're looking so fit and bright."
"I'm terribly sorry to leave you, Dad, but I feel that I'm doing right."
"God bless you and keep you, Young Fellow My Lad, you're all of my life, you know."
"Don't worry, I'll be back, dear Dad, and I'm awfully proud to go."

"Why don't you write, Young Fellow My Lad? I watch for the post each day.
And I miss you so, and I'm awfully sad, and it's months since you went away.
And I've had the fire in the parlor lit, and I'm keeping it burning bright
Till my boy comes home; And here I sit into the quiet night."

"What is the matter, Young Fellow My Lad? No letter again today.
Why did the postman look so sad; And sigh as he turned away?
I hear them tell that we've gained new ground; But a terrible price we've paid.
God grant, my boy that your safe and sound; But oh I'm afraid, afraid."

"They've told me the truth, Young Fellow My Lad. You'll never come back again.
Oh God! The dreams and the dreams I've had; And the hopes I've nursed in vain!
For you passed in the night, Young Fellow My Lad; For you proved in the cruel test
Of the screaming shell and the battle hell that my boy was one of the best

"So you'll live, you'll live, Young Fellow My Lad, in the gleam of the evening star,
In the woodnote wild and the laugh of the child; In all sweet things that are. And you'll never
die, my wonderful boy; While life is noble and true for all our beauty and hope and joy; We
will owe to our lads like you."

CHAPTER 2

A Small Town, a Depression and a War

On October 29, 1929, the United States was enjoying a high plateau of prosperity. The stock market was enticing investors at a record rate and most citizens were living a reasonably prosperous existence.

The 1920s were known as the "Roaring Twenties". The pace of everyday life was faster, morals were looser and parties were the topic of conversation by almost everyone. The Twenties ushered in a truly modern decade of speakeasies, short dresses, jazz music and a new way of life. There had been nothing before or after to match the intellect, science or the prosperity most people were enjoying. It was a new, modern decade that created a new society for the world to follow. It was also an era of ignorance, crime, pettiness and poverty. These changes in our society had far reaching consequences that almost destroyed America. The workweek went from sixty hours to forty-eight hours per week and the masses began to consider "playtime" as important and necessary as "work-time".

Prohibition brought on the decline of social barriers and the commoner rubbed elbows with the rich and famous in their pursuit of alcohol and good times. In the large cities, especially Chicago and New York, gangsters gained control of the distribution of booze, gambling and prostitution. Credit was easy to obtain and the installment plan was created, so people bought thousands of automobiles, radios, homes and other items they fancied and thought they should have. The attitude of most citizens of the time was, "Let the Good Times Roll".

All the good times came to a sudden end on October 29, 1929. The bottom dropped out of the stock market, ushering in what has become known by Americans as "The Great Depression". This was the beginning of the worst economic disaster in American history. Although the crash of the stock market was the starting point of the "Great Depression", it wasn't the sole cause. Rising stock dividends, relatively easy money policies, over-production, lack of stock market regulations and psychology of consumption also played a part in this disaster.

Between October 29, 1929 and November 13, 1929 stock prices hit their lowest point and over thirty billion dollars disappeared from the American economy. America was not alone in the "Great Depression". It demoralized all the industrialized nations, including Germany, Britain and France as well. It also changed the lives of every single one of the men who have a chapter in this book, even though we were only four or five years old at the time. Every family living in America suffered the consequences and it took another twelve years before America began to recover. Literally every household experienced perplexing social and economic problems. There were breakdowns of families, school dropout rates soared, many people became homeless, banks foreclosed on farm property and went broke, and people had to struggle just to eat.

Every one of the men who have a chapter in this book were born during the "Roaring Twenties", and the stock market crash in 1929 brought on hardships never before experienced by Americans. As young people growing up in Glenwood Springs during those difficult days, we really never felt the terrible impact of poverty, as did those who lived in our cities. We were aware of the bread lines in the cities and we were aware that jobs were difficult, if not impossible to find. Consequently, men out of work were riding freight trains all across America looking for employment. Most of these men were good, honest individuals who were desperate to find work in order to support their families. As young people we can all recall that we referred to these men as hobos or bums, and we can also recall they knocked on our doors asking for something to eat. They never begged but rather offered to do some work, any work, just to receive a sandwich. My mother, as well as most other households in our town, always managed to find some task for these men to perform so they would be able to at least maintain their pride and dignity. In retrospect none of us who grew up in Glenwood Springs every realized we were poor. We had no way of measuring poverty because we had nothing with which to make a comparison. No one in our town ever locked their doors even though there was a steady flow of itinerants coming and going through our town. In spite of the abject poverty that held us hostage there was very little crime.

During those dark days one third of Americans were living below the poverty level, but people learned to share and make do with what was available. Somehow, war and prosperity seem to go hand-in-hand. America began a new prosperity of economic growth during WWII and this economic growth has continued to this day. Glenwood Springs also enjoyed a new prosperity of growth and today the population of our little town is over 10,000 citizens. In spite of this growth, Glenwood Springs still beckons to those who grew up here. The magic of the town still prevails and the days of our youth are still deeply imbedded in our lives. Even though those students of so long ago, for the most part lived apart, they have never grown apart. Our love for one another remains intact and as vibrant as ever.

THE HEART'S OF SUMMER
Epes Sargent

The cold blast at the casement beats,
The window-panes are white;
The snow whirls through the empty streets;
It is a dreary night!
Sit down, old friend, the wine-cups wait;
Fill to o'erflowing, fill!
Though winter howleth at the gate,
In our hearts 'tis summer still!

For we are full of many summer joys
And greenwood sports have shared,
When, free and ever-roving boys,
The rocks, the streams, we dared;
And, as I looked upon thy face,
Back, back o'er years of ill,
My heart flies to that happy place,
Where it is summer still.

Yes, though like sere leaves on the ground,
Our early hopes are strown,
And cherished flowers lie dead around,
And singing birds are flown.
The verdure is not faded quite,
Not mute all tones that thrill;
And seeing, hearing thee tonight,
In my heart 'tis summer still.

Fill up! The olden times come back
With light and life once more;
We scan the Future's sunny track
From Youth's enchanted shore;
The lost return; through fields of bloom
We wander at our will;
Gone is the winter's angry gloom,
In our heart 'tis summer still.

James (Bus) Abshire 1944

Deceased

L to R – Bill Bisard, James Abshire, Jake Dwight

K Company Buddies at Reunion 1988

JAMES "BUS" ABSHIRE

A Silver Star Recipient

Bus Abshire was raised in a large family of eight children...four older siblings and three younger siblings. He was born in Salida, Colorado on February 3, 1926 where he started his formal education. When Bus was 9 years old the family moved to Carbondale, Colorado. They resided in Carbondale for one year before moving to Glenwood Springs. Norman Abshire, the youngest of four boys, is the only family member still living. Bus's brother, Junior, was killed in action during the Korean War and all of his sisters are now deceased.

Bus entered grade school in the fifth grade after the family moved to Glenwood Springs. He was the biggest boy in the class and no other classmate ever surpassed him in this category. By the time he graduated from the eighth grade he was six feet tall and weighed 165 pounds. He was an exceptionally gifted athlete and competed in several sports--football, basketball, track, swimming and he helped organize the school tumbling team. He was on the varsity football team and basketball team during his first year in high school.

At the age of sixteen Bus was the Rocky Mountain AAU Champion in the men's division in three different swimming events. He also set two high school world records in two different swimming events. By the time Bus entered his junior year of high school he had grown to 6ft.-3in. in height and weighed 215 pounds.

During his senior year of high school "we" had an unbeatable basketball team, until Bus was called to active duty in the military service in early February of 1944. The starting five of our basketball team were: Bus Abshire, 6ft.-3in., Bill Fender, 6ft.-4in,, Hal Terrell, 6ft.-2in. and the other two team members of the starting five were Bob Simillion and Bill Jackson, both 5ft.-10in. tall. A high school team with that much height in those days was quite unusual as the average height of teen-age boys at the time was not more than 5ft.-9in.

Bus was a happy-go-lucky young man with a perpetual smile on his face. He was generous to a fault that he no doubt learned from having to share with his many siblings while growing up. He was also quick to defend himself and stand up to others when the occasion arose. On more than one occasion Bus and I took one another to task but in the end we always shook hands and parted the best of friends. Every lump we inflicted on one another was worn as a badge of honor. I loved him like the brother I never had and we remained steadfast friends for the rest of our lives. Bus passed away a few years ago and I have truly missed seeing his smiling face, but I can do without the lumps.

Very few boys had access to cars when we were in high school but occasionally one of the boys would be allowed to use the family vehicle on a Saturday night. When such opportunities were available several boys got together and drove to one of the small towns in the area to attend the Saturday night dance and to check out the girls. Invariably such activities led to a fistfight or two with the local boys but these altercations usually ended with a handshake and a drink of homemade "Dago-Red" wine that was always available during such occasions. Bus was a great pal to have along during such outings as his reputation and his size discouraged many of the local boys from becoming overly aggressive toward us. When fights did occur everyone was honor-bound to fight fair. It was inconceivable anyone would employ a weapon, such as a knife, club, gun, or any other kind of weapon. Only bare knuckles were used and seldom was any permanent damage caused. The only way to explain such aggressive behavior, simply stated, is that it was a way to dispel our aggression and live with the frustrations we all experienced during the Great Depression years. One thing is certain---it built character in all of us that has lasted a lifetime. On the flip side of the coin it should be pointed out that a great deal of caring for friends and neighbors was also part of everyone's life and the gentleness everyone learned balanced the aggressive nature that was somewhat prevalent in those days.

The Abshire family moved to Colorado Springs, just as Bus was entering his senior year of high school. Through the efforts of the high school coach and some of the local town businessmen, arrangements were made whereby Bus could remain in school in Glenwood until he graduated in late spring of that year. A room for Bus in a private home was found and many families took turns setting a plate at their table for him. He enjoyed many of his evening meals at my home, as my mother was a very dear and generous person and she loved Bus as if he were her very own. Unfortunately, Bus was called to active duty in February of 1944 and eventually received his high school diploma by mail. This was also the case for several other boys in the senior class that year.

Bus reported to Fort Logan, Colorado in February of 1944 for induction. Immediately thereafter he was sent to an army basic training center. After completing basic training, he was assigned to the US Army 70th Infantry Division, 274th Regiment, King Company.

During basic training Bus was trained as a B.A.R. (Browning Automatic Rifle) infantry soldier since he was a big lad. A B.A.R. is a heavy thirty-caliber gun operated by two men. One man carried the B.A.R. and several rounds of ammunition while the second man carried the bi-pod as well as additional ordnance. According to Bill Bisard, a "K" Company rifleman, Bus was the best B.A.R. man in the company. Bill said, "Bus could run full

31

speed firing his B.A.R. from the hip, which required a lot of strength as well as courage."

The men of the 70th Division became known as "The Trailblazers", and they earned an enviable battle record while fighting the Germans in the Saar Valley area just west of the Rhine River. Their combat record ranks favorably with the many famous fighting units produced during this greatest and bloodiest of wars. The 70th Division was made up of the 274th, 275th and 276th Battalions. All three of these units arrived in Marseilles, France on December 14th 1944. Three weeks later they experienced their first combat when the division was committed to a defensive position near Bischweiler, France. Bischweiler is located a short distance from the west bank of the Rhine River.

Once "K" Company took up their combat positions they fought continuously for eighty-six days in some of the bitterest battles of the war. Powerful German forces were just starting their push into the Ardennes in the north and into the Vosges Mountains in the south of the 70th's position. After the 70th Division was rushed into action they fought a brilliant battle that finally stopped the German offensive. On February 17, 1945, Bus, and "K" Company of the 274th Regiment, surged forward until they had Saarbrucken in their sights. Saarbrucken was the German capital of the rich and long disputed Saarland and the Germans were determined to maintain control of this area.

The Siegfried Line, a strong German fortification, dominated this entire area of valleys, ravines and thickly wooded hills and ridges. The drive on Saarbrucken was a nightmare from start to finish. The entire area was littered with mines and any advance was costly and painfully slow. A complete German Division was rushed into the line to try to stop the advance of the 70th Division, but the 70th held and then continued their advance. They

32

blasted their way through the Siegfried Line until the entire Division had reached the Saar River.

During the 70th's advance between Forbach and Stiring-Wendel, "K" Company of the 274th Regiment suffered 50 percent casualties. (See map). King Company faced 125,000 troops of the crack Nazi First Army. The capture of the Saar River Valley was the prize jackpot and had to be taken. If this area could be taken, the back of Hitler's Germany would be broken. King Company met heavy resistance on their drive to capture the Metz Highway and the town of Stiring-Wendel. Deadly "schu-mines" racked up hundreds of casualties. The "schu-mine" was a simple device consisting of a small wooden box containing four ounces of TNT and a detonation cap that would explode the "schu-mine" when stepped on by a passing soldier.

Right after "K" Company entered the little village of Buschbach, France an interesting incident involving Bus and another young man from Glenwood Springs occurred. Henry Bosco, a member of the Glenwood Springs high school class of 1940, and a member of the 276th Regiment was also fighting the Germans in the same area. Henry and his squad were assigned the task of clearing Buschbach of Germans when they began receiving direct fire from a hill just above the village. Henry said, "I ran for cover down a narrow street and crouched behind a building. I finally peeked around the corner to see if I could detect any Germans in the immediate area and saw another soldier looking at me from around the corner of a building just across the street. I thought to myself, if this guy is a German I've had it." Since Henry didn't draw any fire from the other soldier across the street, he peered around the corner again and he thought there was something familiar about the face looking back at him. Suddenly a voice from across the street said, "Bosco, is that you?" At the same instant Henry said, "Abshire, what the hell are you doing here?" Bus replied, "The same damn thing you are, Bosco." Henry and I had a good laugh when I suggested to him it would most certainly have made the headlines in the local Glenwood Springs paper had they both fired at the same time and done one another in. The front-page headlines might have read, "Two Glenwood Springs boys shoot each other during a battle with the Germans."

Once the village of Buschbach was secured the 274th Regiment began their attack upon Forbach, France, just a few miles north of Buschbach. In quick succession Hesserlling, Lixing and Alsting fell to the 275th and 276th Regiments while "K" Company and the 274th Regiment began their assault on Krentzberg Ridge, near Forbach. This area was so infested with "schu-mines" it was nearly impossible to set a foot down on un-mined ground. Nevertheless, the 274th Regiment captured Krutzberg Ridge, Spichern Heights and then began their push to take the town of Stiring-Wendel.

Taking Spichern Heights was a bloody business but the worst was yet to come for "K" Company. Desperate German defenders tried to regain their previous positions but the 274th Regiment fought off every counterattack. On March 3, and March 4, 1945, the 274th Regiment spread out abreast and began their advance down the hill toward Stiring-Wendel and the Metz Highway. German resistance stopped the 274th's advance almost immediately as they were taking heavy fire from two German bunkers and several well placed pillboxes. King Company was pinned down directly in front of the German guns firing on them from their secured positions.

Even though "K" Company was temporarily pinned down, Lt. Rytting of "K" Company decided to do something about the situation. With a grenade in hand he crawled toward one of the bunkers, only to be seriously wounded by a "schu-mine" before he could toss the grenade. His war ended that day as he lost one of his legs as a result of his wounds. Unfortunately, Lt. Rytting died shortly after being wounded, leaving behind a wife and a new baby daughter he had never seen. Bill Bisard knew Lt. Rytting quite well and the loss of his platoon leader was a terrible blow to Bill. To this day, Bill still gets emotional when he talks about Lt. Rytting and he is quick to say, "Lt. Rytting was one of the best soldiers I ever knew".

Right after Lt. Rytting was mortally wounded while trying to take out the German bunker, Bus and his pal, Ortiz, decided they would take up where Lt. Rytting had left off. They managed to get close enough to the German bunker to toss in a couple of grenades that did the trick. However, both Bus and Ortiz were both seriously wounded in the process. They both spent a couple of months in an Army Hospital recovering from their wounds. Bill Bisard said, "Lt. Crowson always claimed that Ortiz was the toughest and meanest man in his company. All he wanted to do was help German soldiers reach their just rewards. Ortiz and Bus were a perfect team working together".

Abshire was awarded the Silver Star plus the Bronze Star and the Purple Heart. Ortiz received the Bronze Star and the Purple Heart for his bravery during this engagement against the Germans. Their pal, Bill Bisard also received the Bronze Star for his action. Henry Bosco was also awarded the Bronze Star, in spite of the fact he never fired a shot in Abshire's direction during their brief meeting in Buschbach, France.

In the meantime, Lt. Colonel Karl Landstrom, who was directing the assault from his command post from a ridge, ordered up a tank to try to knock out the other German bunker. He then ordered the 274th Regiment to try to bypass the German bunker and pillboxes and to continue their attack on Stiring-Wendel.

King Company was ordered to maintain their present position and continue to try to silence any other German guns in their area. Thus, King Company caught the brunt of the fighting as it seemed every Kraut in Stiring-

Wendel and the Saar Valley concentrated their rockets, mortars, heavy 88s, machine guns and rifle fire into King Company's position.

One of Abshire's buddies, Wendel Rennaker, had this to say about their experience on March 3, and March 4, 1945. "I sure was glad to hear no one has forgotten about our time at Stiring-Wendel, France. I have lived that nightmare over many times. Two of my buddies, Ortiz and Abshire were seriously wounded that day. I got a piece of shrapnel in my knee but I was too damned scared to stop. Ortiz and Abshire both came back to the company after the war was over. We were in Idstien, Germany then. Boy, do I remember that party! Also, the trouble we got into. I was squad leader then so I had my hands full with those two. By that time we had teamed up with another hell-raiser by the name of Guszick. I still carry a picture of those guys around with me."

Bill Bisard also had this to say about "K" Company's experience on March 3rd and 4th, 1945. "Most of the men in "K" Company are no longer with us, including Bus Abshire and his pal, Wendel Rennecker. Jake Dwight, who passed away in 2000, was the man who pulled Abshire to safety when he was wounded. The action during those two days was so intense I thought I'd never live to see my 19th birthday, which was March 4." King Company was finally relieved on March 21, 1945.

Every man who was a member of "K" Company earned the respect of their fellow soldiers as well as the admiration and respect of the enemy soldiers they engaged. During two days of battle between March 3rd. and March 4th, 1945, "K" Company suffered eleven men killed in action and 48 men wounded. A full strength company consists of approximately 180 men but "K" Company's strength was down to 150 men when they went into action on March 3. King Company was awarded 10 Silver Stars, 25 Bronze Stars and one Distinguished Service Cross during those two bloody days in

March. They were also awarded 48 Purple Hearts for wounds received in action during those two bloody days in March, 1945.

By the time Ortiz and Abshire were released from the hospital, the war had ended. The 70th Division was assigned to occupational duties at Idstien, Germany, near the city of Wiesbaden. After Ortiz and Abshire had rejoined their buddies of "K" Company, Bus joined the 70th Division's basketball team. One of his teammates was his pal, Tom Axelrod, another "K" Company member and also a recipient of the Bronze Star. Their team participated in and won second place in the All-European basketball tournament. A member of one of the teams who played against the 70th Division's team was Lyle Call, also from Glenwood Springs. It was just like old home-week when these two men ran into one another.

Tom Axelrod, Bill Bisard and Abshire remained friends for many years. Tom and Bill were both saddened when Bus passed away a few years ago. In the meantime, Tom, Bill and I have become very good friends, even though we have never met face to face. We have discovered that we have a great deal in common. They were both very helpful to furnish details about Bus' combat experiences. I am pleased and proud to have these two men in my life and I hope their friendship will somehow help fill the void in our lives, as we lose more and more of our old WWII pals.

Finally on August 24, 1945, the members of the 70th Division boarded their ship and headed for home. It had been a traumatic experience filled with so many heartaches in which these young men had participated. They formed friendships during those dark days and those special friendships are just as strong today as they were over sixty years ago. The veterans of "K" Company are proud of the part they played in ending the war. It is almost inconceivable to realize a bunch of eighteen and nineteen year-old lads could have accomplished so much. When they finally came home they continued to hone their accomplishments and did their part to make America what it is today.

After being discharged from the service Bus decided to take advantage of the G.I. Bill. He enrolled at Colorado Agricultural and Mechanical College in Fort Collins, Colorado for the fall term in 1946. He graduated with a degree in Physical Education in 1950. He was very active in sports, lettering in both swimming and football in each of the four years he was in school. The A & M "Rams" won the Skyline Conference in 1948 and the team was selected to play in the Raisin Bowl on New Years Day in 1949. Several of his teammates went on to play professional football with several of the pro teams.

After graduation, Bus returned to Glenwood Springs and shortly thereafter he purchased a liquor store from a lady in Basalt, Colorado, just twenty-one miles from Glenwood Springs. Bus wasn't cut out to operate a liquor store, but I for one, was hopeful he would be able to make a success of his venture. Bus, operating a liquor store, equates to turning a blind dog loose in a meat market. He simply enjoyed sampling his products, leaving little profit. Had Bus favored a limerick I'm sure the one that follows would have pleased him:

> I finally found the perfect girl,
> Who could ask for more?
> She's deaf and dumb and oversexed,
> And owns a liquor store.

Bill Eiswerth, (now deceased), a classmate at Glenwood High School and Colorado A & M, was on his way to a family gathering in Basalt, but he made the fatal mistake of stopping at the liquor store before first going to the family gathering. Bus was delighted to see Bill so he closed the store and the two of them retired to the back room to have a drink and catch up on all the news. Bill said, "I never did get to the family gathering but ended up sleeping in the back room of the liquor store with Bus. I think we had a good time!"

Bus sold the liquor store after a few months and accepted a job teaching and coaching high school sports, first in Olathe, Colorado and then Paonia, Colorado. While coaching the high school football team in Paonia he met and married his wife, Ruth. They had two boys and both grew up to be bigger than Bus. After six years of coaching, he accepted a job with Gardner Construction Company as a construction superintendent. Warren Gardner, the owner of Gardner Construction Company, was also a classmate from the high school class of 1943 in Glenwood Springs. Bus spent the remainder of his life working in construction. He managed jobs in Colorado, Utah, Wyoming, Arizona and Idaho for Gardner Construction. Warren Gardner said, "I thought I was a very good construction superintendent, but Bus was the best I ever knew." His passing on February 3, 1990 was a reminder that, "They broke the mold when Bus died." I hope the next time Bus and I meet, he has the community wine jug ready so we can drink a toast of "Dago-Red" to one another and to all of our classmates and WWII buddies.

A VANISHED FRIEND

Charles Hanson Towne

Around the corner I have a friend
In this old world which has no end.
Yet days go by and weeks rush on
And before you know it a year is gone.

So I never see my old friend's face
For life is a sweet and difficult race.
Yet he knows that I like him just as well
As in the days when I rang his bell and he rang mine.

We were younger then
But now we are tired and older men.
Tired of trying to make a name
Tired of playing a foolish game.

So I say tomorrow I'll call on Jim
Just to let him know that I'm thinking of him.
But tomorrow comes and tomorrow goes
And the distance between us grows and grows.

Around the corner yet so far away
Here's a telegram, Sir, Jim died today.
And that's what we get and deserve in the end
Around the corner a vanished friend.

HEADQUARTERS 274TH INFANTRY

APO 461   US ARMY SGC/acg

2 March, 1945

MEMORANDUM:
SUBJECT   : Battle Commendation

This regiment now stands on the German frontier. In this advance to the border, faced by unfamiliar terrain and a determined enemy, all personnel displayed exceptional courage, determination and teamwork.

In the advance which has brought the regiment to the very doorstep of Nazi Germany, historic ground has been taken despite fanatic resistance by the enemy. A portion of the front now held includes the Spichern Heights which is not only the key terrain feature of the strategic Saar Valley but a symbol of German militarism.

Atop Spichern Heights is a German military cemetery in which plots are allotted to the regiments of the Germany army: regiments which have marched in a dozen wars and have cost the world so much in blood. The Nazi held Spichern Heights is a symbol of German armed might and military invincibility. In the storming and taking of this portion of the front, the men of the regiment have not only destroyed and captured many enemy soldiers and taken the key to the Saar Valley but have shattered one of the legends of German militarism.

I wish to commend the entire regiment and attached medical personnel for a job well done, and I feel certain that each of you are ready and capable, when called upon, for the storming across the frontier and destroying the Nazi armed forces which oppose us.

S. G. CONLEY
Colonel, 274th Infantry
Commanding

HEADQUARTERS XXI CORPS

Office of the Corps Commander

APO 101, U.S. Army

SUBJECT: Commendation
    : Commanding General, 70th Infantry
       Division, APO 481 U.S. Army

1. It is my desire to commend to 70th Infantry Division on the capture of Forbach, Stiring Wendel and Saarbrucken and on the crossing of the Saar River. The successful completion of this mission is one in which the 70th Infantry Division may take justifiable pride.

    The courage of your men is evident in their victory in the fact of the enemy's stubborn resistance and employment of natural obstacles. /s/ F. W. Milburn

/t/ F. W MILBURN
Major General, US ARMY
Commanding

Headquarters 70th Infantry Division, APO 461
U.S. Army 7th April 1945

TO: Commanding Officer, 274th Infantry

    All members of the team may be justly proud of the above official recognition of the combat efforts of the Division.

A. J. BARNETT
Major General, United States Army, Commanding

HEADQUARTERS
ARMY GROUP Office of the Commanding General
Washington, D. C.

21, September 1945
SUBJECT: Letter of Appreciation
: Commanding General
70th Infantry Division

Strong devotion to duty permits the fighting men of the 70th Infantry Division to stand proudly with the other courageous American soldiers who swept across Western Europe to crush Nazism and the tyranny which threatened our civilization. To those men and to their gallant comrades who fell in battle, a grateful nation pays deep homage.

The Trailblazer Division is deserving of praise and recognition for an impressive combat salient, crossing the Saar River, capture of Saarbrucken and reduction of the prize Saar Basin. The story of our great victory would not be complete without the chapter written by the 70th Division as it breached the formidable Siegfried Line of defense to permit a junction with the Third Army.

Best known for its skill and tenacity during the bitter fighting in northeastern France after von Runstedt had launched his ill-fated winter drive, the 70th Division was committed to defensive positions in the line less than three weeks after its arrival in France in December, 1944. Activated at Camp Adair, Oregon, on 15 June, 1943, the Division moved to Fort Leonard Wood, Missouri, in July, 1944, to complete its training.

Although the 70th Infantry Division is now being inactivated, the heroism and self-sacrifice of its officers and men will never be forgotten. Thus, it is my privilege to join your fellow countrymen in commending you for your splendid accomplishments.

/a/ JACOB L. DEVERS
/f/ JACOB L. DEVERS,
General, USA

Commanding

HEADQUARTERS 3d BATTALION
274TH INFANTRY
11, March, 1945

SUBJECT: Unit Citation

TO   : Commanding Officer, 274th Infantry, APO 461, U.S. Army

1. Under the provisions of Section IV, Circular 333; War Department 22 December, 1943, it
is recommended that Co. "K", 274th Infantry, be cited for outstanding performance of duty in action against the enemy in the attack of STIRING WENDEL, France, 3 – 4 March 1945.

2. In the above action Co. "K" made the main effort on the right of the 3rd Battalion zone of action. Shortly after crossing the line of departure in KREUTZBERG FOREST at 0700, 3 March, leading elements of Co. "K" ran into an anti-personnel mine field covered by cross-fires from two concrete pillboxes. The approaches to the pillboxes were found to be thoroughly mined. Leaving a detachment to engage the pillboxes while a tank was being brought up to knock them out, "K" Co. moved through dense underbrush around the pillboxes and continued toward STIRING WENDEL. At this time, heavy artillery and mortar fires were place on the woods and this fire continued throughout the action producing heavy casualties. In spite of these fires, "K" Co. moved forward overcoming enemy strong points and pillboxes, and reached their initial objective in the edge of STIRING WENDEL, thus creating a bridgehead into the city. Casualties of "K" Co. on 3 March were 11 killed, 37 wounded and 2 missing in action. The Company Commander and executive officer were among the wounded but continued to perform their duties after receiving emergency medical aid.

3. On 4 March, in spite of the heavy losses and strenuous action of the preceding day, "K" Co. moved aggressively through the assigned zone in STIRING WENDEL, clearing buildings of snipers and capturing five additional pillboxes. Enemy artillery and mortar fires were heavy throughout the day numbering into thousands of rounds.

4. In the action on the above two days, "K" Co. distinguished itself by extraordinary heroism, and exhibited gallantry, determination and unusual esprit de corps in capturing its objectives under unusually difficult and hazardous conditions. The capture of the initial bridgehead into STRING

WENDEL, on 3 March, 1945 by "K" Co. was the key to the success of the battalion in clearing the city on 4 March.

/a/ Karl S. LANDSTROM, Lt. Col., Infantry, Commanding

John Artaz 1943

2001

JOHN ARTAZ
New Guinea, Leyte, Luzon, Japan

John's parents moved to Colorado from Italy in 1907 and settled on a ranch located on Missouri Heights, twenty miles from Glenwood Springs. They had thirteen children, John having been born on May 27, 1925. All thirteen children attended the Luby school, a one-room structure with one teacher. All of the children learned the meaning of hard work. Mr. Artaz raised hay, oats, wheat, alfalfa, potatoes and barley. The children, from the youngest to the oldest, had certain chores assigned to them and they were expected to do their jobs in a timely manner. They worked ten to twelve workhorses doing the plowing, cultivating and putting up the hay during the haying season. They kept milk cows, pigs, chickens and rabbits and planted and tended a large garden. As the children grew older they all learned how to do the plowing, disking, raking and mowing the hay as well as doing household chores.

Bob, who was three years older than John, with John's help, fed the cows and horses and all of the children learned to milk the cows when they were old enough. Mr. And Mrs. Artaz tended to the irrigating as this required a lot of know-how. Mrs. Artaz never had to scold the children because they all accepted the responsibility of completing their work. The family made their own cheese, churned their own butter and made their own soap. They also had plenty of vegetables to eat from their garden during the growing season. They enjoyed canned meat and vegetables during the winter months as these items were canned during the summer months.

The creamery in Glenwood Springs paid $2.00 for a five-gallon can of milk and one of their neighbors made the rounds every day to collect the milk. The children drank all of the whole milk they wanted and the skim

47

milk was fed to the calves and pigs. Nothing was wasted. For Christmas the children received wooden toys their father made and perhaps an apple or an orange. One year Mr. Artaz built a toboggan and everyone enjoyed many hours of fun sledding down the hills and country roads.

When John was about ten years old, the family leased a ranch on Capitol Creek where they remained for the next four years. The house on Capital Creek was considered to be quite modern with the luxuries of inside running water and a carbide gas operated lighting system. This system consisted of a large tank containing carbide. A trickle of water was injected into the carbide tank and a chemical reaction resulted causing gas to form. The gas was piped into the house and they enjoyed light from the gas lamps. Water was piped from a nearby spring into the house and also into a small building called the "milk house". There was a water-trough in the "milk house" where food items were stored in order to keep the food cool.

In 1937 the family moved once again. Mr. Artaz leased a ranch near Glenwood Springs and John started school there in 1938. He didn't care for his new school at first but he soon learned to like and respect his teachers, and it didn't take long before John grew to enjoy his new friends and his new school. John, like all of the other boys his age, found odd jobs in order to earn a few dollars, but mostly he was busy helping his father on the ranch. Consequently, John had little time for sports or after school activities.

When the United States entered the war in December of 1941, many of the boys went into the service. Most of the boys in the class of 1944 enlisted in one of the branches of the service when they turned seventeen. John enlisted in the US Army Paratroopers and in October of 1943, he received his orders and reported to Fort Logan, Colorado for induction and orientation. Seventeen weeks later he came home on furlough before reporting to Fort Ord, California to wait for overseas duty. John left Ft. Ord, on May 10, 1944 when he boarded a troop ship and sailed out of San Francisco just like many other young men before him. After an unbelievable twenty-six days at sea, his ship put into Debodura, New Guinea which was to be his home until November 11, 1944.

John and his buddies had no idea where New Guinea was, nor what to expect when they arrived. However, they soon learned New Guinea was not a South Seas paradise populated with beautiful, passionate women. Their first glimpse of New Guinea was from the deck of their ship as it pulled into Milne Bay. Their first impression was that it was a luxuriant green jungle, and as they pulled alongside the dock, they were regaled with advice from the shore-bound veterans who had arrived a few weeks earlier.

Leaving Milne Bay the ship skirted the shoreline before dropping anchor at Oro Bay where the troops went ashore. After a few miles of dusty roads, they arrived at their new camp located adjacent to an airfield that had been hacked out of the jungle. For the next three months, the 11th Airborne made Debodura their new home until vacating their camp and loading into ships with all of their gear. During their stay in New Guinea the 11th Airborne was occupied in mop-up operations as there were many Japanese still roaming around the area.

They had no idea where their next destination would be, but they realized it must be something big. They departed from Oro Bay escorted by nine Navy destroyers. Seven days later they landed on Bito Beach and joined in the battle to liberate the island of Leyte in the Philippines from Japanese occupation.

Bito Bay was surrounded by rivers and swamps. No vehicles or equipment could move off the beach until the engineers had built bridges across the rivers and swamps. Consequently, the Japanese offered little resistance until November 19 when the men working on Bito Beach saw a lone Japanese plane fly down the beach. This was their first indication that there were Japanese in the area. From that moment on, for the next few months, the 11th Airborne was in constant and continuous combat with the Japanese.

The 187th Battalion was initially assigned the mission of protecting the division's rear area at Bito Beach. But, as the battle grew in intensity the 187th Battalion moved forward into the mountains and engaged the Japanese head on. During one of these engagements with the Japanese, John was wounded but didn't require hospitalization. The 187th regrouped and launched an attack to the northeast where they engaged the Japanese in continuous combat. By December 13, the 11th Airborne had cleared the mountain area and arrived at Anonang to relieve the 2nd Battalion. Then on December 14th, the 187th received orders to move west to Mahonag to block the Japanese supply lines between Mahonag and Anas.

On December 27th, the 187th stormed "Purple Heart Hill" and after bitter hand-to-hand fighting, they destroyed the enemy. The Japanese who had not been killed by artillery, machine gun fire, or mortar fire scattered to the north and the west. Those trying to escape to the north ran into John's 1st platoon of the 187th and were annihilated.

After December 1, 1944 the Japanese on Leyte were starving and attempting to live off the land. They were forced to eat grass, bamboo shoots, coconut and whatever else they could forage from the jungle. As they retreated, they abandoned their equipment, weapons and ammunition along their escape route. Meanwhile, after the success at "Purple Heart Hill" the 11th Airborne Division on Leyte retired to Bito Beach for rest and regrouping. The entire 11th Airborne was once again encamped at Bito Beach by January 15, 1945.

The Leyte campaign had involved 257,766 American military personnel to occupy the island. The total US casualties for the operation were 3,500 US servicemen killed and 12,000 wounded. The 187th Battalion suffered 168 killed, 352 wounded and 12 missing in action. The total number of Japanese casualties was estimated to be 56,263 killed and 386 prisoners taken. About 5,000 Japanese remained on Leyte but were eventually eliminated by the 8th Army during mop-up operations.

On January 26, 1945, the 11th Airborne Division was on the move once again. Their destination this time was the island of Luzon in the Philippines. The 11th Airborne Division landed on Baylayan Bay-Santiago area and immediately went into action. They saw no relief from that moment on until Luzon was finally declared secure in May of 1945. However, mop-up operations went on for some time. John's unit was involved in engagements with the Japanese at Mount Cariliao and Mount Batulao. The enemy occupied the high ground, but after heavy fighting the 187th dislodged the Japanese and occupied the high ground. The 187th also spearheaded the attack on Mount Aiming using bayonets, grenades and rifles. The seizure of Mount Aiming split the Japanese position and the outcome was no longer in question. The 187th was next assigned the mission of protecting Nasgubu and patrolling the US forces main supply lines.

On February 12, General Swing launched a full-scale attack on Nichols Field. Nichols Field was heavily defended by the Japanese when the 187th launched their attack from the south and southeast. John was again slightly wounded but once again did not require hospitalization. By dark, the 187th had captured the airfield, and after this battle, General Swing recommended the entire 11th Airborne Division for the Presidential Unit Citation and it was presented to each and every member of John's Battalion.

Following the fall of Nichols Field, the 11th Airborne Division regrouped for an assault on the last bastions of the Genko Line, still in the hands of the Japanese. The 187th played a key role in this engagement, and by February 21, all resistance by the Japanese had ended. Hundreds of Japanese had been killed during this bitter engagement and the 187th lost several men killed or wounded. The 187th was next assigned the task of helping to liberate the POWs held as prisoners by the Japanese at the Los Banos prisoner camp. Morale at Los Banos was at its lowest and General MacArthur was anxious to liberate this POW camp, as well as all other POW camps in the Philippines. The Japanese had a large number of troops located at Lalakay, only three or four miles from the Los Banos camp, so careful planning was necessary in order to protect the lives of the prisoners. On February 23rd, the raid on Los Banos was successfully executed and all of the prisoners were liberated without any loss of life to the prisoners. Many of the Japanese guards were killed during the liberation, but the Japanese troops at Lalakay, for whatever reason, did not attempt to engage the Americans. Then on February 24, 1945, General MacArthur sent a special communiqué to the men of the 11th Airborne Division that read: "Nothing could be more satisfying to a soldier's heart than this rescue. I am deeply grateful. God was certainly with us today." The 11th Airborne was pleased to be able to count the number of people saved rather than the number of enemy killed.

The 11th Airborne next made a big push to help liberate Southern Luzon. To do this they had to engage the Japanese on the steep slopes of Tayaytay Ridge and on the northern shores of Lake Taal. This area was known as the Lipa Corridor and the 187th was assigned the task of attacking and seizing Tanuan. The order directed the 187th to attack to the east and link up with the 511th. By March 22, the 187th had completed its move from Tanuan to Cuenca and was in position to support the 674th and 675th Battalions. On

March 23, the Japanese launched a banzai attack against the 187th and the battalion lost its commander in this engagement. This was the beginning of the bloodiest combat in the entire history of the 187th Battalion.

The Japanese soldiers in the Philippines were in very poor condition by the 1st of April, 1945. John, like most of his fellow soldiers, believed the Japanese were like robots with little or no feelings. However, after reading a diary found on a dead Japanese soldier John and his buddies changed their minds. The following are the last few entries in this diary:

"14 April, 45: My suffering surpasses even that of death. I finally arrived at Malepunyo. I have just one ball of rice to eat. The enemy air and artillery bombardment is fierce.

15 April, 45: The enemy has concentrated great numbers of troops in Tanuan, San Pablo, and Lipa, and is approaching our front—the enemy artillery bombardment is terrific. We, who are ready to die, are preparing for the enemy attack. My great crisis is approaching. This morning the enemy approached to within 100 meters in front of us. Their rifle and artillery fire is increasing.

Day after day the enemy drop propaganda leaflets that request us to surrender. To hell with them! I'll never surrender even if I must die. No food and no water, only grass and wood. The suffering is great, and there is no communications with Headquarters. Perhaps death is finally upon me.

16 April, 45: I'm hungry. I want to eat rice, fish and vegetables. I want to eat everything. My bowels are growling. If I go down the mountain, I will be able to drink sweet coconut juice, but there are many troops.

Why don't friendly troops come quickly from Manila? There are no friendly planes. Day after day, there are only enemy airplanes. I want to take a bath.

Today again I survived. I wonder when they will attack again. The friends who promised to die together have died, but I am still wandering around the fighting zone. At present only seven men under Sgt. Okamura are left from the squad.

17 April, 45: I'm still alive. This morning another hopeless day has come. I finally started eating grass. Enemy aerial bombardment is fierce. Corporal Sugihi and two others went to headquarters for a message. I pray that they got through safely and will accomplish their mission. My hope is that friendly troops will come from Manila and help us. Malepunyo is cold in the morning and night. Every night I'm thinking of home.

18 April, 45: Hunger woke me. About 1500 hours the enemy approached our rear. The crisis is great now. Artillery shells drop like drops of rain. The end has come. I'm going to die bravely. I pray for the country's everlasting good fortune. I'm completely surrounded. I am going to attempt to cross the enemy lines under cover of darkness. I anticipated going towards Manila. Passing through mountains and ravines I penetrated the enemy front lines.

19 April, 45: Manila is still far away. Today I was assigned as a supply man.

20 April, 45: The enemy is all around. Three men killed and three wounded. The annihilation of the unit is imminent.

21 April, 45: Danger is approaching this ravine. Last night an enemy patrol entered the ravine, but we repulsed them. Enemy bombardment comes closer and closer.

24 April, 45: Another day and no food. At 0800 I started to penetrate the enemy lines with seven other men as a raiding unit. By 1830 I accomplished my mission.

25 April, 45: I'm still alive. The danger is increasing. I heard that headquarters is fighting fiercely, despite being surrounded by the enemy. The enemy seems to have stopped our supplies. Today three men came under my command.

26 April, 45: The enemy is fierce but the morale of my men is high. Three messages from headquarters came through the enemy lines.

27 April, 45: Preparation to move was completed by 0400, and at 0900 we departed towards Mt. Banahao via Tiaong. I wonder if we can get through safely—enemy lines.

29 April, 45: Arrived east of Mt. Malepunyo. I was sent out on patrol. Arrived near Tiaong and hid in the ravine.

30 April, 45: Day has come, and because of the enemy we cannot talk. No food. I hope the enemy will not find us." (This was the last entry in the diary).

On June 30, 1945, the Luzon campaign came to an end and the 11th Airborne Division moved into a reserve area in the Philippines to rest, and receive new replacements. On August 11th, 1945, General Swing received orders for his 11th Airborne "Angels" to prepare to move all combat units along with their equipment to a staging area in preparation for shipment to Okinawa. They were to begin preparations for their next big battle, the invasion of Japan. Before final plans for "Operation Olympic" could be completed, the US had dropped atom bombs on Hiroshima and Nagasaki and Japan capitulated on August 10, 1945. In the meantime, the entire 11th Airborne Division had arrived in Okinawa and was selected by General MacArthur to spearhead the occupation of Japan. The entire 11th Airborne Division flew from Okinawa to Japan and landed at Atsugi Airdrome, near Tokyo on August 30, 1945. They initially occupied an area in and around Yokohama and set up their camp in hangers at the Atsugi Airdrome. They remained at Atsugi until mid-September, 1945 before moving to northern Japan where they assumed responsibility for Akita, Yamagata, Mayagi and Iwate Prefectures. Later, part of the 187th took over control of the island of Hokkaido in addition to their responsibilities for the northern part of the island of Honshu. John remained in northern Honshu with other members of the 187th until he was eventually scheduled to return to the United States.

Prior to their arrival as US occupation troops in Japan, they were subjected to lectures and orientations about Japan, her people and their customs. All US military personnel were warned that no one knew exactly how the Japanese people or the 300,000 Japanese troops still in Japan would react to the occupation. However, not one single incident of resistance occurred. The Emperor had made a speech on the radio asking all of his subjects to cooperate and they dutifully complied.

Many of the Japanese were fearful that the US occupation troops would rape their women, burn their homes and loot their possessions. When this did not happen, many of the Japanese people were genuinely puzzled. One American officer reported that when asked by a Japanese officer why the American troops did not commit such crimes, he felt he didn't give a well-thought-out reply. He simply said, "We just don't do things like that", and that was the end of it.

American prisoners of war who were in prison camps began to leave Japan almost as soon as US troops had landed. General Wainwright and Lt. General Sir Arthur Percival had been held in a POW camp in Mukden, Manchuria and shortly after the surrender of Japan they were both flown to Manila at General MacArthur's orders. They were then flown to Tokyo so they could attend the surrender ceremonies aboard the Battleship Missouri. General Wainwright was captured on the island of Corregidor in the Philippines and General Percival had been captured at Singapore.

In the areas of occupation responsibilities, the 11th Airborne Division was assigned the task of demobilizing Japanese armed forces. On September 2, 1945, Japanese forces numbered 6,983,000 troops scattered all the way from Japan to Manchuria to the Solomon Islands and throughout the Central and South Pacific. The US forces were impressed from the very beginning of the occupation with the cooperation and subservience of the Japanese armed forces and the Japanese people. The entire military structure, as well as the civilian population, reversed themselves from their wartime belligerency to a peaceful acquiescence.

By early fall of 1945, US combat troops began the process of returning to the United States for discharge. In November of 1945, John was due to be discharged, however, he opted to remain in the service for another two years.

Sadly, John lost many of his good buddies during the battle of the Philippines. He doesn't talk about this very much but the memory of these young men is always with him just under the surface. During his years in the service, John made many friends, some long since gone and others still around. John said, "One of these friends was a great guy who wanted to be a baseball player and he had a great arm." He and John went through basic training together, joined the 187th Division together, and went overseas together. His friend was severely wounded on Leyte and was sent home. He never did get to follow his dream of becoming a major league baseball player. He and John still keep in touch and share many special memories together.

At the end of John's two-year extension, he returned to Glenwood Springs and immediately found a job working for the Ford Garage. He also met a pretty red-haired young lady at a roller rink and they have been married for 57 years. John and Estaleen raised three children of their own and adopted a fourth child. They are a close-knit family and they enjoy their many family gatherings.

Over the years, John worked at several different jobs before accepting a position with Mesa College in Grand Junction, Colorado. He organized a training program and taught students auto repair skills. In 1967, John and a partner started a Hertz Rental Agency in Grand Junction, Aspen and Glenwood Springs. He eventually sold this business after having heart bypass surgery in 1984. John loved flying his own airplane but gave this up after his surgery. He and Estaleen enjoy having lunch twice a month with some of his grade school and high school classmates and they are both active in their church

I truly believe John is one of the gentlest and sweetest persons I know. However, under that gentle facade there lives a true warrior.

SOMEWHERE IN NEW GUINEA

Anonymous

Somewhere in New Guinea, where the sun is like a curse,
And each day is followed by another slightly worse.
Where the black dust is thicker than the dirty sifting sands,
And the white man dreams of a greener, fairer land.

Somewhere in New Guinea, where the women are never seen,
Where the sky is ever cloudy, and the grass is ever green.
Where the natives go night howling, and robs a man of precious sleep,
Where there isn't any whisky, and beer "sometime next week."

Somewhere in New Guinea, where the mail is always late,
Where a Christmas card in April is considered up to date.
Where we never have a payday, some never have a cent,
But we never miss the money, 'cause we'd never get it spent.

Somewhere in New Guinea, where the nights are made for love,
And the moon is like a searchlight, to the Southern Cross above.
Which sparkles like a necklace, all through the tropic night,
'Tis a shameful waste of beauty, 'cause there's not a girl in sight.

Somewhere in New Guinea, where the bugs and lizards play,
And 100,000 mosquitoes, replace each one you slay.
Oh! Take me back to Colorado, let me hear that coyote yell,
For this Godforsaken outpost is a substitute for hell.

(Concerning the poem, John said, "You heard rumors about the South Sea
Islands, their beauty, and their glamorous women—well, I guess we must
have landed on the wrong island.")

Jay Brutsche 1943

2001 Deceased

JAY BRUTSCHE

A Seabee at Iwo Jima

Everyone's heard the well-worn phrase, "You can't judge a book by its cover."

I never thought a lot about this phrase until I interviewed Jay Brutsche for his chapter in this book. It was then I discovered the true meaning of this saying. I discovered that Jay was not only the book cover, he was also the book within the cover!

Once we had gotten past the first few minutes of the interview, Jay reverted to his normally quiet, gentle self, and I had to literally drag every response to my questions out of him. I asked him four questions, "Jay, were you in the service, did you go overseas, did you do anything exciting while overseas and what was it you did that was exciting?" After each question Jay hesitated before answering, "Yes", but nothing more. At this point I was getting a bit impatient so I said, "OK, Jay, what was it you did that was exciting?" After one more pause he replied, "Well, I made the invasion at Iwo Jima." It was now my moment to pause as I tried to recover my composure and retain control over my emotions. I almost fell out of my chair as I had no idea this quiet little fellow had been involved in such a horrendous battle that cost the US Marines, Navy, Army Air Force and the Seabees 26,000 casualties over the thirty-two days it took to dislodge the Japanese from their fortifications on the tiny island of Iwo Jima.

Jay was born on July 17, 1925 in Glenwood Springs. He was one of the smallest boys in our class and when he graduated from high school he was still quite diminutive, stood about five feet five inches tall and weighed all of 120 pounds. Jay didn't participate in any sports but rather concentrated his energy into his love of music. Jay was an outstanding clarinet player and was a member of the school band, school orchestra and pep-club band. He attended all of the basketball and football games with the pep-club band. Jay admired several of the bigger boys in our class as we were the "school-jocks" and we were Jay's "role-models". However, when Jay informed me he had made the invasion at Iwo Jima, we immediately switched roles and Jay became my hero and my "role-model". He is living proof that one doesn't have to be a football or basketball jock in order to prove his manhood or display his courage.

When Jay was sixteen years old he developed a serious back problem and spent an entire year in Children's Hospital in Denver. He managed to keep pace with his classmates in Glenwood Springs through an educational program organized by the hospital. After his release from the hospital he returned home and became even more dedicated to his love of music and his clarinet. The school band director took Jay under his wing and arranged for him to receive special music lessons. During Jay's last year of high school he was selected as a member of the local symphony orchestra which was made up of talented high school students from Western Colorado, as well as many adult musicians residing in the area. Thus Jay was able to continue his love of music and he eventually became a member of the 90th Seabee Construction Battalion's Band.

Jay, like most of the other boys at that time, found odd jobs during the summer months in order to earn a little pocket money. He, like the rest of the boys his age, realized his parents didn't have extra money to spare, as the entire country was struggling to survive "The Great Depression".

Jay worked in local restaurants as a dish washer, did yard work wherever he could find it, sold newspapers and accepted almost any other work he could find in order to earn a little money. Between his junior and senior year of high school he found a job working at a Dude Ranch in Snowmass, Colorado, fifty-miles from Glenwood Springs. He worked ten hours a day, seven days a week, and was glad to receive $2.00 a day plus board and room. He never went to town that summer so he was able to save what was considered a small fortune at that time. Jay did manage to fall in love with the owner's daughter during that summer but he never got around to sharing his feelings with her.

Before graduating from high school Jay tried to enlist in the regular Navy but was turned down due to color-blindness. He enlisted in the Navy Seabees in June of 1943 and was sent to Camp Perry, Virginia. After completing boot camp training, his next stop was at Port Hueneme, California where he received advanced training in construction techniques. From Port Hueneme Jay was sent to Red Hill, Hawaii where he received two months of jungle training, as well as training in demolition. Finally, along with the 90th Seabee Battalion he boarded ship and sailed out of Pearl Harbor into the vast Pacific Ocean. They made two stops, one at Eniwetok and the other on the island of Saipan, before sailing on to the little volcanic island of Iwo Jima where Jay received his first baptism under fire in actual combat.

During WWII over 325,000 men served with the Seabees. They participated in construction projects and actual combat on six continents and over 300 islands throughout the Pacific. They built bridges, airstrips, roads, hospitals, gasoline storage tanks, warehouses and accommodations for Marines and Army personnel. The Seabees motto is "WE BUILD, WE FIGHT", and the 90th Seabee Battalion more than lived up to its motto.

Iwo Jima, which means "Sulfur Island" in Japanese is of volcanic origin and lies east of Okinawa 653 miles and south of Japan just over 600 miles. It is approximately 12 square miles in size and was strongly fortified by the Japanese. The Japanese had built an airstrip on the island and were in the process of building two more airstrips when the Marines and the Seabees landed on February 19, 1945. The landing by the 90th Seabee Battalion was at "Red Beach", the same area where the 5th Marine Division had landed and was dominated by Mount Suribachi, the highest point on the island, (550 feet}. Their first assignment was to clear the beach of all wrecked trucks, jeeps, landing craft, heavy guns, tanks and other equipment that had been destroyed by Japanese guns and mortar rounds. The 90th Seabee Battalion was stuck on this beach for two days finding it almost impossible to find safety from the carnage that was taking place around them. Jay said during those first few days he never thought he would make it back home alive.

As soon as the Seabees had cleared the beach they split into two groups. Jay's group crossed the narrow neck of the island while the second group started improving the three airstrips. They were able to begin reconstruction of these airfields within three days, as the Marines had cleared this area of Japanese by then. It was understood by the Seabees, as well as by the Marines, why these airfields were so desperately needed for a place where crippled B-29 bombers could land after their raids on Japan. The airfields were also needed for P-51 Mustang fighter groups. The Mustang with its wing-drop-fuel-tanks could rise up from Iwo Jima and escort the B-29 bombers to Japan and back. The group of Seabees who started work on airstrip number one was under constant fire from the Japanese but they got the job done in spite of the losses they suffered. Even with the airstrip area cleared of the enemy it still wasn't a secure place for the Seabees to work.

The Japanese continued to harass the Seabees and Japanese snipers were a serious threat, forcing the Seabees to lay low, but whenever the shooting stopped they went right back to work. The 90th Seabee Battalion worked on airfield number one day and night, and although there was still a lot of work to do, it was made serviceable within one week. On March 4, two weeks after the initial landing on Iwo Jima, the first damaged B-29 made an emergency landing on Iwo Jima. The Seabees were still working on the field, but in spite of the rough surface the pilot made a successful landing while the battle continued to rage. Thereafter thirty-five more crippled Super-fortresses made emergency landings during the battle. Consequently, the Marines and the Seabees received daily reminders of why they were fighting for this miserable little sulfur-choked bit of volcanic rock. Jay was proud to tell me that he and every other service man who witnessed this first emergency landing of a crippled B-29 Super-fortress felt they had done their jobs well.

Once the airfields on Iwo Jima were finished, the Army Air Corps' B-29s were able to organize massive raids on Japan, including Hokkaido, the northern most Japanese island in the chain. Because they could refuel at Iwo Jima on their return trips to home bases on Guam, Tinian and Saipan, they were able to carry heavier bomb loads. Marine officers questioned if the loss of life suffered by the Marines and the Seabees was worth the effort. But, they realized the war would be shortened considerably due to the massive raids on Tokyo and other major Japanese cities. It was estimated that the US military would lose up to one million men should it become necessary to carry out the invasion of Japan, not to mention the millions of Japanese who would have perished.

Japanese General Kuribayashi had a total of 21,000 men under his command on Iwo Jima. By the time Iwo Jima was declared secure by American forces, 20,000 of Kuribayashi's men were dead. Contrary to previous battle strategies employed by the Japanese on Kwajalein, Tarawa and other Pacific islands, General Kuribayashi did not engage the Americans man to man on Iwo Jima's beaches. He realized pillboxes on a beach stood little or no chance against the concentrated weight of American air, naval and amphibious assaults. Instead, he built his defensive fortifications well back from the landing beaches and concentrated his long-range firepower directly

65

onto the beaches. His strategy was to hold his positions and let the enemy come to him. He reasoned that this would offer the best chance of surviving the impending landing of US forces that he knew was soon to come.

General Kuribayashi built subterranean fortifications into the volcanic rocks of Iwo Jima up to a depth of seventy feet. The heat was so intense it was impossible for his men to work for more than a few minutes at any given time before having to return to the surface for a breath of fresh air. His labor force included several hundred Korean conscripts as well as his own troops, but he completed the project within one year. He imported engineers and mining specialists from Japan to oversee the project when finished, would included several miles of tunnels, large storage rooms, and dozens of smaller warrens. Kuribayashi also built over 150 concrete pillboxes in the area of Chidori near the beach. By early 1945 Kuribayashi had an intricate underground network of caves, bunkers, command posts and hospitals, all connected by sixteen miles of tunnels. One tunnel was 800 yards long and featured fourteen entrances. These installations were well stocked with water, food and munitions. The labyrinth of caves and tunnels were equipped with electrical power to operate radio equipment, field telephones and internal communication equipment. Finally, the entire system of underground fortifications was covered over with concrete blockhouses, pillboxes and earth for the purpose of concealment, as well as a buffer against bombs and heavy gunfire from US invasion forces. In all, Kuribayashi had over 800 gun positions, hundreds of mortar pits and dozens of machine-gun emplacements ready for action when the US Marines and Seabees landed.

Once the landing beaches had been cleared, Jay's group followed in the footsteps of the 5th Marine Division and crossed the narrow neck of the island. Even though the distance they had to traverse was less than one mile, the area was exposed to enemy fire from Japanese gun positions dug into Mount Suribachi. The Marines had silenced the enemy guns from dozens of Japanese pillboxes. However, these same pillboxes were back in action within minutes because each bunker and pillbox was inter-connected by Kuribayashi's maze of tunnels. Consequently, the Seabees came under heavy fire as they crossed the neck of the island and suffered many casualties in the process. Jay was shocked at the sight of so many dead bodies, but seeing a hand stretched out of the black sand has never left him to this day.

The eerie sight of hot steam pouring in thick clouds out of dozens of holes and the terror of constant explosions was almost more than he could bear. Nevertheless, Jay and his 90th Seabee Battalion buddies managed to deal with their fear, even though that fear never left them for a second during the entire time they were on that horrible spit of land in the middle of nowhere. Jay said, "Any man who has seen combat and claims he never felt fear is either crazy or is a liar." Jay's courage was not the absence of fear!

After the 90th Seabee Battalion reached their assigned area on the opposite side of the island they dug in for the night. Jay dug his foxhole deep, as it was to become his home for the next two weeks. He recalled how at night it was like attending a Fourth-of-July party with constant explosions lighting the sky and thousands of tracer bullets flying in every direction. Each night Jay dug his hole a little deeper and stacked sandbags around the edge of his foxhole whenever he could find a sack to fill with sand. Two weeks passed before Jay finally received a hot meal and had the chance to take a bath, albeit in salt water. He and his fellow Seabees lived on K-rations and a canteen of water each day. Getting that first hot meal was almost like being home for Christmas dinner.

Jay's first assignment after digging his foxhole was to locate and remove unexploded mines, shells, grenades and any other deadly explosives from construction areas. The 90th demolition crews also had the responsibility of blowing up Japanese pillboxes and blasting shut cave entrances. This was a very dangerous assignment but saved many lives.

The Seabees and the Marines shared a strong bond of respect and friendship not shared by any other two branches of the armed forces. The Seabee's dead were buried with the Marine's dead during every engagement they shared throughout the Pacific area, and Iwo Jima was no exception.

The scars of war imposed upon Iwo Jima and in Jay's mind left a lasting impression upon him and those who served with him. As the years passed, Mother Nature healed Iwo Jima, but Jay's scars are still there. "It was an unforgettable experience! Living in such hell caused young men to do things they would never have otherwise considered doing," Jay said.

During one of my visits with Jay he shared some of the horrors he experienced while on Iwo Jima. Even though General Kuribayashi never ordered his men to mount a bonzai attack until the very end of the battle, there were nevertheless several smaller scale attacks. Jay recalled one attack that took place early one morning. A group of about 300 Japanese mounted a charge against the Marines who were dug in near the area where the 90th Seabee Battalion had established their first construction camp. The Marines killed most of the enemy before they reached the Seabee camp, but a few Japanese managed to penetrate the Marine's positions and suddenly they were right on top of the 90th Battalion. Before Jay realized what was happening he found himself face to face with a Japanese soldier. "The Japanese soldier didn't have a gun, but was threatening to throw a hand grenade at me that he was waving above his head," Jay said. Even though Jay was almost frozen with fear, he raised his rifle and shot the Japanese soldier dead. On another occasion, Jay and three other Seabees found five dead Japanese soldiers in a large shell hole. One of the Seabees jumped into the hole and began searching the bodies for souvenirs. Suddenly one of the Japanese soldiers, an officer, raised his pistol and pointed it at Jay and his buddies. Without hesitation, they opened fire with their rifles and killed the Japanese officer before he could fire a shot. After relating these stories to me, Jay put his head in his hands and sat quietly in deep thought for a minute or two. He eventually said, "It was either them or me!" He witnessed another small bonzai attack against the Marines a few days later. The Marines killed most of the Japanese but took a small group of Japanese prisoners. The Japanese bonzai attack had killed several of the Marines, leaving the surviving Marines very angry. Without so much as a second thought, the Marines marched the Japanese prisoners to the edge of a large concrete water cistern the Japanese had built and shot every one of them. After disposing of the bodies in the cistern they told Jay to keep his mouth shut about what he had witnessed or he would end up in the cistern with the Japanese. "I have never spoken of this matter in all these years until I related the story to you. Now I'm glad I finally told someone," Jay said quietly.

Once the construction area had been cleared of explosives Jay's 90th Battalion group began building a torpedo storage dump. In the meantime Motoyama Airfield was converted into a major American airfield. In a matter of days the 90th Battalion had also turned the other two airstrips into serviceable airfields and built maintenance facilities as well. By August 1945 more than 2,400 B-29 Superfortresses found refuge there.

Another priority project the 90th Battalion undertook was the construction of a huge gasoline tank farm that could feed the fuel-thirsty B-29 bombers and the P-51 Mustang fighters. The 90th Battalion construction crews blasted the terrain, smoothed and surfaced the airfields, built fuel pipelines from ship to shore and accomplished dozens of other jobs by toiling day and night. In support of the Marines, the 90th Battalion built and operated a concrete batch plant to furnish concrete to all the island's projects. A steady stream of dump trucks moved this vital commodity to various jobs from one end of the island to the other, all the time under fire from the enemy. They built storage facilities, ammunition and ordinance depots and field hospitals, as well as having the responsibility of issuing equipment.

Once Iwo Jima was secured, the 90th Battalion remained on the island in support of the invasion of Okinawa and continued to support the bombing raids on the Japanese home islands. After the last Japanese soldier had been dug out of his hole, Iwo Jima settled down into somewhat of a peaceful mode. There was time for relaxation and the chance to enjoy a semblance of normality.

Time Magazine combat correspondent, Robert Sherrod, a veteran of earlier landings on other Pacific islands said, "The Marines and Seabees who fought on Iwo Jima died with the greatest possible violence. Nowhere in the Pacific war had I seen such badly mangled bodies. Many were cut squarely in half." The toll suffered by the Marines, Seabees and other supporting forces came to an appalling total of 24,050 casualties. Six thousand nine hundred Americans and 20,000 Japanese soldiers lost their lives on Iwo Jima. The US Marines captured a total of 216 Japanese soldiers and most of them were wounded.

The overall US casualty rate for the Marines and Seabees was about 30 thirty percent of the forces employed, but many rifle battalions surpassed 7seventy-five percent casualty rate. News of the savagery of Iwo Jima shocked the American public, but there was no time to indulge in recrimination. The invasion of Okinawa began four days after Iwo Jima fell. As it turned out, the Okinawan campaign was equally as bloody as had been the fighting on Iwo Jima. There were still battles to fight and, presumably, the assault on the Japanese home islands themselves was bound to be the bloodiest and costliest of all.

After Iwo Jima had settled into a fairly normal daily routine, Jay and his mates spent their spare time exploring the island. During one such expedition, Jay found a diary hidden in one of the many caves that had been written by a Japanese officer. Jay had the diary translated by an interpreter and the first entry is dated January 1, 1945, about six weeks before the Marines and the Seabees hit the beach on Iwo Jima. The last entry in the diary is dated March 26, 1945. Presumably that was the last day of this Japanese officer's life.

TRANSLATION OF JAPANESE OFFICER'S STORY

(Found by Jay Brutsche in a cave on Iwo Jima)

(The wording of this diary is just as the translator wrote it)

Note: By official translator--this diary for which I am writing for you will have a few subjects left out of 19, February to 28th of March for intelligence reasons.

January 1, 1945:

Arrived on garrison position of our imperial home defense number 8d. Haven't had time to correspond home but we accompanied a great of worries for the American axis in the Pacific. I have just left the Philippines. It is a very good place. I haven't had time to write from there to here due to censorship regulations.

January 2, 1945:

Placing myself to superior command. I have been promoted from lance or super lieutenant over battalion Todisho Dadamine.

January 3, 1945:

An honor was cited to lieutenant Kurata-san for bravery on the Philippines Islands. He was cited with the Deiehe Neiha Beijo Ban or medal of honor. Today we have honored him with the Imperial Sword of Kawanato's Shrine. The goddess of all spiritual guidance.

January 6, 1945:

We have left a great many heroes of our Japanese supermen army divisions for the defense at the Philippine Islands.

January 8, 1945:

We will not in any way lose this war with a shameful defeat. Gladly to say we are having a great amount of power and sacrifices before we win, and bloodshed will be teared off in pieces all over the world.

January 9, 1945:

Today we are having a shrinal prayer for our victory in the Pacific.

January 21, 1945:

USA armies who are fighting in Germany are finding a hot reception from our allied country, Germany. Lieutenant General Von Rundstedt's defense in France showed the axis that our power has not dwindled but just beginning. Adolph Hitler, our superior commander (Europe) has just given up his very thought of this drastic war. We have just begun he says and will begin with heavy blows to axis.

January 22, 1945:

I am observing the anniversary of little Kaido. Please give him my regards on his birthday. Mitlake Jous Tunachine (greetings from a far flung shore).

January 23, 1945:

Received orders from commanding general of the third Imperial Japanese Army and marine garrison to confiscate all important papers due to foreseen battle. The axis are rapidly advancing towards position. The axis think we are crumbling from doubt, due to lack of power and machinery but what a surprise we have for them here. Though we have no way of protecting and reconquering our losses in the Pacific we have duly sworn to sumari--Crises to our Imperial Emperor Seiko Sai administer to war, Kolso, that defenses that we strung throughout the Pacific will not in any way betray our fatherland.

January 24, 1945:

I am writing an important diary today concerning the arrival of Tadamichi Kuribayashidorn of the Internal Tax Commissioner for the territories of Japan. Stated that in behalf of all Emperor Chieftains that Lt. General

Kuribayashi has further implied his wholehearted support for the defense in the area and around Japan.

January 26, 1945:

A field inspection was made to our defense Commander today, our Imperial Marines and Army has fully showed the General what he expects.

January 27, 1945:

Air raids is beginning to be quite a game for the axis. Today we have shot down 18 heavy bombers and 14 fighters. Very little damage were done to our shore installations. Light casualties were inflicted on our personnel and they were quickly replaced.

January 29. 1945:

We are on alert. Continuous raids are going on every day. We are in our defense areas every day and night. Fighters of all sizes. Seems that the axis are losing her planes due to because of planes that they are using. Our planes are bombing Saipan too in order to destroy the evil bird NASHINA-DESO-KUDO-WASA-DER. (This refers to the B-29 Superfortresses). The kind of planes they have are larger than the airfields they can build for them. Caves are the only ground protection from the continuous air raids that they are pulling every night.

February 1, 1945:

We spotted naval crafts about 6,400 yards away from our shore batteries. Too far away from shore batteries to open fire in order to not give our positions away. But to commence firing at air attacks, we sent to meet foes fleet. They scattered wildly with heavy losses. All our planes returned safely. Reinforcements have landed on position number 8d. They are 8th garrison region who have gallantly fought axis in Kwajalein. In 1943, the 21st division who have just arrived from China. The 8th, 9th, and 16th medical with one woman of the AUX aid unit AAIV 671 FA. (Shore batteries) 7721 N. F. Marines and Army veterans of New Guinea and our unit the 67th F.A. first B.N. Imperial Region. The 11th O.M. B.N. are doing a fine job of supporting us with machines and food.

February 10, 1945:

American nurses on the Philippine Islands have cooperated splendidly in amusing and aiding our wounded and well in Lingyan as Lieutenant Sodono Kawaguchi stated that sexual intercourse and diseases after courses were extremely fine. One or two American women (civilians) were sent to Japan for Imperial purposes. They volunteered wholeheartedly.

February 15, 1945:

To continue to receive word Admiral Kusunoka Watanobe was killed in a naval battle along the China coast.

February 16, 1945:

We're stationed in a new area we're the fourth to the tenth Southeast of our position.

February 18, 1945:

Enemy surface crafts, hundreds of them were sighted south by southwest of our position.

February 19, 1945:

An alarm is given to open fire within distant range as I have said an invasion has started. The battle is on. We have expected the time to happen and the axis are using all sorts of power to land on our positions. Surface crafts would fire, enemy planes would take over when surface crafts would finish firing. Our defense commander is in direct communiqué between positions. We are highly setting up land mines and booby traps for the axis.

February 20, 1945:

I cannot recognize the kind of troops that the enemy are using but, stupidly enough they are advancing to their death trap. Some of my scouts have recognized that they were marines of the Axis. We are ready for them.

February 21, 1945:

As my assistants say, if the Marines have landed on the islands in the Pacific, then they are dumb enough to land on this position. Lets give them what they came for. Our dauntless defenders are holding out greatly. Locations and defense on this island were a great surprise to the enemy. Fire of all Col. We have been firing day and night at the enemy. Dead enemies are strung along the north and southeast shore of our position like rats. Many more enemies are trying to land on, but they are paying for what they have done to our men. We shoot eight of theirs. We are digging underground to relieve pillbox number 8 and we are jolted by more enemy troops.

February 23, 1945:

We have gained back positions number 4 from the enemies, but scarcely enough ammunition, we did not have enough ammo.

February 24, 1945:

We haven't slept for four days now, since the time of the invasion orders were given out to retreat and to counter attack with all might.

February 25, 1945:

Two o'clock this morning we were given a conference call. Col. Saguri Doi c/s to General Kuribayashi informed us that our defense would be the caves on position 8d. We were given enough ammo to carry and bonsai on the enemy, as long as the enemy would remain for the reception. I cannot mention the strength, but gladly to say we have them guessing. 21:00 A.M. on a scouting job tonight. Rather to say, we are going to the enemy positions around areas. Orders are to demolish enemy held pillboxes and operate in and movements of the enemy. Sniping is done during the day and infiltration during the night. I am back in position 4c. The enemy is trying to build a road leading southeast to replace their men and equipment quickly. Of what I have seen and accomplished was an enemy depot. The men were working day and night to destroy and delay all possible reinforcements. The enemy is trying to pull out. I have killed two Marines and Seabees laboring along the beaches. While two of my men covered me I infiltrated in the area and destroyed the enemies equipment.

February 27, 1945:

The second night we did the same thing of what we are supposed to do, and if so, more. But, the sentries were alerted. This time barricades and machine guns four squads and about 100 to 185 yards intervals. Their barricades consisted of two concentration and tightly strewn barb wires on the outline. About two to three feet upon our objective was gasoline dumps, food and water was not available. The enemy used rifle type finder flares held four radius of a circumference. A description of a parachute with sixteen strands of cords.

February 28, 1945:

Last night two of my scouts were killed. They were laced (by two CB men) they were good at scouting. Things were building much faster then we expected, but some of our Imperial units are delaying most of them throughout the areas. The enemies are increasing along the shores. Four batteries were knocked out, and our men retreated towards positions 4c to assemble and form a new counter attack against the enemy.

March 1, 1945:

Enemy tanks forced to share anti-tank mines and land mines stopped most of them. They looked as though they were heavily armed with guns. Some of our pillboxes still in use were giving a hot time. Enemy tanks are advancing towards positions number 4c and AGL84. Their firing was directed into the inner positions of the 1st division who are holding out against enemy advances along the Northwest positions forming a "V" shape like barricade from the West tip shores Southeast of position 8d. Flame throwers were scarcely used by the enemy. Lt. Jima Sugimi, a well observed disciplined officer is an expert of enemy weapons of which most of them are ingenuinely invented for war purposes. Lt. Sigma stated that axis Americans are a war tested county. These weapons show the immense power to conquer and demolish the poor innocent victim of the world. He also said the war lords of American and their partners joined in the drive for mastering the Pacific, and the whole world for sinister purposes.

March 9, 1945:

Haven't much more to write from here on. There is lots of fighting today. Most are separated and the main fighting units are disorganized along the patrol of light axis marines have scouted the area thoroughly. Through their bravery in our positions we had our KAMA 1920 rifles, lots of ammo which was stored up in this cave, surprisingly so. These caves were build for gasoline and anti-aircraft use. No food or water which is a great trouble to get. We managed to live on our traveling rations.

March 23, 1945:

I've killed or demolished two of my men because they were of no value to the unit. One of them was seriously wounded, the other suffered from a punctured lung. Orders from Col. Doi was to demolish all useless personnel which cannot recover or fail survive after so rough a travel. Left position 4c to 5c, now in position 8d-1. My men are gathering all weapons and spare parts that they can find. Last night we managed to secure some drinking water from an enemy. Area booby traps were laid or attached to their valve gauge. When disengaging the valve, the booby will effect a great explosion.

March 25, 1945:

We are concealed from enemy patrols during the day here. Today, four enemy patrols were a few feet away from our position. Firing ceased, to not draw attention. Every day they passes this very spot and it seems that our concealment was perfect. Today I received a message from Col. Doi in behalf of the 21st division. An attack was to be made on enemy positions. Col. Doi will take 500 to the Western half of position 80 and General

Kuribayashi will resume the attacking orders from position 8d-1 NC North Central part of the Northeast was our prey. Very few rifles or any intentional weapons will be used. In our unit we are recorded to destroy nearby defending positions of the enemy for who are thinking that a surprise will be attempted. My orders was to draw the attention, if possible to the right flank, to the left flank from position 8d-V. We are allowed to wear marine dungarees, infiltration shoes, saber knives, small arms, grenades. Charge and work caps to avoid attention so heavy rifles will be carried. Such as submachine guns, heavy mortars and light machine guns.

March 26, 1945:

No identification tags will be worn. This task will be a suicidal attempt to lessen the enemy if possible, and dislocate their units and communiqués. General Kuribayashi is ready to throw the charging orders and if accomplished, of which I doubt very much. We can resume and reestablish our joys or SNIKO-FUJI-SAI. Death to the defense of all out of place."

(End of diary entries) (Translated May 1, 1945).

Jay was still on Iwo Jima when the A-bomb was dropped on Japan. Right after Japan capitulated, the 90th Seabee Battalion began the process of sending their men home for discharge. The first men selected were those men over forty-two years of age. Thereafter the men who had accumulated the highest number of points were sent home for discharge. The point system was based on time in service and campaigns in which they had participated. Jay's participation in the battle of Iwo Jima was adequately stated by his Commanding Officer, George S. Brockway. He said to all of the men who served under him, "May you ever bear with pride this patriotic service you have so unselfishly contributed. May you long cherish in your memories the many experiences you have gained in the adventures of this organization. As you leave, my best wishes go with you. Your performance has been in keeping with the highest Navy tradition." The 2,400 Army Air Force pilots who were forced to land on Iwo Jima between its capture and V-J Day (Victory in Japan), along with their 27,000 crewmembers, had no doubts either. One said, "Whenever I land on this island, I thank God and the men who fought for it."

Jay, along with many of his Seabee buddies, boarded a transport ship on August 28, 1945. As the ship's crew pointed the bow of the ship toward San Francisco and the Golden Gate Bridge, Jay stood on deck in silence and looked back at Iwo Jima. For the past 56 years the physical topography of that terrible place has faded into a dim image in Jay's mind. However, Jay is quick to say, "The experience of surviving that place is still vivid in my memory, just as if it happened yesterday. The loss of so many young men on Iwo Jima, many of them my friends, has had a devastating impact on family members of all those who perished there."

After two weeks at sea, Jay and his 90th Battalion Seabee mates landed at the Naval Receiving Center at Treasure Island, California where they remained under quarantine for the next three weeks. Their next stop was once again Port Hueneme. They had originally boarded ship at Port Hueneme that took them to their devastating assignment on the island of Iwo Jima.

Jay spent one week at Port Hueneme before receiving a ninety-day leave. He immediately headed for Glenwood Springs where he spent two weeks visiting family members and friends. His next destination was Muskegon, Michigan to visit his sister, Bonnie and her husband, George Smeltzer. He spent the balance of his leave in Muskegon where he met Ann Pearson whom he eventually married in 1950. Jay returned to Port Hueneme at the end of his ninety-day leave where he received his Honorable Discharge on March 6, 1946.

Not until 1968 were Iwo Jima and Chichi Jima returned to Japan with appropriate pomp. Even though the US admitted the islands were Japanese it retained full control until then. On February 19, 1985, exactly forty years after the battle of Iwo Jima, a reunion was held on the island to honor the war dead of both the US and Japan. Two hundred and seventy US Veterans and family members and one hundred Japanese representatives met there to commemorate a "Prayer Monument' that reads as follows:

"We commemorate our comrades, living and dead, who fought here
with bravery and that our sacrifice on Iwo Jima will always be
remembered and never repeated."

Once again a group of US Veterans returned to attend Iwo Jima commemoration ceremonies held there in 1995. They were joined by a group of Japanese Veterans on a similar remembrance of peacemaking. Many of the Marines and Seabees were returning to the island for the first time in over fifty years to revisit the past and reflect on how their war experiences affected them over the years.

After receiving his discharge Jay returned to Glenwood Springs for another two week visit with family and friends. He then returned to Muskegon, Michigan where he found a job working for Borg-Warner-Norge Division building refrigerators and aircraft parts. In 1953 Jay and Ann left Muskegon and moved to Clifton. He found a job working for the Atomic Energy Commission Radio Metric Laboratory located in Grand Junction,

Colorado. He remained in this position until 1957 when he accepted a position with the Climax Uranium Mill in Grand Junction. He held this position for the next thirteen years before he went to work for School District fifty-one in Grand Junction where he remained for eighteen years before retiring.

Jay and Ann had five children, three boys and two girls. They adopted their sixth child, another girl, to even out the family at three boys and three girls. After forty-nine years of marriage Ann passed away with cancer. Jay was devastated at the loss of his beloved Ann, but he managed to adjust to his loss and went on with his life. Jay said, "Sometimes I really get lonely but after Iwo Jima I think I can survive almost anything." Jay developed an interest in photography and spends a lot of time roaming around his beloved Colorado Mountains. Jay passed away in a nursing home n Grand Junction, Colorado in 2005. In my mind's eye, Jay was a special and unique individual who defended his country with honor. He is truly one of my special heroes. "NO, YOU CAN'T JUDGE A BOOK BY ITS COVER."

GOD SAVE THE FLAG

Oliver Wendell Holmes

Washed in the blood of the brave and the blooming,
Snatched from the altars of insolent foes,
Burning with star-fires, but never consuming,
Flash its broad ribbons of lily and rose.

Vainly the prophets of Baal would rend it,
Vainly his worshippers pray for its fall;
Thousands have died for it, millions defend it,
Emblem of justice and mercy to all.

Justice that reddens the sky with her terrors,
Mercy that comes with her white-handed train,
Soothing all passions, redeeming all errors,
Sheathing the saber and breaking the chain.

Borne on the deluge of old usurpation's,
Drifted our Ark o'er the desolate seas,
Bearing the rainbow of hope to the nations,
Torn from the storm-cloud and flung to the breeze.

God bless the Flag and its loyal defenders,
While its broad folds o'er the battle-field wave,
Till the dim star-wreath rekindle its splendor,
Washed from its stains in the blood of the brave!

Louis Columbo 1944

1990 Deceased

LOUIS COLOMBO

Battered Bastards of Bastogne

Almost sixty years have passed since I last saw my good friend, Louie Columbo. I thought about him often over the years and wondered what became of him. After I decided to write this book I began a search to locate Louie and eventually found his half-brother, John Bartlett, who lived in Denver. (John passed away shortly after I visited with him). John was several years older than Louie and did not live with Louie's mother and stepfather while Louie was growing up. Nevertheless, John was able to furnish details about Louie's life that I had missed over the years. John also gave me the phone number and address of Louie's wife, Katie, who lives in Pinehurst, Idaho. When I phoned Katie, I was sorry to learn that Louie had passed away on July 22, 1996. He had open-heart surgery in 1967 and while still in the hospital recovering from the surgery, he suffered a stroke. The stroke debilitated Louie and he lost his ability to speak. Louie was never able to work again after the stroke, but he was lovingly cared for by Katie until the day he died. I didn't stay in touch with Louie over the years and I now regret my failure to do so. All I have left of Louie are my early memories and the details about his life that John and Katie have so graciously shared with me.

Louie was born in Glenwood Springs, Colorado on October 4, 1924 and lived on his grandfather's small ranch with his mother and stepfather until the family moved to Butte, Montana. Louie was about fourteen years old at the time. Louie's father passed away when Louie was ready to enter school in Glenwood Springs. The loss of Louie's father caused many difficulties for Louie and his mother.

Louie's Grandfather had migrated to the United States from Italy before the turn of the century, but he retained some of the skills he had learned in the "old country". He was an expert at making homemade wine and enjoyed smoking cigars that were shaped in a twist. I don't know where he found those cigars but Louie and I discovered that one had to have a strong constitution to successfully smoke them. We learned this lesson one weekend when I was visiting Louie at the family's ranch. Louie's mother and grandfather had gone to town to shop, so we decided it would be the perfect opportunity to partake of the nectar of the grape. We proceeded to sample grandfather's homemade wine, which tasted very good and before we realized it, we had overindulged. Eventually we reached a point where we thought we should also enjoy a couple of grandpa's cigars. After we had consumed more wine and smoked the cigars down to a stub, Louie informed me that his grandpa always chewed the cigar stub. When the cigars stubs where about two inches long, we proceeded to indulge ourselves with what we perceived to be a "good chew". At the time, chewing on a cigar stub seemed reasonable to me but that was the last "chew" of tobacco I ever tried. Of course we washed everything down with some more of grandpa's wine, and the next two days were spent in bed where I was convinced that I was going to die. Louie was just as sick as I was, and unable to function for a couple of days. Neither one of us ever told our parents or Louie's grandpa what we had done. In retrospect, I now realize they had sorted out our subterfuge from the beginning. Louie's mother, his grandfather or my parents ever expressed the slightest concern about our near demise. To this day I cannot stand the smell of cigar smoke, but I still like to tip a glass of wine now and then. I will always remember to toast Louie with a glass of wine, but I'll never again indulge in the displeasure of smoking another cigar.

Sometimes on weekends Louie hitched an old gray horse to a buggy and drove the three miles into town to collect two or three of his pals. We usually made a few trips up and down main-street just to check out the action before returning to grandpa's ranch. We could always find interesting and fun things to do for entertainment, and all of us looked forward to visiting the ranch.

It was around 1939 or 1940 when Louie's family left Glenwood Springs and moved to Butte, Montana where they lived for two or three years before moving to Pinehurst, Idaho. Louie's stepfather worked in the mines in both Butte and Pinehurst. By then Louie was old enough to find part time employment in the mining industry while he was in high school. He learned to drive trucks and operate other types of heavy equipment, and he began an apprenticeship program as an electrician. Louie met his wife to-be, Katie, while attending high school in Pinehurst.

Louie enlisted in the US Army on December 28, 1943, and said goodbye to Katie and his family before reporting to the Army Induction Center in Spokane, Washington. After a short stay at the Induction Center, Louie was assigned to the 101st Airborne, 502nd Paratroop Division. The 101st Airborne Division was known as the "Screaming Eagles", a nickname befitting a tough group of soldiers. He was sent to Ft. Bragg, North Carolina for further training and after qualifying as a paratrooper he received his silver jump wings. His unit then sailed for England on September 12, 1944, arriving on September 23, 1944. He was stationed near Chilton and Hungerford and his unit lived in Nissen huts and tents or were assigned quarters in English homes. After seemingly unending training and numerous practice jumps in the bleak and cold English countryside, the 502nd finally received orders to prepare for combat assignments in Europe. In September of 1944, the 502nd jumped into combat at Eindhoven, Holland in support of the Allies and their plans to maintain control of the port of Antwerp, Belgium. The Allies called this plan "Operation Market Garden". There were plenty of supplies in England but the Allies needed control of Antwerp in order to land the supplies on the continent. The 101st was assigned the task of capturing and holding open a corridor so that British armor and tanks could drive north to relieve the British paratroops who had landed at Arnhem. Unfortunately the British armor and tanks failed to arrive as scheduled, causing the 101st to go it alone. Nevertheless, the 101st managed to liberate several Dutch towns and repulse numerable German counter-attacks. There were many instances of hand-to-hand combat as brutal fighting raged in the streets of Dutch towns and villages. The landing by the 101st Airborne at Eindhoven gave valuable time for British forces to complete their assault on Arnhem and by the end of November, 1944, Antwerp was still in Allied hands. The first supply ship dropped anchor in Antwerp's harbor on November 28, 1944. As a result of this engagement the 101st suffered a high casualty rate. Finally, the 101st Airborne was withdrawn from Holland at the end of November and sent to Camp Mourmelon le Grand, France for rest and refitting. Less than three weeks later, the 101st was rushed north into Belgium to counter the German Ardennes counter offensive. Their assignment was to throw a cordon around key roads leading to Bastogne, Belgium. During this engagement the 101st Division was surrounded by the German push into the Ardennes, but they refused to yield the town of Bastogne to the Germans. The German ring around Bastogne was finally penetrated and broken on December 26, 1944 by elements of Patton's 3rd Army.

Louie was seriously wounded on December 31, 1944 during the fighting at Bastogne. He was evacuated to a hospital in England where he spent two months recovering from his wounds. Louie's half-brother, John Bartlett, was also serving in Europe in 1944, and he was able to visit Louie in the hospital.

The 101st Airborne Division became know as "The Battered Bastards of Bastogne" for their brave and unrelenting courage during the Battle of the Bulge. For their heroic defense of Bastogne, the 101st Airborne Division was awarded the Distinguished Unit Citation, also known as The Presidential Unit Citation. This was the first time this citation was ever awarded to an entire Division and Louie was one of the deserving recipients. During WWII the 101st Airborne Division spent 214 days in combat and were additionally awarded two Medals of Honor, forty-two Distinguished Service Crosses, 516 Silver Stars and 6,977 Bronze Stars. They captured 29,527 enemy soldiers, but in comparison, 336 men from the 101st were taken prisoners by the Germans. The price of victory was high for the 101st Airborne Division. The Screaming Eagles lost 2,043 men killed in action against the Germans and 7,976 men were wounded in action. When the Battle of the Bulge finally ended a total of 1,193 men were listed as MIA (missing in action) for a total of 11,203 casualties.

When Louie was released from the hospital in England, he was no longer considered physically fit for combat, and was assigned to the 353-Second Ordnance in Marseilles, France. His duties there included demolition work and driving truck to deliver ammunition, small arms and heavy artillery shells to combat troops. The supplies were loaded onto trucks at the port of Marseilles, and trucked to combat areas in other locations in France and Germany. Shortly after V.E. Day (Victory in Europe), Louie began his journey home. He departed from Marseilles, France on February 26, 1946. After arriving in the United States he reported to Fort Douglas, Utah for separation. He received his discharge on March 16, 1946 and two days later he was back in Pinehurst, Idaho. After a lengthy recuperation period he found work as an electrician with American Smelting and Refining Company. Louie remained with American Smelting until the day he suffered his heart attack and stroke. He rose to the position of Supervisor of the Welders and Electricians and was a proud and loyal employee for this company.

Louie and Katie were married in September of 1946, and were blessed with three children, David, Carlette and Nanette. Louie and Katie was a loving couple, and after their marriage they were never again separated until Louie's death on July 23, 1996. Like so many WWII veterans, Louie never talked very much about his war experiences to Katie or his children. He simply kept his feelings private, not even sharing them with his son. Katie said, "We had four grandchildren and two great-grandchildren and Louie was a wonderful grandfather to all of them. Louie was always with me when he was alive and he is still with me now, in my heart and in my memories."

He was a great friend when we were young boys, and he is one of my heroes today. He was awarded many honors for his dedicated service to his country. Not only was he one of the proud recipients of The Presidential Unit Citation, he also won his Silver Wings as a paratrooper, the badge of a Sharpshooter with the M-1 rifle, the Combat Infantryman badge, the Purple Heart for the wounds he received in combat, the Victory Medal and the European Service Ribbon with three Bronze Battle Stars. What an accomplishment for a quiet young man I knew when we were boys with no cares or concerns.

All of the young men who served in the 101st Airborne lived moments in hell. Jack E. Kline said it well in his poem, "They've Done Their Hitch in Hell".

THEY'VE DONE THEIR HITCH IN HELL

Jack E. Kline

We're sitting here and thinking of the things we left behind,
We'd hate to put on paper what is going through our mind.
We've dug so many foxholes, cleared many miles of ground,
A hotter place this side of hell we're sure cannot be found.
There is a certain consolation though, so listen while we tell,
When we die we'll go to heaven,
'Cause we done our hitch in hell.

We've built up three kitchens, for Jerry bombed out two,
And there we meet three times a day to draw our daily stew.
We've dodged the red-hot shrapnel from the dirty Jerry bombs,
We've sweat and bled and hollered just to see our moms.
When our work on earth is finished, our friends behind will tell,
Those boys all went to heaven,
'Cause they done their hitch in hell.

We take our atabrine daily, those bitter little pills,
To build up our resistance to fevers, aches and chills.
"Put out those lights and cigarettes," we hear each sergeant yell,
"This ain't no Sunday picnic,
It's another hitch in hell."

When the final taps have sounded and we shed our earthly cares,
We'll pass in grand parade, we all, upon those golden stairs.
The angels there will greet us and their harps they'll gladly play,
We'll draw 100 dollars and lose it in a day.
We'll hear Gabriel blow his trumpet and St. Peter loudly yell,
"Front seats you guys from the 101st,
'Cause you've done your hitch in hell."

Leroy Comrie 1944 Deceased

LEROY COMRIE
Bikini Atoll

Leroy was one of my classmates but I had difficulty learning much about him during my research. His sister, Helen, was the only family member I was able to locate and she could furnish only limited details about Leroy's life after high school. Leroy was born on November 13, 1926 in Glenwood Springs, and his school days passed routinely from kindergarten through high school. He was an average student and studied standard subjects. Even though he was small and rather short in stature, he held his own with the bigger boys in his class. His sister, Helen, said, "He got tired of being knocked around during football practice by the big guys like Hal Terrell, Bus Abshire and Walt LaForce , but he stuck with it in spite of his size." During his senior year he developed into an aggressive and determined football player and dealt out more than he received in spite of his small stature.

Leroy played in the high school band and it has always puzzled me why the band director chose Leroy to play the tuba. His tuba was almost as big as Leroy himself but he didn't complain or seem to mind. He enjoyed playing in the band concerts and he loved to go to the band tournaments held in Grand Junction, Colorado. He was also very active in the Methodist Youth Fellowship and the Boy Scouts.

Helen remembered the time Leroy came home from a Scout meeting and his mother detected the odor of tobacco smoke as he came into the house. Needless to say, Mrs. Comrie was more than a little bit upset with him. After Mrs. Comrie got to the bottom of the matter it turned out that Leroy and two of his classmates had gotten their hands on a pack of cigarettes and decided to "light up". Rex Sidener, Leroy's future brother-in-law, and Robert

Bainbridge, the Methodist preacher's son were the other two smoking participants. According to Helen's recollection, all three of the boys, "just went along for the ride".

Helen claims that Leroy really was a lover at heart, never a fighter. She remembered the time Leroy came in the back door of their house in tears. He was about eight or nine years old at the time. When asked by his mother what the problem was, he sobbed, "Willie McDonald led me down the alley by my ear!" He received no sympathy from the family on that occasion. Willie McDonald was also in the class of '44 and has a chapter in this book.

Like the rest of the boys Leroy's age, he found odd jobs in order to earn a little money. He sold newspapers and magazines door to door and also had a paper route delivering the Denver Post. Every young person in those days had to find ways to earn extra money, as none of our parents were financially able to supply pocket money or an allowance, as many parents do today.

After graduation in 1944, Leroy enlisted in the Navy and was trained as an electrician. He served aboard navy ships in the Pacific area until the war ended. He remained in the Navy for a time after the end of the war, and was with the fleet that tested the atomic bomb on the Pacific island of Bikini.

On July 1, 1946, as peace began to ease world tensions, Bikini Atoll experienced its first Atomic Test Blast. The test was planned and carried out by the US Government and was known as "Operation Crossroads". Two separate Atomic Bombs were detonated. The first bomb, called "The Able Test", was dropped on 100 unmanned US ships moored in careful arrangement just off the coast of Bikini Island. The second blast, called, "The Baker Test", took place on July 25, 1946. It was the same kind of bomb used in "The Able Test", except this time the bomb was exploded ninety feet underwater. A massive mushroom cloud of debris from the ocean floor spewed into the air and rained down radiation on the dummy fleet. Six of these ships sank right after the "Baker" blast. This was an experiment few people today know about or remember, but it was a memorable experience for a young man from Glenwood Springs.

Just prior to the first blast, 200 Bikinians were forced to leave their homes for what they thought would be a few months. But with the first ever, underwater nuclear detonation, radioactivity rained down on the island and the other fifty-seven islets that made up the atoll. US scientists were stunned, but the damage was done. The experts didn't have a word for what was happening, so they settled on the logical "fallout" term that is now a common word in the English language. The islanders became nuclear nomads, as the United States moved them to three different atolls and islands during the next two years. They nearly starved to death on one of these islands before they were eventually resettled on Kili, a tiny, solitary island 425 miles south of Bikini. It had no reef and no lagoon, so fishing was out of the question for the new residents and they were once again faced with starvation.

Twenty-two years later the Atomic Energy Commission finally declared Bikini Atoll "safe". Some of the Bikinians headed home, but others who had seen the effects of radiation refused to return. The Bikinians who opted to "go home" were once again forced off their beloved Bikini Atoll in 1978 when it was discovered that the radioactive element cesium 137 was still present, and they ran the risk of radiation accumulating in their bodies.

While the 200 Bikinians were getting ready for their first exodus, preparations for the US nuclear testing program advanced rapidly. Leroy took part in the program involving 242 naval ships, 156 aircraft and 25,000 radiation-recording devices. The Navy also imported 5,400 rats, goats and pigs to the island for experimental purposes. More than 42,000 US military and civilian personnel were involved in the testing program at Bikini. The history of the Bikinian people from that day on has been a story of their struggle to understand scientific concepts as they relate to their islands. Since starvation became a serious problem for the Bikinians who had been moved to the island of Kili, the Trust Territory Administration donated a forty-foot ship to be used for transporting copra (dried coconut meat) between Kili and other atolls in the area. In 1951 the ship was washed onto the Kili reef by a heavy surf and sank along with a full load of copra, but little was done by the US Government to relieve the situation, and starvation continued to be a critical issue for the islanders.

Early in the morning of March 1, 1954, the Bikinians hope of returning to their beloved island of Bikini was once again dashed. The US Government again detonated an atomic device on the surface of the reef in the northwestern corner of Bikini Atoll. The area was illuminated by a huge and expanding flash of blinding light and a raging fireball of intense heat shot skyward at more than 300 miles per hour. The fiery gusts blasted the surrounding islands and stripped the foliage from the trees. Ships stationed forty miles east of Bikini monitored the test and reported massive clouds of radioactive material had been generated by the fifteen-megaton blast. Radioactivity was so high that the US Government ordered all personnel aboard the ships to vacate the area immediately.

By late 1969 the Atomic Energy Commission stated, "There's virtually no radiation left on Bikini and we can find no discernible effect on either plant or animal life." However, this conclusion was theoretical. In 1972, the AEC announced that radiological contamination was still present on Bikini Atoll. Consequently, the Bikinian Council voted not to return to Bikini. In September of 1978, Trust Territory officials arrived on Bikini and once again removed the people who had returned to the atoll. Finally, in the 1980s the people of Bikini received two trust funds from the United States government in compensation for giving up their island to the US government for nuclear testing. In the 1990s the Bikinians began a Tourism Program on Bikini. By the year 2000 most of the original islanders who had been forced from their island were gone and a new generation of Bikinians have now replaced them. Nevertheless, Bikini is, and always will be home to those displaced island people.

After discharge from the Navy, Leroy was bitten by the wanderlust-bug, and spent time at odd jobs in Arizona and California, but did not communicate with his family very much during those years. In April of 1951, he married his high school sweetheart, Barbara Duffy, and they settled in Southern California. Leroy found a job driving a delivery truck for UPS and he began to communicate with his sister, Helen, and her husband, Rex Sidener, once again. In 1955 Rex and Helen, along with their two children, moved from Alaska to California and stayed with Leroy and Barbara while Rex looked for a job. Helen assumed the job of cooking the meals and doing the cleaning while the other three worked at their jobs. Helen recalls that Leroy used to say, "No cake out of a box is fit to eat...they all taste like cardboard." But Helen and Barbara conspired and made many cakes with Betty Crocker's help and Leroy would smack his lips and say, "Now this is how a cake should taste!" Helen said that he never knew the difference or found out otherwise.

By 1960, Leroy was driving a semi-truck for Safeway and was listed on the "extra-board". This meant he could be called out for a trip at any time. That was in September and he and Barbara had just made plans to build another new home. Just as Leroy had settled down for a much-needed nap, after returning from a long trip, he was called out to make another out-of-town delivery. On his return trip home he drove off an overpass onto a railroad bed near Victorville, California and was killed instantly. There was no evidence of mechanical failure or any effort to avoid an accident so it was determined that he had gone to sleep at the wheel.

With his death and no surviving children, the Comrie name ended abruptly. As for the 200 Bikinians who were forced to leave their beautiful island of Bikini in 1946, life as they knew it also came to an end. The Bikini people have long seen the irony in the conduct of the Trust Territory agreement that allowed the bombing of their homeland and forced them into starvation on other distant atolls. Most of those 200 islanders who were relocated to other islands in 1946 have now passed on. The new generations of Bikinians have lost their culture, and their way of life has become a struggle. One can only ask why has this problem burned with such vigor in the minds of paranoid politicians and why didn't the United States live up to all of the promises they made to the Bikinians in a timely manner?

If Leroy was alive today he would most certainly share the plight of the Bikinians and work to improve their lives.

I'M ALWAYS WITH YOU

author unknown

When I am gone, release me, let me go.
I have so many things to see and do.
You mustn't tie yourself to me with tears.
Be happy that we had so many years.

I gave you my love, you can only guess
How much you gave to me in happiness.
I thank you for the love you each have shown.
But now it's time I traveled on alone.

So grieve a while for me if grieve you must.
Then let your grief be comforted by trust.
It's only for a while that we must part.
So bless the memories within your heart.

I won't be far away for life goes on.
So if you need me, call and I will come.
Though you can't see or touch me, I'll be near.
And if you listen with your heart, you'll hear
All of my love around you soft and clear.

And then, when you must come this way alone.
I'll greet you with a smile and "Welcome Home."

Lester Donegan 1944

2004 Deceased

LESTER DONEGAN

The Battle for Mindanao

Lester Donegan was born on August 11, 1926 in Glenwood Springs. He spent his childhood there living on his father's 160-acre farm at the edge of town. Lester had an interesting time growing up in Glenwood Springs. In addition to his farm chores he worked in the repair shop his father operated to service the John Deere agricultural equipment he sold to ranchers and farmers in the area. The family kept many animals on the property and it was Lester's job to feed and take care of the livestock. Lester never found the time to participate in athletics or other school activities due to his already busy schedule.

Lester was an ambitious young man and was always involved in some scheme whereby he could earn a few dollars. When not otherwise occupied at the farm or in his father's shop, Lester found jobs working on threshing crews during harvest time. A threshing machine is a large piece of self-propelled agricultural equipment that separates the grain from the stalk and chaff. He also picked tomatoes and potatoes for farmers in the area when time permitted.

In 1939 his family moved to California, leaving Lester in Glenwood Springs to look after the farm and take care of the animals. This was quite a responsibility for a boy of twelve or thirteen to undertake. Lester's grandmother was also left at the farm, so she was the only family Lester could rely upon for the next two years until his family returned to Glenwood Springs and the farm.

In 1942 Lester purchased a used tractor on credit from a local dealer. Somehow he convinced the dealer to sell him the tractor with the promise that he would make monthly payments. Such a business arrangement would be impossible today unless the person making the purchase was at least 21 years of age. Lester was sixteen years old at the time but he had no trouble keeping himself and the tractor busy. He found jobs plowing "Victory Gardens" for people throughout the area. WWII had started and many people planted vegetable gardens as a way to help the war effort and put a few extra groceries on their tables. Lester also found jobs for himself and his tractor working in the fields during harvest season, and plowing fields in the spring of the year. He proudly told me, "I never missed making one single payment on my tractor."

It wasn't all work and no play for Lester, as he did on occasion find time to have a little fun and hang around with his pals. Lester reminded me of an incident that took place when we were juniors in high school. One night Lester and I and some of our classmates were looking for something to do when someone suggested we mount a raid on Mr. Baker's apple orchard. It seemed like a great idea at the time so everyone sneaked into the orchard. Mr. Baker's son, Bob, climbed a tree to dislodge a few apples. Before he could dislodge one single apple, a shot rang out and Bob fell out of the tree. He hit the ground running, as did the rest of us. All of our effort went for nothing as we didn't manage to get away with one single apple. After we had put a considerable amount of distance between the "trigger-man" and ourselves we stopped to assess the damage. The only person who suffered any bodily harm was Bob. Whoever the "trigger-man" was had apparently loaded a shotgun shell with salt, which caused a great deal of discomfort to Bob for a couple of hours. We concluded that it would have been ironic if it had been Bob's own father who pulled the trigger.

After some discussion we decided to report this incident to my father, who was the Sheriff of Garfield County. This decision turned out to be a very poor decision on our part. All we got for our efforts was a severe lecture from my father. He even threatened to put us in jail for trying to steal Mr. Baker's apples. He told us that in his opinion we had received exactly what we deserved. That ended any further thought of trying to learn who pulled the trigger. We just conveniently and wisely forgot the entire affair and never discussed the matter amongst ourselves again. In fact, I had almost forgotten the entire episode until Lester reminded me of the "Big Apple Raid".

After graduating from High School in 1944, Lester enrolled at Mesa Junior College in Grand Junction, Colorado. He and Bob Bainbridge, also a classmate from Glenwood Springs, immediately became close friends, as they were the only two boys from Glenwood Springs registered for classes at Mesa Junior College. Bob's father was the Methodist preacher in Glenwood and he had purchased an old car for Bob so he would have a means of transportation while attending college. One night Lester and Bob decided to drive to the edge of town and help themselves to a few tomatoes from one of the local gardens. Apparently, Lester hadn't learned his lesson from the "Apple-Raid" a year earlier, as the results of their "Tomato-Raid" also had dire results. A local policeman discovered them in the act of liberating the tomatoes and their efforts to escape led to disaster. Bob's old car didn't have any brakes so they ended up crashing through the front of a country store causing a considerable amount of damage. Lester is still trying to decide if it would have been wiser for him to run around with a sheriff's son rather than a preacher's son!

One month after entering Mesa Junior College, Lester received his draft notice in October and was sent to Camp Joseph Robinson, Arkansas for basic training. After basic training, Lester reported to Fort Ord, California for amphibious training before he boarded a troop ship and sailed off across the Pacific. His ship made short stops in New Zealand, Australia and New

Guinea before landing on the island of Leyte in the Philippines. He was assigned to the 24th Division, 21st Regiment and experienced his first combat when the 24th Division made the invasion on the island of Mindanao in the Philippines in 1945. Lester was soon promoted to the rank of Sergeant and was assigned as head scout for the 21st Division Regimental Combat Team.

In the summer of 1945 Lester and his Regimental Combat Team participated in two separate invasions on the island of Mindanao. They made a significant contribution to the conquest and the capture of Mindanao and were particularly effective in defeating the Japanese holding that portion of the island lying east of the Zamboanga Peninsula. To accomplish this, the 24th Division landed along the shore of Illana Bay on the eastern coast of Mindanao before defeating the Japanese who were entrenched in an area east of the Zamboango Peninsula.

The Eighth Army was assigned the task of capturing that portion of Mindanao lying east of the Zamboanga Peninsula. The battle force was made up of troops from the 24th and 31st US Infantry Divisions. Also assigned to this task force were troops from the 162nd and 108th US Regimental Combat Teams, along with personnel from X Corps and Filipino troops from the Bugo-Del Monte Area Command.

McArthur's plan called for the 24th and 31st Infantry Divisions to land along the shores of Illana Bay on the west-central coast of eastern Mindanao. It was thought that the Illana Bay area was lightly defended by the Japanese, therefore the 24th Division would stand a good chance to achieve success in that area. A good landing area existed at Malabang on the northeastern shore of Illana Bay. It was estimated that the Japanese maintained a weak garrison at Illana Bay so Malabang was chosen as the spot for the main landing assault.

After successfully landing at Malabang, Lester and the 24th Division advanced by land and water to secure Parang and Polloc Harbor, some twenty miles from their landing area. After reaching Parang and Polloc Harbor, the 24th struck south to Cotabato and blocked the mouth of the Mindanao River, thus, securing the mouth of the river. Shortly thereafter, the 24th learned they had their work cut out for them.

Fortunately for the 24th Division, the 30th and 100th Japanese Divisions were in poor shape and hopelessly isolated. They were short of artillery shells, small arms ammunition, transportation, and their communication equipment was practically non-existent. They had some stocks of food but since the 24th Division had captured the roads leading into the Japanese held territory, food soon ran out leaving the Japanese forces destitute. Nevertheless, these Japanese troops were determined to hold out to the last man. The 30th and 100th Japanese Divisions made frantic preparations to engage the US 24th Division but they were only able to hold out for two days. From the overall theater of operation's view, the 24th Division would be involved in mopping up operations from this point on. However, tactically speaking, the 24th Division was about to experience a frontal attack by the Japanese that was as rough as any engagement the US Army had thus far experienced in their efforts to retake the Philippines. The Japanese frontal attack upon the 24th Division was their last major effort in eastern-central Mindanao. By dark of the second day of the attack the 30th and 100th Japanese Divisions were beaten units. They withdrew into the mountains and from that point on they were ineffective as a fighting unit until the end of the war. This engagement cost the 24th Division 350 men killed and 1,615 wounded. The Japanese 30th and 100th Division lost roughly 4,500 men killed and 30 captured.

Filipino-American operations to secure the Saranganti Bay region began on July 4th when scout patrols (including Lester's squad) landed in the area to assess Japanese strength. The following day the main body of the 24th Division loaded aboard Allied Naval PT boats and landed in force on the southeastern shore of the bay. By July 11th, the 24th had joined forces with the Filipino Guerrilla units and delivered M1 rifles and ammunition to the guerrillas. On July 24th the main force of the 24th Division joined up with their advance group and began their push to eliminate Japanese forces in the area. With all elements of the Saranganti Bay Task Force in place, events began to move rapidly. Within a few days the combined US forces discovered the main body of Japanese hiding out along the river valleys and in the mountains. Organized Japanese resistance collapsed on July 25th and operations entered into the mop-up and pursuit stage.

Two days before the Japanese finally surrendered to Allied Forces, Lester's luck ran out. While engaged in mop-up operations he was wounded in the hip by a Japanese shell-burst. He was evacuated to an Army Hospital on the island of Leyte in the Philippines. By the time Lester was released from the hospital his unit was already in Japan occupying an area around Okiyama. Once he was released from the hospital he hitched a ride on a US Army plane and made his way to Okiyama to join his unit. He was immediately assigned to an MP (Military Police) unit but shortly thereafter he suffered a heart attack and was sent to Osaka General Hospital in Japan. He was then transferred to a hospital ship bound for San Francisco. Upon arrival in San Francisco, Lester was admitted to Letterman General Hospital for further treatment. After his release from Letterman General Hospital, Lester was sent to Beaumont General Hospital in El Paso, Texas where he was finally discharged on the last day of May 1946.

Even though the battle to capture Mindanao was not considered to be a major engagement, it was a major disaster in terms of lives lost. The 24th Infantry Division lost 540 men killed and 1,885 wounded for a total of 2,425 casualties. The 31st Infantry Division, 108th and 162nd Regimental Combat Teams and the Bugo-Del Monte Filipino Unit lost 465 men killed, 995 wounded for a total of 1,460 casualties.

Right after Lester was discharged from the service he returned to Glenwood Springs where he spent the next year trying to decide what he wanted to do with his life. Eventually he enrolled in an Aircraft and Engine Mechanic school in Denver, and accepted a position with Monarch Air, the forerunner of Frontier Air Lines. Lester kept this job for about a year before joining Elwood Edwards Agency, the second largest Hudson automobile dealer in the US. He remained at the Elwood Edwards Agency for three years before accepting a position as Service Manager with West Colfax Dodge Agency in Denver. He remained with this company for two years before starting his own business. He owned his own auto repair shop in Denver for several years, but finally sold the business in 1994 and moved to Guffy, Colorado. Lester claims he retired after selling his business but he, like most of the rest of the men of his generation, remained as busy as ever doing whatever he can find to occupy his time. No doubt the circumstances of the times in which we grew up instilled a work ethic in us that we cannot escape. All of us from our generation still consider a man's word and a handshake to be a contract that must be honored. We will take this attitude with us right up to our final moment on earth and as we take our final breath. If I were to offer Lester any advice it would be, "Buy your apples and tomatoes at your local market". Lester is gone now by his memory lives on in my heart.

AMERICA THE BEAUTIFUL
Katharine Lee Bates

O beautiful for spacious skies,
For amber waves of grain,
For purple mountains majesties
Above the fruited plain!
America! America!
God shed His grace on thee.
And crown thy good with brotherhood
From sea to shining sea.

O beautiful for pilgrim feet,
Whose stern, impassioned stress
A thoroughfare for freedom beat
Across the wilderness!
God mend thine every flaw,
Confirm thy soul in self-control,
Thy liberty in law!

O beautiful for heroes proved
In liberating strife,
Who more than self their country loved,
And mercy more than life!
America! America!
May God thy gold refine,
Till all success be nobleness
And every grain divine!

O beautiful for patriot dream
That sees beyond the years
Thine alabaster cities gleam
Undimmed by human tears!
America! America!
God shed His grace on thee,
And crown thy good with brotherhood
From sea to shining sea!

Raymond Heisler 1944 Deceased

RAYMOND HEISLER
Extraordinary Courage

This story is neither a success story nor a story of failure. It is one of endeavor and determination seldom experienced by most people. It is an experience of pain and suffering, of defeat and humiliation, of cowardice and weakness and of hate and bitterness. It is also the story of my friend and classmate, Raymond Heisler, a severely handicapped person.

Raymond was born in Glenwood Springs, in 1924 into an average American family. His life would not have been different from any other had it not been for an accident involving his parent's car before he was born. The steering wheel had come loose from the steering column causing the car to plunge over the bank and into the Colorado River. Raymond's Mother, who was eight months pregnant with him at the time, escaped from the car and floated down the river. She sustained many broken bones in her arms, legs and ribs as well as other injuries. Raymond's father was badly hurt too, but somehow he managed to get Raymond's mother out of the river. As a result of the accident Raymond was a completely paralyzed child at birth. Only his eyes would move.

Science is seldom able to determine the specific cause of injuries or how to cure them. Whatever the cause, Raymond knew even at age three he could not speak or move. His mother resolved to take him all over the United States to find help, but the doctors told her Raymond would be paralyzed for the rest of his life and it would be best for all concerned to let him die, an option she never considered.

Raymond's childhood was a period of great struggles and much difficulty. His mother pulled him in a wagon to public school. He was the only handicapped student there. He had good teachers who were willing to help his mother and for this she was eternally grateful. Raymond couldn't remain in school all day so he went home at noon where he was confined to his bed for the rest of the day. In spite of his physical handicap and poor health, Raymond managed to graduate from high school in the upper thirty percent of his class.

His Mother and Father worked with him for many hours each day until he was about twelve years of age. That was when he began to move his arms and took his first step. What a joyful day for his mother and father, as well as for himself! There were still more struggles ahead for Raymond, especially in trying to learn to speak and communicate. Walking was still a hardship, but most of the time he was free to chatter and mouth words to his hearts content when at home. In fact, Raymond's father thought him to be a chatterbox, but desperately wanted Raymond to grow into a normal child, but this was not to be.

The transition from elementary school to secondary school, and the growth from adolescence into puberty brought more changes to Raymond's life. A marked tendency toward more frequent problems, as he tried desperately to make people understand him, was almost overwhelming. He encountered situations he found very difficult to respond to, especially in classroom recitation and Boy Scout activities. Every situation that demanded the use of speech was embarrassing for him, so he adopted a general policy of avoiding speaking altogether, a well-known line of least resistance that he made his priority for several years.

Although Raymond took small non-speaking parts in high school plays and participated in small group discussions and in curricular or extracurricular activities, he had to write everything he wanted to say on a piece of paper. His affliction left him in a hellish dilemma as the harder he tried to talk the less likely he was able to talk. Such efforts only increased his muscular tension, making him physically and psychologically unable to utter the words to form an intelligent sentence. Perhaps this was the reason Raymond turned to manual arts. He loved working with wood and creating all sorts of art projects. He was very skillful at manual arts, which later became his salvation in life.

All throughout Raymond's life he developed many acquaintances, but they were not the close associations he desired. However, there were some exceptions, as he did form a few close relationships with some of his classmates.

As far back as grade school I had an overwhelming feeling of compassion for Raymond. He needed an extended hand of friendship and not pity. Perhaps that was the first time I began to accept the role as his mentor, which lasted right up to the day he died on March 18, 2000.

Unfortunately, there were those who seemed to delight in teasing Raymond and making fun of his handicap. Such cruel and thoughtless activities caused a great deal of distress for him and often brought him to tears. I detested those who teased Raymond, as I considered it to be a form of abuse. Most of Raymond's classmates did not engage in such perverse activities, but there were always those few bullies who did. Raymond did his best to deal with these situations, but up to the day he passed away he had to contend with the few ignorant individuals who delighted in making his life even more difficult than it already was.

When Raymond and I were sophomores in high school one of the school bullies was teasing Raymond one day so I decided to intercede. At the time I weighed about 140 pounds and the bully, an upper-classman, weighed around 200 pounds. I took it upon myself to suggest to the bully he should try teasing someone who could defend himself. The bully took this as a challenge and asked me if I thought I could defend myself against him. I told him I could at least give him a better run-for-his-money than Raymond could. We then made arrangements to meet after school to settle the matter. The fight lasted about thirty-five minutes, and according to my "Second", I was down seventeen times but I refused to give in. Finally, the bully asked me if I had had enough. I told him that he might be able to get the best of me physically, but that mentally he would never win the fight. Fortunately for me, the bully said, "Ok, that does it, I quit." With that he put his arm around my shoulder and helped me go home since both of my eyes were almost completely closed by then. That was the last time the bully ever teased Raymond. He either realized how disgusting he must have appeared to his classmates or he wasn't keen about having to expend all his energy dealing with me again. After that, the other school bullies left Raymond alone. Thereafter, the bully I had fought became a staunch friend to both Raymond and me. I never again found it necessary to engage in another fight in defense of Raymond, and the best part of the entire affair was, the bully and I formed a life-long-friendship. I hesitate to mention his name because of the respect I now have for this man and his wife. In fact, this individual eventually became a very successful businessman and a truly sophisticated gentleman. He and I, along with our wives, enjoyed many years of friendship and traveled together to many exciting and interesting places throughout the world.

During our high school days many of the boys turned out for football as well as for other sports. The first day of football practice during our junior year of high school Raymond appeared on the practice field all decked out in a football uniform. I have never forgotten the beautiful smile on his face or how proud he was to be a member of our team. All of Raymond's teammates immediately realized it would be necessary to avoid any physical contact with Raymond as his body was so frail and his balance left a lot to be desired. About one week after practice had started Raymond walked off the field and disappeared into the locker-room. Upon investigating, we discovered Raymond sitting alone in the corner of the locker-room in tears. He had realized that his teammates were avoiding contact with him. He had so desperately wanted to be just like the rest of us. The coach resolved this matter by appointing Raymond Football Manager. The team then voted to award Raymond his "G" letter and thereafter he proudly wore his letter-sweater almost constantly. I think I was just as proud of Raymond as he was of himself. This was a great accomplishment for Raymond when one considers the severe difficulties he faced every single day of his life.

Raymond was exceptionally skillful at Manual Arts. Whenever our teacher, Mr. Latson, assigned us a project we all managed to complete our assignments. If the assignment was constructing a waste-paper basket or building a birdhouse, Raymond's work stood so far above the rest it could not be compared. He always won first place at the fairs, but it was a complete mystery to me how he could manage such beautiful woodwork given his handicap and the difficulty he had coordinating his hands and body movements. Not one single person in our class ever approached the skill-level Raymond managed to display.

There seemed to be an intangible, insurmountable barrier that existed between Raymond and the world, a gap that could have been bridged if only he had had the capacity of speech. During meals he found it impossible to communicate a single spontaneous remark, so he frequently ate dinner in silence. He managed to talk better in the presence of "Mother's love" than he did with friends. Raymond found it uncomfortable having to meet people in social situations, but he knew it was something he would have to overcome. He realized that if he ever gained control over his speech and body movements he would have to learn to meet people, and not flee from them.

One month after Raymond graduated from high school he visited the local employment office in hopes of finding work, but without success. He tried to get into all branches of the armed forces, but they turned him down. Raymond displayed his worst attempt at speaking when applying for a job. Nevertheless, he was eventually hired by DuPont Company, and was employed in their plant in Hanford/Pasco, Washington. The position was connected to a secret project, the development of the atom bomb.

Raymond left home for Washington the day after his brother, Calvin, departed for the Naval Air Cadet Training Program. He didn't know a soul in Washington but while involved in this project he improved his speech and body movements. During this period Raymond made a vow that if he ever gained the capacity of speech he was going to do something to help others who were afflicted with a handicap. After two years of employment, the company released him in order that he could continue his education. He then went to Wichita University and the Institute of Logepedics, a speech clinic in Kansas. His wonderful teacher made every effort to help him master the art of speaking. His progress was painfully slow but he did experience some improvement. It was the first time he ever talked on the telephone.

Raymond faced his experiences and his handicap straight on, and he learned some valuable lessons as a result. He learned that life is rough, cold, and hard, and that society has no place for the weakling, that it tends to hurl to the ground and grind to dust. He learned that people have to fight for everything they want in life if they expect to overcome physical handicaps and win academic success. He learned how difficult it was to overcome economic hardship and develop intellectually in society. In short, for everything worthwhile, Raymond found that the business and economic world has no time to wait for the speech defective and physically impaired.

He discovered that, in general, people are selfish and often give the handicapped little consolation. Consequently, he learned he had to find his strength in God if he ever hoped to succeed in his test of life.

Raymond was all too familiar with the meaning of humiliation, fear, and the dread of being handicapped. He knew what it was like to be half a man and not to be able to carry out normal activities. He knew what it was to hate privilege, snobbery, bigotry, selfishness, cruelty, and intolerance. Raymond felt a deep bond of allegiance between himself and all who suffered.

He also learned that all individuals have something of value in them if only they would search for these values, and that a sincere, genuine quality is the basis for a satisfactory human relationship. He learned not only to appreciate the aesthetics in life, but also those that are ugly, because they are important as well. He learned that self-criticism is the most stinging of all criticisms, and the only true achievement for him was in the realization of God's ideals and teachings. He learned to put his faith in God and his confidence in his fellow man.

During Raymond's years at Wichita University he worked his way through school as a carpenter's helper. He received a scholarship from the Elks Club for improving himself in all realms of his handicaps. This was a wonderful gift and Raymond never forgot to give praise to God and thanks to the Elks Club for their generosity. He left the University because his instructors felt his handicaps would preclude him from becoming a doctor, which he so desperately wanted to be. A dream he could never realize!

Raymond then enrolled in Pasadena College in California and started preparing himself to become a missionary. But they too, didn't have the faith to believe he could achieve his goal, so he left there as well. Undaunted, he then went to New Tribes Missionary Boot Camp for several years to learn how to live by faith for his needs and how to live in the jungle and desert as if he were in a real mission environment.

The next stop, in his search for self, was at the American Soul Clinic where he continued his education. After two years, he was told he could go to Africa. Raymond raised his fare and support by hitchhiking all over the United States giving sermons, primarily through the use of a blackboard, with limited speaking. He hitchhiked the equivalent distance of traveling around the world three times while raising his financial support. He had many experiences during this phase of his life, and was twice a guest on national ABC television to give his testimony to God. This was a very taxing and difficult time for him, due to his ill health, frail body, and the difficulty he had communicating through the spoken word.

Eventually, he sailed to Africa on the ship, Christopher Columbus. When he reached Africa, he was met by a group of missionaries with whom he worked in Africa, Spain, Italy, and Egypt. This experience lasted for five years before he contracted malaria. He didn't want to return to the United States so he begged to stay in Africa. His heart was in Africa working with the Arabic and French speaking people, but he was too sick to continue. He was flown home and after a few months back in the United States Raymond said, "God healed me of malaria and it never returned."

Raymond still wanted to go back and work for the United World Mission so he prepared himself by learning the skills needed to help construct buildings and hospitals. Unfortunately he was unable to go, even though his clothes, equipment, records and tools had already been sent to South Africa. He wired the staff there and instructed them to go ahead and use his belongings that represented most of his worldly possessions. He eventually overcame the keen disappointment he felt by not being able to return to Africa.

All that Raymond accomplished, even though little in his opinion, could have been much more if people had only given him more of a chance. Even today most people do not try to understand, and shy away from forming a friendship with a physically challenged person. They are afraid to get to know them and accept them as equals. God gave Raymond many talents he tried to use, but people in general seemed to look upon him as unintelligent or unbalanced. It was very hard for him to prove he could do things, perhaps even better than an unchallenged person, because of the patience he had learned. Raymond had knowledge of electrical work, carpentry, plumbing, weaving, crocheting, sewing and gardening. Through God's mercy, the love of his parents, friends, classmates and associates, Raymond learned to be a survivor.

Eventually Raymond settled in Lancaster, California where he resided for many years. My wife, Leta, and I visited Raymond several times while he was living there in a small house on the outskirts of town. The house was so full of items he had collected over the years it was difficult to move around from room to room. His income consisted of a meager monthly Social Security check, which he supplemented by mowing lawns and doing yard work. A local church group adopted Raymond and, upon occasion, some of the ladies of the church group would visit Raymond, bring him food and look after some of his most pressing needs. He owned an old van and a power mower and a few garden tools, but this work was quite difficult for him and he often lost his balance and fell, yet he persisted.

His mowing business was a success as he had contracted to take care of several yards and gardens in the area. He operated Heisler Gardening Service from 1965 until shortly before he passed away in March of 2000.

His gardening work was featured in Better Homes and Gardens magazine, and he received many top honors for his flower garden. Thus, he managed to sustain himself with his limited income, since he was too proud to ask for help.

Every five years the Garfield County High School graduates from the classes of 1939 through 1945 held a reunion in Glenwood Springs. Raymond desperately desired to join his classmates at one of these reunions but he didn't have the funds available to participate. I decided to remedy this situation, so I sent him an airline ticket and made a hotel reservation for him. Knowing that Raymond possessed a great sense of humor, I decided that this would be the perfect opportunity to tickle his funny bone and provide him with a good laugh. I wrote him a letter that I mailed to him along with the airline tickets. The letter included instructions regarding his itinerary. I called his attention to the fact that he had a 45 minute lay-over in Las Vegas and that he should use this time to avail himself of some of the charms being offered by a few of the ladies who resided in Las Vegas. I also pointed out that should he fail to accomplish this goal on his way to the reunion, he would notice that he had a two-hour layover in Las Vegas on his return trip. I even went so far as to jokingly suggest to Raymond that it usually took me only 15 minutes to accomplish this feat whenever I had a layover in Las Vegas. I told him that this is what "lay-over" meant. Where I made my mistake was in failing to consider Raymond would misplace my letter and the tickets among the items he had stacked in his house. Since he belonged to the church group in Lancaster, he contacted them, and they sent a delegation of six women to search his house for the tickets. Of course, they found the tickets along with my letter, which they read. The phone rang that very evening and when my wife, Leta, answered she was immediately put upon the defensive by the woman on the other end of the line. The caller

121

wanted to know in no uncertain terms just what kind of a reunion it was that Raymond was going to attend. Of course Leta didn't know about the letter, but she realized that I had no doubt put my foot in my mouth, so she told the lady on the phone she should speak with the person who wrote the letter. It took me about ten minutes to explain the letter and another ten minutes of intense begging, but eventually the lady relented and agreed to help Raymond get to the airport. It turned out that I had more difficulty dealing with my wife than I had in dealing with the lady on the phone.

Raymond arrived in Grand Junction, Colorado, some eighty-five miles from Glenwood Springs, on schedule. Louis Pappas, a member of the class of 1942, and I met his flight and when Raymond deplaned we were both shocked at his appearance. His clothes were ill-fitting and shabby and he was desperately in need of a haircut. After collecting his luggage we loaded him into the car and headed for Glenwood Springs. Upon arrival we checked him into the hotel and took him to the barbershop where we got him a nice haircut. Our next stop was at a clothing store where we bought him a new suit, shirt, tie, shoes, etc. Once we got him all dressed up, he really looked dignified, and immediately he became the "Prince-of-the-ball" with all of his classmates, as well as the entire hotel staff. He was treated with dignity and respect, and it became obvious that many of his classmates had harbored a guilty conscience over the years for some incident that had involved Raymond when they were young.

I'll never forget the tears that came to Dorothy Green Bale's eyes when she told me, "I once threw a snowball at Ray that struck him in the face and made him cry." She went on to say, "Now, I have the chance to make this up to Raymond", and she certainly did do just that, as did many of the others who attended the reunion. Raymond later told me that he had never before experienced so much love from so many people in his entire life. This brought tears to my eyes as my heart went out to Raymond. I just nodded my head and tried to swallow the burning lump in my throat.

Raymond had a great deal of difficulty swallowing his food so he was embarrassed to find himself in situations where he had to eat in front of people. He soon realized that all of his classmates understood his situation so he relaxed and enjoyed himself to the fullest.

It was a sad and tearful occasion when the time came for everyone to return to their respective homes and to say goodbye to Raymond. Everyone found it difficult and painfully moving to say "ALOHA" to Raymond. We realized it would no doubt be the last time most of us would see him again. I have used the word "ALOHA" because it has a multitude of meanings. It means hello, goodbye, I love you, and come again.

Needless to say, Raymond didn't follow my instructions during his two-hour layover in Las Vegas on his return flight to Lancaster. But, I'm certain a smile crossed his face when he thought about my advice. Shortly after Raymond arrived back in Lancaster, I received a letter from him to thank all of his classmates for the expressions of love he received during the reunion. He also informed me that someone had stolen his lawn mower and yard tools during his absence. The loss of the income Raymond derived from his lawn-mowing jobs financially devastated him and forced him to apply for County Aid. Raymond ended his letter to me with the words, "I love you."

Shortly after Raymond completed the necessary documents and had submitted them to the proper county authorities I received a phone call from a woman who represented the County Agency that was responsible for approving financial aid. She asked me if Raymond was really handicapped and if I thought he deserved assistance. I had a difficult time controlling my temper, but kept it under control as I explained Raymond's life-long struggle. I told her that if there was ever a person who deserved help it was most certainly Raymond. I explained to her that he was too proud to accept a "hand-out" or "charity" but the time had come when he really needed help. I told her if she had taken the time to visit Raymond personally we would not now be having this conversation.

The very first Christmas after the reunion in September, Louie Pappas and his wife, Sheila, along with Louie's sister, Helen, invited Raymond to spend Christmas with their family in Henderson, Nevada. Helen had been a classmate of Raymond's at Glenwood High School. Louie sent Raymond an airline ticket (without any instructions regarding his itinerary), and he arrived on schedule to join the Pappas family for a gala Christmas celebration. I later received a letter from Louie that expounded on Raymond's visit. The following words are those Louie shared with me:

"After the class reunion in 1990 at which time Ray Heisler was the special guest, my wife, Sheila, and I decided without hesitation to invite Ray to spend Christmas with us in Henderson, Nevada. We phoned him in October of 1990 and asked him if he would do us the honor of spending Christmas with us. He started to cry and between sobs he let us know that he would be very, very happy to accept our invitation. We purchased the airline ticket and sent it to him the following day. On the day of his arrival we picked him up at the Las Vegas airport and we couldn't believe the smile on his face when he arrived. Ray then started to cry again as we ran to greet him. He told us that this was one of the happiest days of his life. Over and over he thanked us for inviting him to spend the holidays with our family and for giving him the opportunity to be a part of our family. We, in turn, thanked Raymond for honoring us at this auspicious occasion.

"During dinner on Christmas day we knew that Ray had a problem with the way he ate, but he bowed his head, folded his hands and said, "Please forgive my manners". Christmas day was really fun and joyous. For

Christmas, Ray gave Sheila and Helen a set of chimes he had made. The chimes had doves on the top of them and to this day those chimes still hang in our home as well as in my sister's home.

"Ray had a lot of fun on Christmas Day playing out on the lawn, laughing and waving to the vehicles that came by. He also enjoyed playing with our dogs. Ray was overcome once again with tears when our grandson, Daniel Medrano, his mother and father, Rudy and Samantha, gave Raymond an album that contained pictures of the 1990 reunion. He said he would always remember this Christmas as we put him on the plane on December 26th for his return to Lancaster, California. Just before boarding the plane Raymond turned around, gave us a big smile, threw us a kiss and waved goodbye. That was the last time we ever saw Raymond, but that moment will always live in our hearts. We think of him every time we hear the chimes ring or hear the soft coo of a dove. Raymond will always be in our hearts. May his soul ever rest in peace. Lou, Sheila and Helen."

Raymond is gone now, but some of his family members brought him home and he is buried in the local cemetery in Glenwood Springs. My wife, Leta, and I, along with some of Raymond's other classmates, were there to pay our respects and to say ALOHA to Raymond as he was laid to rest. His old bully tormentor, and good friend of mine, has also passed away. I like to think this bully of years ago is once again with Raymond because I know in my heart that Raymond will be with a loving classmate and a first-class friend who will continue to protect him and give him all of the love and respect he has so painfully earned.

In retrospect, I sometimes think that Raymond was my mentor rather than the other way around, because what I learned from him has been an important part of my life. Even though Raymond could not talk he could speak volumes with his eyes and his actions. The suffering he experienced throughout his life instilled a humility in me that will be a part of me for the rest of my life. Raymond was gifted with qualities that most of us lack and I am proud to say that he was a special, affectionate and benevolent friend and he loved completely without expectations of receiving riches in return. I, for one, would be pleased to experience my relationship with him all over again, because such friendships bring a joy that only comes around once in a lifetime.

"Raymond, old friend, I love you also!" Hal Terrell

EVICTUS

William Ernest Henley

Out of the night that covers me,
Black as the Pit from pole to pole,
I thank whatever Gods may be
For my unconquerable soul.

In the full clutch of circumstance
I have not winced nor cried aloud.
Under the bludgeonings of chance
My head is bloody, but unbowed.

Beyond this place of wrath and tears
Looms but the horror of the shade,
And yet the menace of the years
Finds, and shall find me, unafraid.

It matters not how strait the gate,
How charged with punishments the scroll,
I am the master of my fate,
I am the captain of my soul.

Wendell Hutchinson 1944

2001

WENDELL HUTCHISON

Sinbad the Sailor

Wendell arrived in Glenwood Springs in November of 1942 and left in May of 1943. In a way he was the equivalent of a weekend guest in town, but it was not unusual for him to have lived in only one place for such a short time. During his first sixteen years he lived in eleven different houses, eight different towns, four different states, and attended eight different schools, so his brief stay in Glenwood Springs was more like the norm.

His first glimpse of the beautiful town of Glenwood Springs was in August of 1942. His father and uncle took him to Glenwood Springs when they closed a deal to purchase the local flourmill just outside of town. Wendell's father had been involved in many get-rich-quick schemes but this time he was sure there would be a major food shortage in the country after the war ended. Therefore he concluded he would have a corner on the flour market.

Just prior to moving to Glenwood Springs, Wendell and his family lived in South Pasadena, California. During the summer months his parents operated a Dude Ranch located on the White River near Meeker, Colorado. Thus Wendell had spent many enjoyable summer months in Colorado before moving to Glenwood Springs.

With no regard for his schooling or school term his family sold the house in South Pasadena, packed their belongings, and moved to Glenwood Springs so his father could take charge of the flour milling operation. Wendell was fascinated with the milling process and soon learned how all of the machinery worked. The mill was located directly on the Roaring Fork River and the machinery was hydraulically driven by a large diameter paddle wheel. River water was delivered through a ditch that originated many yards upstream. This primary source of power drove the many conveyors, grinders, shakers and sieves. The mill generated its own power for lights and supplied electricity to drive the electric motors and mechanical vibrators. The grain was delivered in 110-pound gunnysacks that produced ninety-eight pounds of flour. The grain was dumped onto a conveyor located in the basement and from there conveyed to a silo. From the silo the grain started its journey by gravity through a crusher, screens, sifters, then to the roller mills. One could usually tell where the Miller was because every time he passed a metal duct he would tap it to make sure no flour was hanging up in the duct. The entire design was nineteenth century in a modern 1940 environment. Wendell believes the flourmill could have been a success but certainly no bonanza, as his father believed. No doubt Wendell's interest in the mill machinery was one of the reasons he eventually obtained a degree in engineering.

Eventually Wendell's father sold the mill, packed up the family belongings and moved back to California. Since the food shortage never developed, Wendell's father once again started looking for another way to get-rich-quick. Many years after Wendell's father sold the mill, it was discovered the mill had exclusive water rights. Wendell's father didn't recognize the value or the subsequent importance of owning these water rights. Eventually the water rights became far more valuable than the flourmill itself.

Unfortunately for Wendell, his stay in Glenwood only lasted until May of 1943 when he was on the move again. Wendell said this was the first time he regretted having to leave a town. He fell in love with Glenwood Springs immediately after his first glimpse of his new surroundings. Wendell was about twelve weeks behind his classmates scholastically when he entered

130

school in Glenwood Springs. However, he was impressed with his teachers and soon caught up with the rest of his classmates. Wendell's chemistry, English and history teachers were especially helpful to him. He applied himself in school and soon became an excellent student. He tried out for the basketball team and, even though he claimed he couldn't get the ball to go through the hoop, he made the varsity traveling team.

Wendell is quick to point out he found his fellow classmates most congenial and soon made many friends and was readily accepted into the class social life. "It was like I belonged, or had lived in Glenwood Springs all my life," Wendell said. He became a bona fide classmate and joined his many friends for ice-skating, sleigh riding, skiing, and party functions. "Living in Glenwood Springs was a wonderful experience for me", Wendell said. He still values the memories of those days when he lived there.

Wendell recalled when the local American Legion sponsored a shooting gallery in the basement of the Legion Hall. The Legionnaires wanted to prepare the young men for war, so they encouraged them to join the group and learn the art of firing a pistol and a rifle. They taught us to fire from a standing position, a kneeling position and a prone position. Those who qualified were given a certificate of accomplishment issued by the National Rifle Association.

Wendell was fascinated with guns and enjoyed shooting tin cans with his twenty-two caliber rifle. One day he and his good pal, Bus Abshire, decided to go hunting. They took along Wendell's twenty-two caliber rifle as well as his father's 45-90 rifle. The 45-90 rifle is not what you would call a target rifle, but more suited for shooting buffalo or elephants. At first, the only game they saw was a mama grouse and her cute little chicks. They didn't bother the grouse because they were looking for more interesting game. Without considering the consequences, Wendell raised the twenty-two

131

caliber rifle and with one lucky shot he became an experienced hunter or a felon as he had just brought down his first deer. Fortunately, they both lost interest in firing the 45-90-rifle but rather concentrated on taking turns carrying the deer. They carried the deer to a farmer's barn and obtained permission to dress the deer in the barn. They gave the farmer some of the meat and decided to take the rest of the venison home. Bus Abshire was afraid to take his share home for fear he would get into trouble for hunting out of season, so they stored his share in the pump house at the flourmill. A couple of days later Bus finally got up the nerve to take his share of the meat home.

Because of rationing, meat was in short supply. When meat was available you had to have a ration coupon to present to the butcher before you were allowed to buy the meat. Occasionally one could find a rancher who had recently slaughtered a steer and if you were lucky, he might sell you some of the meat. There was a bulletin board at the local locker plant where one could offer to trade an item for a few cuts of meat or vegetables. With such a barter system everyone managed to eat quite well in spite of rationing.

There was a manpower shortage because so many of the young men had already joined the service. Consequently, one could get excused from school for a few days if they would agree to fill some of the labor requirements. In the spring of 1943 Wendell found a job cleaning an irrigation ditch for a local farmer. This project required more than just a weekend to complete, so Wendell and a couple of his friends got excused from school for an entire week. They had to furnish their own shovels and find their own ride to the farmer's property. This job was hard work as all the weeds, silt and debris that had accumulated in the ditch the previous season had to be removed. Nevertheless, Wendell concluded that it was a welcome reprieve from school and a little pocket money (fifty cents an hour) was a welcome necessity.

Wendell's pal, Bus Abshire, was a fairly aggressive type who wouldn't hesitate to instigate something out of the ordinary. He had discovered a way to sneak into the Hot Springs Swimming Pool at night. It cost fifteen cents to gain admission, but since few boys seldom had fifteen cents to spend, Abshire's "under-the-fence" method served quite well. Wendell recalled it was snowing the first time he went under the fence, but he thought it was wonderful to be able to swim in the natural hot water pool in the winter and not get caught. It is interesting to note that the cost of admission to the pool today is $7.50.

Glenwood Springs featured a very nice golf course, but none of the boys could afford the green fees. Wendell and a couple of other enterprising young men took it upon themselves to build their own private golf course. They laid out the course in the local cemetery between the headstones. They buried tin cans for the green cups and designated certain areas as tee-boxes. The entire course was played with one club that served as driver, iron and putter. No doubt the divots rattled a few bones, but those of us who played the "Marble Orchard" golf course thought it was like having our own private County Club. We had to learn how to duck golf balls as they ricocheted off of headstones, but this was good practice for what was to come later after we had joined the service.

One day Wendell, Bus Abshire, Stanley Rogers and Warren Gardner decided to go to Grand Junction, Colorado to check out the girls. Grand Junction is ninety miles west of Glenwood Springs, and since it was a larger town, these enterprising young men concluded that there were more girls living there than in Glenwood Springs. The boys advised Mrs. Abshire of their plans and her reply was, "You have no business in Grand Junction", so that was it...no further discussion was necessary, as Mrs. Abshire was more aggressive than her son, Bus. Wendell said he could have told his folks he was going to Alaska and they might have reminded him to be home by 6:30 PM as that was when they ate their evening meal. Incidentally, Wendell admitted going to Grand Junction anyway, in spite of Mrs. Abshire's admonishment. However, Wendell did not say if they were successful in their search for girls.

Wendell's mother wanted him to go to college and study engineering. She continuously reminded him that he should get an education and not follow in his father's footsteps. Toward the end of his junior year of high school he applied to Colorado University for the fall term. To his amazement, he found they would accept him without a high school diploma. Since he would be eighteen before graduating from high school, he realized he would be drafted into the service and end up in the infantry. He believed if he had a year of college under his belt the opportunity for further education in one of the branches of the military might be possible. Since Colorado University had agreed to accept him, he reasoned the University of California would accept him as well.

Wendell felt far removed from the war while living in Glenwood Springs, but this was not the case once he moved back to Pasadena where he hoped to further his education. Rumors that Japanese submarines were surfacing and firing on oil refineries near Santa Barbara were rampant. Several of Wendell's Japanese American friends and their families were relocated to internment camps inland, as a direct result of such rumors. A number of the local Japanese Americans who were truck garden farmers had their homes and property confiscated by the United States Government. Wendell happened by the Santa Anita racetrack, which was used as a collection center, and witnessed many of his Japanese friends being loaded into trucks for transportation to inland internment camps. There was a steady stream of new arrivals all day long. These innocent neighbors were being guarded by US soldiers with guns.

Rationing throughout the United States was a way of life during the war. Certain food items were rationed, such as meat and sugar. Tires and gasoline were also strictly rationed and one had to have a ration stamp to purchase any of these items. California had installed air raid sirens up and down the west coast and Block Wardens were recruited to patrol specific areas in order to insure no lights were visible from homes in these areas.

Wendell's father found a job working in a shipyard and his oldest sister worked at the Lockheed Vega Aircraft plant. Getting to and from their respective jobs used the family's entire gasoline ration, so there was little thought of enjoying a Sunday drive in the country.

Wendell was less concerned with the war and more concerned with getting an education, but the University of California would not accept him without a high school diploma. He solved this problem by attending a private school where he took several courses, and even received a credit in gym for walking to school every day. He received his high school diploma in August of 1943 and immediately started classes at the University of California that fall. While he was enrolled at the University of California, Sam Chappel, an ex-classmate from Glenwood Springs, visited him. Sam was taking basic training in San Mateo, about twenty minutes from Berkeley. Sam was in the Merchant Marine Cadet Corps and he thought it was great. Wendell became intrigued with this program as well. The idea of attending three months of basic training in San Mateo, California, six months sea duty, then a year at the Merchant Marine Academy in Great Neck, New York appealed to him. His objective was to obtain a license to operate and navigate a ship. Consequently, Wendell enlisted in their engineering program and received an unlimited license to operate any size ship, steam or diesel, and he also obtained a commission as an ensign in the US Naval Reserve through a special program offered by the US Navy. Wendell is still very proud that he became an officer in the US Navy Reserve.

During his sea duty he was assigned to a 10,000-ton tanker that transported high-octane gasoline to various war zones. Once the tanker was loaded with aviation fuel it headed for the island of Saipan, where they unloaded several thousand gallons of fuel. As his ship was leaving Saipan, the Japanese mounted a bombing raid on Christmas Day, 1944. On New Years Day of 1945, Wendell watched another Japanese raid on the Island of Guam from the deck of his ship. They held their fire for fear they would draw attention since they were carrying a flammable cargo of aviation fuels. His ship made calls to Hawaii, Saipan, Guam, Majuro, Enewetok, New Guinea and then through the Panama Canal to Aruba and Curacoa. His ship then returned to Panama where he was taken off the ship and flown to Key West, Florida, en route to the Merchant Marine Academy in New York for additional training.

By the time Wendell had completed his second tour of duty at the Merchant Marine Academy the war had ended. He then opted to go to sea once again, and spent the next year sailing all over the world. He made several trips up and down the west coast before shipping to Hawaii, Japan, Saudi Arabia and through the Suez Canal to Naples, Italy. From Italy his ship sailed into the Persian Gulf to Iran, then all the way to Sydney, Australia before docking in Wellington and Auckland, New Zealand.

During the war Wendell saw a lot of devastation, hitched a ride on a B-17 bomber when it bombed one of the Japanese held islands, and bummed a ride on another flight that participated in a skip-bombing mission. He thought visiting New York was quite exciting. He enjoyed several week-end passes in New York, swam at Jones Beach, played at Coney Island, went to the top of the Empire State Building, saw Grant's Tomb, marveled at some of New York's museums and attended several plays and musicals. He also heard Frank Sinatra perform on stage at the Orpheum. He even marched down 5th Avenue in the Armistice Day Parade on November 11, 1945. Last but not least, he managed to find time to spend a few weekend passes at a girl's College in Massachusetts. I can only speculate about the activities he organized during these visits.

This was quite an experience for an nineteen year-old young man. He saw a lot of ocean, but only spent a day or two in each port. He read a lot of books while at sea and completed an Integral Calculus course as a way to pass time. Wendell said, "I had many regrets that I didn't get to finish high school in Glenwood Springs at Garfield County High School. I can't say my wartime experience was a hardship case. It was an enriching experience which helped make me more worldly, enhanced my education, and prepared me for later responsibilities in life."

Following his year of sailing around the world, Wendell returned to California to find that all of the love letters he had written to Suzanne Saxby had been taken seriously and they immediately became soul-mates. He attended one summer session at Berkeley only to find he and Suzanne had serious intentions so Wendell was hooked. He was also broke, and out of work, so the only answer was for him to go back to sea once again as a Marine Engineer in order to earn enough money to allow him to marry Suzanne and enter college full-time. He sailed for one more year and managed to save enough money to get married and enter college.

Berkeley was so crowded with returning WWII veterans that Wendell decided to enroll at UCLA. While attending UCLA he held down a part time job while Suzanne worked for the Atomic Energy Commission on campus. After graduation, Wendell worked as an engineer for Shell Chemical

Corporation before accepting a position with Fluor Corporation. While working for Fluor Corporation he gained valuable experience designing refineries, chemical plants, and power generation plants. Wendell also worked as an estimator for Tidewater Oil Company and later worked for Humble Oil Company and Rockwell Corporation. Wendell said, "I loved designing buildings and working with subcontractors."

As the years have passed, Wendell has never lost his wonderful sense of humor. Like so many other WWII veterans, he remembers the fun times and the good times and tries to forget the memories of the bad times. He keeps such memories to himself and pushes them deep into the recesses of his mind.

Wendell values his past experiences and he is proud of the part he played in "His Little Part of History."

LAND POETIC

Author Unknown

I've traveled the U.S. highways
A million miles and more
From the majestic Pacific mountains
To the tranquil Eastern Shore.

I've seen lakes and rivers wide,
The mountain rills and streams,
A flower wild by the countryside,
A beauty beyond my dreams.

I've seen the plains in the great Midwest,
The tumbleweeds and thistles,
The deserts bare with beauty rare
And heard the Eastbound's whistles.

I've heard the call of the meadowlark
And seen the brown trout running.
I've seen the coyote, heard his bark,
And watched the bathers sunning.

I've seen amigos in the shade
And quaint adobe huts
And all the refreshing verdant glades
And dried-up creekbed ruts.

I've seen the redwoods great and tall,
The beauteous rocks and caverns
And heard the wild dove's mating call
And the singing in the taverns.

I've seen the mountains
capped with snow,
The Black Hills of South Dakota,
And felt the sting of the winds that blow
In Maine and Minnesota.

I've watched the cowpokes round 'em up
On the widespread open ranches.
Drunk coffee from a campfire cup,
Smoked a peace pipe with Comanches.

I've seen canals and locks
And inland waterways,
Fishing piers and docks
And spacious coves and bays.

I've watched the motorboats at play,
Seen riverboats and barges,
The placid lakes and rattlesnakes
And grand canyons and gorges.

I've seen the many Army camps
Defending our great nation,
Skyscrapers tall tow'ring over all
And a movie on location.

Then on Sunday morningtide
I've seen the church's steeple
And the wooden pews inside
Filled with thankful people.

In this great land we have it all:
There's nothing that we miss.
Let's thank the Lord that we've been born
To live in a land like this.

Bill Jackson 1944

2001 Deceased

BILL JACKSON

Japanese Stragglers on Guam

Bill was born in Riverton, Wyoming in May of 1927. His parents moved to a ranch on Four Mile Creek, eight miles south of Glenwood Springs in 1937. The living conditions by today's standards would be considered very primitive. They had no electricity, and no running water, but they did have mail delivery. There was no school bus service, so Bill and his brother, Charles walked or rode a horse three miles to and from school. The schoolhouse was a one-room structure that accommodated grades one through eight. One teacher taught all eight grades, so Bill took both the seventh and the eighth grade the same year. The schoolhouse also served as a community center and several times each year dances or parties were held for all the people who lived on Four Mile Creek. Everyone from eight to eighty attended these functions. Bill said, "It's surprising how well one can live without the material things that are considered necessities today."

The family always had a large garden and grew vegetables that were either canned or stored in a root cellar. They raised their own beef and pigs and also ate a lot of "government beef" (deer and elk)". They smoked ham and bacon, made sausage and rendered the pork fat for cooking. They always shared a bountiful table and enjoyed their lives to the fullest. The three Jackson brothers, Bill, Charles and older brother, Carter, learned the value of honest work habits. Their house was heated with a pot-bellied stove and a Monarch kitchen range, both fueled by wood or coal. It was enjoyable to sit by the fire in the evenings, but it was quite cold in the mornings before the fires could be built. Bill's parents built a new home in 1940 and installed a coal burning furnace and running water. Bill and his brother, Charles, along with the help of neighbors mixed and poured the concrete foundation by hand, which was no trivial task. Electricity didn't come to Four Mile Creek until after the war in 1948.

Bill and his brother, Charles, attended high school in Glenwood Springs and Bill recalled many memorable moments during those years. He played the trombone in the high school band and was a member of the varsity basketball team. He enjoyed the basketball trips the team made during his junior and senior years. Bill and his brother, Charles, were very close. They were competitive, they fought, but they were defensively loyal to each other. Like the rest of the high school boys his age, Bill found full-time summer work and part-time work during the school year. Men who were normally available to put up hay for the neighbors had already gone into the service, so Bill helped take up the slack by haying for the neighbors in the summer. He also worked part-time during the school year at a local hardware store in Glenwood Springs. He graduated from high school when he was sixteen years old, and since most of his friends and classmates had already joined the service, Bill enlisted in the US Navy when he turned seventeen. He was sent to boot camp at Great Lakes Training Center near Chicago. While in boot camp he was visited by his brother, Charles, who was attending a Navy electronics school at Navy Pier in Chicago.

After graduating from boot camp, Bill went directly overseas. He served aboard the USSR-3 floating dry dock that was based at Apra Harbor, Guam in the Marianas Islands. His unit was attached to the submarine fleet and he found it interesting to explore many of the submarines that docked in Guam for overhaul and repairs.

There are two types of dry docks. One is a stationary structure and the other is a floating dry dock that functions much the same way as any ship. The floating dry dock Bill was assigned to was completely self-sufficient, with quarters for a complement of 120 men, along with their own mess facilities.

After a vessel enters the chamber of a floating dry dock, water is pumped out leaving the vessel guyed and resting on supporting blocks that are anchored to the floor of the dry dock. This allows the crew to inspect the vessel and make necessary repairs. To re-float the vessel this procedure is reversed and the vessel is once again ready for sea duty.

After the war ended, Guam was a boring place for any young man to be stationed. Guam is the largest of the fifteen islands in the Marianas group located in the Central Pacific. The island is approximately thirty miles long and from eight to sixteen miles wide. The topography of Guam is quite rugged and is dominated by three mountains ranging in altitude from 576 feet to 1,334 feet. The landscape is covered with heavy jungle vegetation and coconut trees. The temperature is hot and humid and there are numerous rivers and streams that rise in the higher elevations.

Guam was a US possession when Japanese forces landed at 0400 on December 10, 1941. The Japanese main forces consisted of 5,500 men, far superior in numbers to the few hundred US forces stationed on Guam. Captain McMillian, aware of the overwhelming superiority of the enemy, decided not to endanger the lives of the few American service men or the civilians by holding out against the Japanese. Thus, Guam fell into the hands of the Japanese at 0600 on December 10, 1941.

The small losses suffered by the Japanese and the Americans on December 10th gave little indication of the high price both sides would pay when the US forces re-took the island. Immediately after the Japanese captured Guam they began building defensive fortifications and their total strength grew to well over 20,000 troops,

On July 11, 1944 the US Naval forces began a massive ship bombardment of Japanese installations in preparation for their own landing. This bombardment went on continually until July 21st, when the Army, Navy and Marine forces began their invasion of the island. Organized resistance by the Japanese ended on August 8, 1945. A little over a year after the Americans had recaptured Guam, it was estimated that 18,377 Japanese had lost their lives and 1,250 prisoners had been taken. After August 10, 1945 it was further estimated that an additional 8,500 Japanese had been killed or captured. The final cost in US lives was 2,124 dead and 5,250 wounded.

For many months after Japan had capitulated, small bands of Japanese continued to resist. As time passed, resistance amounted to nothing more than an occasional shot or two being fired, or some minor sabotage. Nevertheless, it wasn't safe for American service men to wander around in the jungle to search for war souvenirs. The only excitement Bill looked forward to took place when a Japanese straggler occasionally lobbed a mortar shell in their direction from high on a hill above the harbor. This broke the monotony and gave Bill and his pals something to look forward to with great anticipation.

On June 11, 1945 Major Sato surrendered bringing thirty-four men with him. Two weeks later Lt. Colonel Hideyuki Takeda led a group of sixty-seven officers and men in to surrender. Small bands continued to surrender during the following year until it was finally declared there were no more Japanese stragglers hiding in the jungle. However, on May 22, 1960, Ito Masashi and Minakawa Bunzo were captured after holding out for sixteen years. Sgt. Ito Masashi wrote a book about their experiences and their repatriation back to Japan. The name of the book is the Emperor's Last Soldiers. The capture of these two Japanese soldiers ended any further thought there might be other stragglers still hiding in the jungle on Guam.

But in June of 1973, Sgt. Shoichi Yokoi was captured after holding out for twenty=eight years. He claimed he did not know the war had ended, and he was waiting for Japan to retake the island and rescue him.

After Sgt. Yokoi returned to Japan he received all of his back pay for the twenty-eight years he had remained on Guam. The total amount Sgt. Yokoi received wasn't enough to buy a new suit of clothes. Inflation certainly would have been devastating to Sgt. Yokoi had the Japanese Government not compensated him quite generously for his undying loyalty to his country. It is ironic to note my family was living on Guam when the two Japanese soldiers surrendered on May 22, 1960. It is even more ironic that my wife and I had returned to Guam on a business trip the day after Sgt. Yokoi had been captured.

In 1961 the US Navy organized several demolition teams to clear live Japanese and American ammunition from the island. During a period of six weeks, these teams recovered ninety-six tons of live ammunition, including hand grenades, large unexploded navy shells, land mines, small arms shells and a Japanese Zero fighter plane found in a swamp near the capital city of Agana. This plane was completely intact with air still in the tires. One demolition team discovered a live 500- pound bomb in a Guamanian village being used as a flower planter.

Guam eventually became a tourist mecca, and in 1995 one million tourists visited the island. More tourists visited Guam than any other island in the Central Pacific other than Hawaii. Guam is a very popular destination for Japanese honeymooners. Bill would certainly be surprised if he was to visit Guam today. Tumon Bay was nothing more than jungle during the war, but now it is the Waikiki of the Central Pacific. Hotels extend from one end of Tumon Bay to the other and are mostly owned by the Japanese. What Japan could not win by war, they have managed to buy. This is an ironic turn of events that no one could have foreseen in 1944 and 1945.

Guam features fine golf courses and tennis courts and there are many travel agencies available to organize sightseeing excursions for the tourists. Agana, the capital city of Guam, has the largest K-Mart store in the world and is a very popular destination for the Japanese. There are many restaurants, bars, clubs and specialty shops in and around Agana. Since Guam is a duty-free port, one can buy pearls, cameras, electronic goods from Japan, Swiss watches, Hong Kong clothing, Asian jewelry and island handicrafts. Entertainment of every variety is featured in the tourist hotels, but the Japanese soldier with the mortar is long gone.

Bill was discharged in July of 1946 with the rank of Signalman Third Class. In addition to his signaling achievements he gained experience driving a variety of navy small boats, an experience that came in handy years later when the three Jackson brothers and their families enjoyed on their annual house-boating trips to Lake Powell, Utah.

Bill returned to Glenwood Springs and like the rest of the young men recently discharged, he was at loose ends for a while. The family ranch had been leased to a neighbor for three years, so when the lease expired, Bill bought the ranch from his parents. He married his sweetheart, Frieda, in 1947 and settled down on the ranch to enjoy "the good life".

While working part time for United Lumber Company in 1948, there was a devastating fire in Glenwood Springs involving a group of petroleum storage tanks. The lumber yard probably would have been a total loss had it not been for Bill's heroic fire-fighting efforts. Bill suffered from smoke inhalation for the rest of his life as a result of that experience. In 1948 Bill and Frieda had a baby girl, Ann, and in 1950 they became parents of a son, Bill, Jr. While Bill ran the ranch, he also worked part-time for the Soil

Conservation Board and for the State of Colorado as a brand inspector. In 1970 Bill sold the ranch and retired, but he was not content with retirement. He and Frieda then traveled extensively with Argonaut Farm's show horses. As Bill's health failed, he was put on oxygen full time curtailing all of his activities. Sadly, Bill passed away on May 27, 2002 after a long illness, but his love for his family and friends never wavered for a second right up to the moment he drew his last breath.

GOVERNMENT ISSUE
Author unknown

Sitting on my GI bed,
My GI hat upon my GI head,
My GI pants, my GI shoes—
I wish they'd give me GI booze.

They issue everything I need,
Paper to write on, books to read,
My belt, my socks, my GI tie,
I'm what is known as a GI guy.

They issue food that makes me grow—
GI want a long furlough.
I eat my food from GI plates,
Buy all I want at GI rates.

It's GI this and GI that,
It's GI work that breaks my back.
Everything here is GI issue—
GI wish I could kiss you.

Charles Jackson 1944

2001

CHARLES JACKSON

The China Prince

My first memories of Charles were that he was a quiet, polite boy blessed with a bit more intelligence than the rest of the boys in our class. He was interested in everything mechanical and electrical but when we were young I thought his perpetual smile was his greatest asset, and it endeared him to all. Quite simply, I remember him as a dedicated student who wanted to get everything out of his education he possibly could.

When Charles first moved to Glenwood Springs he was twelve years old and was in the sixth grade. His brother, Bill, also the class of '44, was in the fifth grade. Their folks had bought a ranch on Four Mile Creek and living there was initially quite primitive. The house was big enough and built with round logs. The previous owner had wallpapered the inside, stretching the wallpaper across the depression between the logs, so every time one bumped the wall the wallpaper would tear. His stepfather often said there were several places where one could throw a cat through the wall. They had no electricity or running water, although they did have a battery powered telephone. They also had a radio, but listening to it was strictly limited because radio batteries were very expensive. (The energy-conserving transistor had not yet been invented).

The family obtained their drinking water from Four Mile Creek that ran right by their house. One of Charles' jobs was to carry water from the creek into the house in a bucket. He kept an axe handy during the winter so he could chop a hole in the ice. This method of obtaining household water seemed adequate until his mother learned that the creek ran through an upstream neighbor's pigpen. His mother immediately vetoed the water supply, so they developed a spring located about a quarter of a mile from the house. They installed a redwood collection box near the spring and, after filling a fifty-five gallon drum with water, they hauled it to the house. Charles' stepfather built a one-horse cart out of an old abandoned cultivator that was used to haul the drum full of water to the house. Charles' job was to harness old Orphy, a twenty-year old mare, to the cart and go to the spring and fill the fifty-five gallon drum with water.

Several years later, his folks learned they could buy used pipe from the oil fields at a reasonable price, so they installed a pipeline from the spring to the house. Due to the rocky soil, burying the pipeline was very difficult and labor intensive. The pipeline had to be buried in order to keep it from freezing during the winter. They used dynamite to break the rocks and a lot of "elbow grease" to dig the trench. The pipeline worked fine, but as long as they lived there, they could observe rainbows on the surface of the water in a drinking glass because the oil never stopped leaching out of the pipes.

To keep food cool in the summertime, they used an old-fashioned icebox. They had an ice pond about a quarter of a mile from the house and in the winter, when the ice was thick enough, they sawed out blocks of ice. The blocks of ice were then hauled on a horse-drawn sled to the icehouse and buried in sawdust. The sawdust kept the ice from melting, thus the ice lasted throughout the summer. The tricky part of extracting the ice from the ice pond was getting the blocks of ice out of the water. "It was always a contest to see if you could pull the block of ice out of the water before it would pull you into the water," Charles said.

Acquiring the sawdust was a problem. Charles recalled the time he and his brother, Bill, drove a team and wagon several miles up Four Mile Creek to the Lyke Brother's sawmill to get a load of sawdust. Charles claims one hasn't lived until he has ridden several miles on a primitive road in a wagon with steel and wooden wheels and no springs.

For household fuel they burned coal and wood. When they first moved to Four Mile Creek, they would go to the Diamond Coal Mine, several miles from their home, for a load of coal. The two boys drove a team and wagon to the mine for a few years before the family acquired a 1942 Dodge truck. The truck simplified the coal and sawdust hauling operation and made life a bit easier for Charles and Bill. For wood they used quaking aspen and oak ties from the abandoned Colorado Midland Railroad, that ran through their property. At first they had to cut the aspen with an axe and bucksaw. A bucksaw is like today's bow saw but with a wood frame instead of steel.

One day, Charles' stepfather learned that an upstream neighbor named Pony Moore had been to a sale and bought an old four horsepower stationary engine that weighed about 300 pounds. Pony couldn't get the engine to run so Charles' stepfather asked Charles if he could repair the engine so it would run. Charles said he could, but he didn't bother to tell Pony or his stepfather that he had already worked on the engine and had it operating like clockwork. Charles' stepfather then made a deal with Pony to cut his wood if Pony would give him the engine.

Charles' stepfather built a thirty-inch diameter saw-system by mounting the engine on skids and connecting the engine to a circular saw blade with a flat canvas belt drive. Charles' job was to keep the engine working. This system worked wonderfully well when cutting aspen wood, but when sawing oak ties it was necessary to cut halfway through the Oak tie, then allow the engine to build back up to speed before completing the cut. Incidentally, that old engine helped them justify acquiring more than their usual four gallons of gasoline a week, which was all that was allowed by the wartime rationing board.

"The entire family took a bath every Saturday night whether they needed it or not", Charles said. The coal-fired kitchen stove had a water reservoir attached to it and this heated a portion of their bath water. The rest of the water was heated in a copper boiler on top of the stove. Because of the hot water problem, more than one person would use the same bath water.

Their first bathtub was a circular galvanized tub about three feet in diameter. Eventually the family ordered a fancy rectangular sheet metal bathtub from the Montgomery Ward catalogue. That tub represented the height of luxury, and was the envy of many of their neighbors, even though the water still had to be heated on the kitchen stove. Charles remembered how ridiculous it seemed when they were taught in health class at school that they should bathe at least twice a week.

Charles and Bill had wonderful parents. Their mother was born into a prominent Philadelphia family, but she decided to go west for the experience and the excitement of living the life of a pioneer. She fell in love with the West and never went home. In 1937 she married their stepfather, Elmer Sinclair, who was a westerner. Charles claims both of his parents deserve a large share of credit for any success achieved by the Jackson brothers. No doubt many other members of the class of '44 can justifiably make this same claim. Charles' stepfather expected them to work like adults, even though they were boys. It was difficult at first, but they soon learned that their stepfather's way was the right way and the fair way.

Charles worked hard at home, but when he was twelve years old he had the opportunity to work for a neighbor shocking grain for one dollar a day. He remembered at the end of the fifth day he went home with five crisp one-dollar bills and he thought he was filthy rich.

Some years later, after many of the young farm workers had gone into military service, the Jackson brothers were much in demand by their neighbors to help put up hay and harvest other crops. The Jackson family didn't own a tractor so Charles and Bill enjoyed working for the Hammerick

154

family because they got to drive the Hammerick family's tractor. Mrs. Hammerick, along with Charles and his brother Bill, made a wonderful hay bailing crew. Bill drove the tractor, Charles ran the blockers and Mrs. Hammerick tied the bails.

The engines on the tractor and bailer made so much noise they could only communicate by sign language. One time Bill started holding his nose and making wiggley signs with his arms trying to tell them something. From Bill's vantage point on the tractor he could see the input feeder to the bailer, and he was trying to tell them they had just bailed a big bull snake.

In 1940 the family built a new house that had hot and cold running water and a regular bathtub. They had a hot water tank that was heated by a water jacket built into the coal-fired kitchen cook stove. This system was considered to be quite modern at the time. They built their new home out of spruce logs and pine lumber that was harvested and sawed by the Lyke Brothers sawmill located in Four Mile Park. The sawmill was a magnificent antique and it held a great deal of interest for Charles. It was powered by a turn-of-the-century steam traction engine connected to the mill equipment by a flat belt drive.

The Lyke brothers hauled the logs and lumber to the new house location on WWI vintage White trucks. The larger of their two trucks had pneumatic tires on the front and solid rubber tires on the rear. It had a single-band type brake system that worked on the drive shaft (no wheel brakes). Charles recalled riding on top of the load of logs and lumber down the steep, crooked Four Mile road. The load was top-heavy and it seemed to him they were gaining speed all the time as the single brake band was leaving a trail of smoke behind them. As they approached each curve, Charles had a mental picture of the truck overturning with him ending up under the load of logs and lumber.

He and his brother, Bill, did a lot of the excavating for the basement of their new house. They used a hand operated Fresno scraper pulled by a team of beautiful Percheron draft horses. Bill drove the team of horses and Charles operated the Fresno. A Fresno is quite like a large shovel with a central handle. The operator of the Fresno follows along behind the team of horses pulling the Fresno. Once the Fresno bucket is full of excavated material it is emptied by lifting up on the handle. When one considers that a full Fresno bucket of excavated material could weigh two or three hundred pounds it becomes quite obvious such work for a small young boy had to be very difficult indeed. Digging the basement required the use of a lot of dynamite and both Charles and Bill learned to be proficient with this task as well.

When Charles was quite young he became interested in building radios. He built his first radio when he was nine years old and was still living in Wyoming. He had one radio project or another going on from then until he graduated from high school. Another project he undertook was to generate electricity for their house. He found an old abandoned automobile generator and a washing machine gasoline engine he used as the power source. He connected the engine to the generator with a "V" belt drive, and connected the generator to a 6-volt automobile battery. Next he hooked a 25-watt light bulb to the batter--lo and behold, he had created an electric light. It wasn't a mind-bending system but it was certainly an improvement over the oil-burning lamps and candles the family was using at the time.

Charles and Bill completed grade school at the Four Mile School, a one-room structure with one teacher teaching all eight grades. There was a barn next to the schoolhouse where they could stable their horse while they were in school. They rode horse-back to school as did other children who lived on Four Mile Creek. Both Charles and Bill started high school at the same time as Bill had completed the seventh and eighth grades in one year. Their grade school teacher wasn't much older than her students but she taught them well so they were prepared when it came time to attend high school in Glenwood Springs.

While Bill and Charles were still attending classes at the Four Mile School they probably didn't get as much discipline as they deserved. Charles recalled one funny story involving his brother, Bill. The teacher hung a cowbell out of the window which she would shake vigorously to call the children back inside after recess or lunch. Predictably, the cowbell came up missing one day. Because Bill was usually involved in most mischief at the Four Mile School, he naturally was blamed. However, this time Bill was innocent. As a way of punishment, the teacher kept Bill inside the school building during lunch and recess while the rest of the children went outside to eat their sack lunches and play. Suddenly, Bill exited the schoolhouse at high speed, shouting, "I didn't hide your----bell." The teacher was in hot pursuit and gaining on Bill with every step. The other students had a grand view of this event from a small hill near the schoolhouse. Bill, in desperation, attempted to cross the creek, but a moss covered slippery rock stopped him cold and the teacher captured him. That night, a tearful teacher called Bill's mother and sobbed, "I thrashed your child;" Her response was, "I'm sure he deserved it, what did he do?" No one ever learned what really happened to the bell but it did re-appear the following day.

In high school, Charles joined the "Radio Club", and enjoyed his first chance to work with other people on his favorite hobby. He was also in the school band and played the cornet. Charles became a very good musician and occupied the first chair position in the cornet section. He never participated in sports, but he went to all the football games with the band.

157

Charles' interest in science sometimes got him into trouble. He and a classmate discovered that phosphorus could be dissolved in carbon disulfide forming a solution that would spontaneously burst into flame upon drying out. They learned one could dip a piece of paper into this solution, place the paper in a book while still wet, and it would behave until someone opened the book to that page. Once exposed to the air the paper would burst into flame. They should have dropped their experiment right there, but they had to find a practical application for this new discovery. They doped a piece of paper, put it in a book and at an appropriate time presented the book to one of the girls during study hall. They advised her there was a note for her on a certain page. When she removed the note from the book it burst into flame. The English teacher witnessed the event and to make a long story short, the two of them ended up in a serious discussion with Professor Igo, the principal. Even though it was obvious Professor Igo saw the humor in the event, he made it very clear it would not happen again. Incidentally, all of the high school students were in agreement that Professor Igo was the finest individual they ever had the privilege of knowing.

Another memorable occasion had its good news and its bad news. Bob Baker, who had the reputation of being very tough, started picking on Charles in mechanical drawing class. Charles invited Bob to meet him in a vacant lot after school to settle the matter. Charles later agreed this was a dumb move on his part but it was the honorable way disagreements were settled in that day and age. The entire high school was interested in the fight and everyone turned out to see the impending action. The fight lasted long enough to be very interesting to the observers, but the bad news was that Charles lost the fight. However, the good news was, Bob and Charles ended up very good friends thereafter. At least Charles proved to be quite agile during the fight as he managed to land several telling blows with his face directly into Bob Baker's fists.

During Charles' senior year he lived in town and worked part time as a janitor at the William's Hotel and occasionally at the coke bottling works. Charles recalled the times he helped load a rail car with cases of coke. The entire crew worked all night loading the rail car. It was very tiring and labor intensive work for the entire crew. During one of those late night jobs, the boss noticed the crew was getting tired so he broke out a bottle of 100-proof Yellowstone Whiskey. Charles was carrying cases of coke through a narrow passageway when he noticed the passageway kept shifting from side to side. He later concluded it must have been the coke they were using for a chaser that caused the problem with his equilibrium.

In April of 1944, Charles would turn eighteen and therefore be eligible for the draft. Everyone that age was aware of this and realized they might end up being killed in the war. Nevertheless, everyone was enthusiastic about a new adventure for a cause that was so clearly RIGHT. No one in the class of '44 tried to avoid serving our country. Most enlisted after turning seventeen. Charles was interested in the Navy's Radio Technician Program, so he enlisted when he turned seventeen. The Navy allowed him to remain on inactive duty until he had finished high school. Charles had passed an electronics test when he first enlisted and this earned him the rank of Seaman First Class even before he reported for active duty.

In July of 1944 he reported for active duty at Great Lakes Naval Training Center where he completed boot camp. After completing boot camp, Charles attended a one-year electronics training program at Wright Junior College in Chicago, Illinois. He was sent to the Naval Training Center in Gulf Port, Mississippi for more training before finally graduating at Navy Pier in Chicago as an Electronic Technician's Mate Third Class.

Being in the service in Chicago was a wonderful experience for Charles. Often, after finishing a meal in a restaurant or having a drink in a bar, Charles and his mates would discover some civilian had paid the tab. The civilians in Chicago were solidly behind the war effort and the service people were considered the heroes of the day. While stationed in Gulf Port, Mississippi Charles found that the attitude of the public was quite different from what he had experienced in Chicago. In Gulf Port everyone seemed to still be fighting the Civil War and the Union was still the enemy.

The war ended on August 8, 1945, just before Charles graduated from electronics school at Navy Pier in Chicago. On that day, the entire Navy Pier facility "went over the hill" to celebrate. No punishments were meted out and no AWOL charges were made against any sailor for having taken such a liberty. The celebration included kissing girls in the middle of a normally busy intersection, stopping trolley cars by pulling the trolley wheels off of the overhead electrical wires and dancing in the streets. Charles thought that he would soon be able to go home without having to go overseas but he learned that the powers-that-be in Washington had other ideas. Washington decided that wartime military personnel would be discharged gradually in order to minimize the impact on the country's economy, so instead of going home Charles was sent overseas.

Since the war had ended, a lot of the Navy's electronic equipment was shut down, thereby reducing the need for Electronic Technician's Mates. Consequently, Charles was first sent to the Island of Samar in the Philippines aboard a troop ship to serve in some other capacity. Right after clearing the harbor in San Francisco, the infamous ground swells were encountered, and seasickness was the order of the day. As they sailed farther southwest toward Samar the weather turned hotter and seasickness continued to plague the troops. The ship's ventilation system didn't work, so everyone abandoned

160

the normal sleeping quarters below deck in favor of sleeping topside under the stars and on the hard steel deck.

From Samar Charles was sent to Tsingtao, China aboard an LST (Landing Ship Tank). An LST is a very slow vessel designed to transport military tanks and military personnel. Charles believes that LST really stands for "Large Stationary Target". When the LST arrived in the China Sea there were still a lot of mines scattered around in the ocean. The crew on the LST sank several of the mines with a 20mm cannon, but the knowledge that these mines were out there floating around caused all the shipboard personnel some serious concerns. Charles slept at the front of the LST tank deck and, had the LST hit one of these mines, Charles knew he would have been blown to "kingdom come". While still aboard the LST, they went through the tail end of a typhoon, which was quite an exciting experience. Even though Charles never saw combat, he learned the sheer terror of being in a dangerous situation.

When Charles first arrived in Tsingtao, China he was assigned to help inventory a warehouse full of equipment that had been stored there in anticipation of the invasion of Japan. Immediately after the inventory had been completed, they received orders to dump everything into the ocean. Charles said he never did understand why anyone bothered about doing an inventory unless the idea was to keep the personnel busy and give them something to do.

Charles was eventually assigned to shore duty in a Shore Patrol unit while in Tsingtao. This assignment lasted for about nine months. There was a large military presence in Tsingtao at the time and even though China was not the enemy during WWII, the American military operated very much like an Army of Occupation. The Shore Patrol worked in pairs, one Marine and one Sailor. They had the authority to enter any restaurant to determine if it was sanitary. If such an establishment proved to be unsanitary, it was put off limits to all US military personnel. Charles remembered an incident when the owner of a restaurant actually requested the Shore Patrol to raid his establishment and threaten to put it off limits just to frighten his Chinese help into keeping the establishment clean.

Prostitution was legal and the Shore Patrol was also charged with the responsibility of checking the "cat-houses" to determine the sanitation conditions of these establishments. The Shore Patrol had the authority to put these pleasure houses off limits as well if they were found to be unsanitary. It was interesting to Charles that the Navy advised their personnel never to pay more than fifty cents for the services of a prostitute in these houses. Charles is quite adamant that he never indulged in such activities. He claims he couldn't say for sure if those who did indulge did so for a mere fifty cents. Occasionally, when a US military person was found in one of these houses, it might was declared off-limits. When this happened, the prostitutes would create all kinds of fascinating ways to deceive and distract the Shore Patrol in order to protect their client from being discovered.

In the 1930s, Tsingtao had been a very luxurious resort city frequented by Europeans, especially the Germans. Quite a number of White Russians who had fled communism were also permanent residents. Just prior to WWII, the Japanese Army came to the Tsingtao area and stayed throughout the war. Charles lived in the Grand Hotel, which had been one of the luxury hotels before the war. He slept on a Japanese steel frame cot that was about six inches too short for his 5ft. 10in. body, so he didn't enjoy the luxury that existed before the war.

During the Japanese presence in Tsingtao a lot of the farmers were driven from their land into the city. As a result, Tsingtao was swarming with people who were suffering in total poverty. Charles saw a lot of children begging in the streets, and many young women who resorted to prostitution just to keep their families from starving. The Chinese scrounged the American Military's trash heaps for food. Even the remains of half a grapefruit became a prized find for a hungry Chinese.

Inflation was rampant in Tsingtao. A rickshaw ride across town cost 100 yuen, the equivalent of 10 cents in US currency. Charles said, "Chinese men are uninhibited, and don't hesitate to cry when they are happy. The offer of a few American coins would bring a smile, but the smile would turn to a scowl if paid in Japanese yuen". Charles soon learned American cigarettes were the best medium of exchange. Cigarettes cost military personnel rifty cents a carton and a carton of cigarettes would buy just about anything. Charles found it interesting that the Chinese seemed much more susceptible to cigarette addiction than Americans were. He found it even more interesting that little children, seven and eight years old, smoked and inhaled deeply when they could get their hands on a cigarette.

There were always several US Navy and Allied ships in the harbor, and many sailors would go on shore for liberty, some for the first time in weeks or even months. These military personnel would have a great time on shore and then try to smuggle bottles of booze back to their ship, which was strictly against Navy regulations. One of the less popular jobs assigned to the Shore Patrol was to confiscate the booze anyone tried to smuggle back to their ship. This was for their own safety as bottles might break while being transported in the small boats through choppy water going back to their anchored ships. Needless to say, Charles didn't make very many friends performing this activity. Charles recalled a confrontation he had with some British Navy personnel that turned physical. They had been told they had the authority to confiscate booze from all Allied personnel but this particular group of British sailors from Her Majesty's Navy thought otherwise. That was when Charles learned why Shore Patrol personnel carried nightsticks. Rather than engage in a fistfight with an intoxicated sailor, the best solution was to crack that individual across the shins with the nightstick. No doubt this way of settling an altercation was much better than had been the choice Charles made when he challenged "Bob Baker" to a fistfight. Using a nightstick was much more conducive to maintaining his health than trying to duke it out with a person who might be considerably bigger.

By April of 1946 Charles had enough points to go home so he packed his belongings and got ready to leave. The day before he was to depart China, all Electronic Technician Mates were declared essential, This was a strange declaration indeed, since they had been declared redundant only a few months earlier. After cooling his heels for a couple more months, Charles finally received orders he was to be sent back to the United States for discharge. During the trip home they received word that the Chinese Communists had attacked Tsingtao, so he felt his departure from China was quite timely. One of the happiest times of his life was when the troop ship sailed under the Golden Gate Bridge.

Charles decided to spend at least one semester in college, to satisfy his mother's wishes. He registered for classes at Colorado A&M (now called Colorado State University) in Fort Collins, Colorado. Much to his surprise he really liked school so he continued on with the help of the GI Bill and completed his bachelor's degree in electrical engineering. The GI Bill paid for his books and tuition and $75.00 per month subsistence allowance. Married men were paid $105.00 per month plus their tuition and books. While still in college, Charles married a delightful lady, Helyn, from Fort Collins, Colorado and their daughter, Jean, was born two years later.

After graduation in the spring of 1951 Charles accepted a position with Westinghouse in Lima, Ohio, where he designed electric motors for use in the aircraft industry. During this time he earned several patent awards. Eventually Charles and his family moved to Albuquerque, New Mexico where he worked on designing army fusing and firing systems for nuclear weapons at Sandia Labs. Charles and Helyn's two sons, Richard and James, were born in Lima, Ohio when Charles was employed by Westinghouse.

During the ensuing years Charles continued his graduate work through the University of Pittsburgh's extension program. In April of 1981, Charles retired from Sandia Labs and became involved in other interests. Charles and Helyn enjoyed ballroom dancing and competed in many dance contests held by the Arthur Murray Dance Studio. Charles also became a member of his local barbershop quartet and performed solo concerts throughout the Albuquerque area. After being together for over fifty years, Helyn passed away in March of 2002. Like the rest of the WWII veterans, Charles continues to carry on just as he did during his years of service to his country.

Charles put it quite adequately when he said, "I believe that adversity brings out the best in all of us. We spent our childhood during the Great Depression, and then the US went to war in a very noble cause. Most of us had to wait until long after the war to escape from conditions that, by today's standards, would be defined as poverty. We had great reasons to fear the future because we really didn't know for certain if we would win the war, and when we were faced with military service, we didn't know whether or not we would survive the war. But somehow we remained optimistic, thereby becoming 'One Small Part of The Greatest Generation'. I am proud to have grown up in that generation and of being a contributor to this book. I truly regret that much of the world is still in poverty and lives in fear of the future. Hal and Leta Terrell and others on the Class Reunion Committee have had a lot to do with perpetuating the closeness of our class, as well as with other classes, by promoting and implementing our many wonderful class high school reunions."

I am not surprised that Charles and Heyln led such full and productive lives. I think their success is a direct result of their upbringing when they were children. I am pleased, honored and proud to say Charles is a dear and valued friend. Perhaps the following poem was written with Charles in mind.

FORTY YEARS AGO

Francis Huston

I wandered back to the old town, Tom
I sat beneath the tree
In the old school house playground
That sheltered you and me.

There were none there to meet me, Tom
And few were there to know
Who played with us upon the green
So many years ago.

The grass is just as green, Tom
Barefoot boys at play
Were sporting just as we did then
With spirits just as gay.

And the Master sleeps upon the hill
Which covered oer with snow
Afforded us a sliding place
So many years ago.

The old school house is gone now
The desks replaced by new ones
Much the same as those
Our penknives once defaced.

But the old stone blocks have disappeared
The bell no longer swings to and fro
But 'twas music just the same, dear Tom
'Twas so many years ago.

The boys were playing some old game
Beneath the same old tree
I forgot the name just now
But you've played the same with me.

'Twas played with knives
By throwing so and so
The loser had a task to do there
So many years ago.

The river is running just as swift
The willow on its bank
Are larger than they were. Tom
The stream appears less wide.

But the grapevine swing has disappeared
Where once we played the beau
And swung our sweethearts, pretty girls
'Twas so many years ago.

The spring that bubbled 'neath the hill
Nearby the spreading beach
Was very low, 'twas then so high
That we could scarcely reach.

And kneeling down to drink, Dear Tom
I started so
To see how sadly I am changed
Since so many years ago.

Nearby that spring upon an aspen
You know I carved your name
Your sweethearts just beneath it, Tom
And you did mine the same.

Some heartless wretch has peeled the bark
'Twas dying sure but slow
Just as she died whose name you carved
So many years ago.

My lids have long been dry, Tom
But tears came to my eyes
When I thought of her, the one I loved
Those early broken ties.

I visited the old cemetery
And took some flowers to throw
Upon the graves of those we loved
So many years ago.

Some are in the cemetery laid
Some sleep beneath the sea
But none are left of our old class
Excepting you and me.

And when our time has come, dear Tom
And we are called to go
I hope we meet with those we loved
So many years ago.

William "Willie" McDlonald 1943

2001 Deceased

WILLIAM McDONALD

Peleliu, Okinawa, China, Korea

Willie, by virtue of birth, became a citizen of Glenwood Springs, on October 30, 1925. He was an only child, but his father and mother never spoiled him by allowing him any special privileges. He was given certain tasks to do and he was expected to accept the responsibility of doing these jobs in a timely manner. Willie's father owned and operated a shoe repair shop in Glenwood Springs and one of Willie's jobs was pulling heels off shoes brought to Mr. McDonald's shop for repairs. Willie said, "I was about six years old when I started helping my dad in the repair shop. I never found it necessary to search for other jobs as did so many of the other boys."

Money was very hard to come by during the Great Depression years so most citizens opted to have their shoes repaired rather than invest in a new pair of shoes. Mr. McDonald's shoe repair shop was a very lucrative business leaving very little idle time for Willie to enjoy his life as a small boy. His father was also involved in a partnership arrangement with a gentleman by the name of Ted Moore. They owned a small ranch where they kept a string of twenty to thirty saddle horses. Mr. Moore operated a stable where tourists wanting to enjoy a day exploring the beautiful Colorado Mountains could rent a horse. By the late 1930s, America began to show signs of economic recovery so a few tourists began returning to Glenwood Springs for a holiday. Many tourist who visited Glenwood Springs, and the western slope of Colorado, enjoyed horseback riding on the many mountain trails and exploring the wilderness areas nearby. The Flat Top area was easily accessible from Glenwood Springs and offered tourist the opportunity to enjoy hundreds of square miles of alpine scenery, dozens of pristine lakes, sparkling streams, and mountain parks displaying a maze of colorful wild flowers. Wildlife was abundant and offered tourist the added pleasure of viewing deer, elk and other animals up close and in their own habitat. Willie was about eleven years old when the tourist business began to recover. He was delighted to find himself looking after the horses rather than having to help his father in the shoe repair shop. During the summer months several horses were stabled at Grizzly Creek, six miles east of Glenwood Springs, and right in the heart of the Glenwood Canyon. Grizzly Creek is one of many beautiful mountain streams flowing into the Colorado River. Eons of years ago the Colorado River created the beautiful and spectacular Glenwood Canyon, in itself a must for all tourist who visit the area.

Every morning Willie's mother drove him to Grizzly Creek where he saddled the horses and took them another six miles up the Glenwood Canyon to a trailhead known as Hanging Lake. This was where the tourist would mount their horses to begin a day of excitement and pleasure. Willie remained at the trailhead at Hanging Lake until the horses were returned in the evening. He then collected the fees from the tourist and took the horses back to Grizzly Creek where he stored all the tack and took proper care of each animal before meeting his mother for the return trip home.

Willie entered high school with the same group of peers he had been with since grade school. It was at this point in his life when he began his search for other odd jobs. One summer he found a job working for the City of Glenwood Springs. He drove a trash truck around town picking up the trash citizens discarded in the alleys behind their homes. He also worked with a crew of men trimming trees along the city streets. Another summer job was working as a grounds-keeper at the local golf course.

When Willie was thirteen or fourteen years old a forest fire broke out on Oasis Creek, just a few miles from the McDonald/Moore ranch. Willie was hired by Garfield County to deliver supplies to the fire fighters as he had

172

access to twelve horses. For the next three weeks he and his classmate, Rex Sidener, made two trips each day with a string of packhorses to deliver supplies. Willie said, "This was really hard work—we started at daylight and finished by eight in the evening. We then had to take care of the horses, That took another two hours. But, we both made what we considered to be a fortune during those three weeks."

By the time Willie was a junior in high school he was five feet, nine inches tall and weighed 180 pounds. He was very muscular, built like a tank, and exceptionally strong. His strength and his build made him a valuable asset to the high school football team. He could play any position from center to running back. He didn't believe in wasting energy by running around an opponent so he just ran over them instead. Football, tumbling, swimming and wrestling were the sports Willie participated in. His outstanding swimming skills were eventually to play an essential role in his life.

December 7, 1941 brought changes in Willie's life, just as it changed so many other lives. America suddenly found itself involved in a world conflict with Japan, Italy and Germany. Without hesitation, Willie enlisted in the US Marine Corps on October 30, 1943. He reported immediately to the San Diego, California Marine Base for twelve weeks of boot-camp training. After completing boot camp, he remained in San Diego where he attended a six-week Sea School training program. Sea School trained young Marines as armed guards to staff US Embassies and Legations throughout the world as well as ship's complement and courier duty.

While in boot camp training, Willie met Vernon Duffy, another Glenwood Springs young man, who was also taking boot camp training. Willie never ran into Vernon again even though Vernon was involved in the invasion of Okinawa, as was Willie. However, Willie did learn while he was still in Okinawa that Vernon had been killed in combat.

After a short furlough, the last of March 1944, Willie reported for duty at Camp Pendleton, California. When members of the Marine Corps reached this point in their transformation from civilian to Marine they each received training as a rifleman. This training also included a special military occupation course. Willie chose the field of communications and specialized as a radio operator.

In the month of May 1944, Willie was transferred to the Fleet Marine Force, put aboard a troop transport ship that sailed out the port of Los Angeles headed for Oahu, Hawaii. Within a week after arriving in Hawaii, Willie was assigned to the Thirty-first Replacement Battalion being formed on the Hawaiian island of Kauai. By the end of June 1944, the Thirty-first Replacement Battalion had been fully formed. It was at this point when Willie first taught swimming to his fellow Marines who were not good swimmers.

Non-stop physical and technical training was the order of the day from the first day on Kauai until the Thirty-first Replacement Battalion boarded a Merchant Marine troop ship and headed for the recently recaptured island of Guam, MI. As planned, all of the new replacement personnel were used in the mop-up operations. This gave the green troops some idea of what was yet to follow.

The First Marine Division was rebuilding at a miserable "rest camp" on Pavuvu in the mid-Solomon islands. Meanwhile, Willie's records were being reviewed at Thirty-first Battalion Headquarters. To his surprise, he and three other corporals were sent by air to the First Marine Division Headquarters at Pavuvu. The few weeks attending Sea School had gotten Willie, and the three other Marines, posts as couriers. For the next several weeks Willie was sent to many places in the Pacific, including Australia and New Zealand, carrying military pouches from place to place.

By this time, the US Navy had made itself felt with carrier strikes against the Philippines and the Palau Islands. Their carrier strike successes led Halsey to contact Admiral Nimitz with strong recommendations that the planned invasion of Peleliu, one of the islands in the Palau group, be called off. Halsey believed the invasion of the Philippine operation should be moved up. In hindsight of more than sixty years since the Peleliu campaign, history has shown that Halsey was probably correct. Many historians believe the Peleliu battle need not have been fought at all.

Air reconnaissance of Peleliu indicated the island was fairly flat and lightly defended by the Japanese. General William Rupertus, the First Marine Division commander, was aware it would be difficult to capture Peleliu, but he also determined that complete success could be accomplished within a short period of time. However, the Japanese had heavily fortified Peleliu, which resulted to one of the bloodiest battles of the Pacific War.

D-Day on Peleliu was September 15, 1944. The First, Fifth and Seventh Regiments of the First Marine Division landed on their assigned beaches. Defending Peleliu was Colonel Kuinio Nagagawa with a force of 10,500 battle-hardened veterans from years of fighting in China. Commander Nagagawa took masterful advantage of the islands rough topography. He had constructed a maze of underground tunnels well connected to concrete bunkers. All of the Japanese fortifications were well hidden and difficult to locate once the Marines had landed. The First Regiment, under the command of Colonel Chesty Puller, landed on White Beach One and White Beach Two on the left flank. They were responsible for securing the northeastern peninsula of the island. The Fifth Regiment with a new commanding officer. Colonel Bucky Harris, hit Orange Beach One and Orange Beach Two at the center of the invading forces. The airstrip was their immediate objective. The Seventh Regiment, with Colonel Herman

Hanneken at the helm, landed on Orange Beach Three with two battalions, the Second and Third.

On D-Day plus four, the First Battalion, Seventh Regiment landed on White Beach Two to reinforce the First Regiment. It was at this point when Willie and his buddies of the First Battalion, Seventh Marines were thrown into the battle. Willie said, "Once we hit the beach on Peleliu my romantic ideas of what war and combat were all about changed immediately. I came ashore in an amtrack and was immediately welcomed by a barrage of Japanese mortar fire. I thought, what a way to visit a South Seas Island---nothing like the movies." Even after the reinforcements had landed on Peleliu, maintaining the momentum of the assault was a difficult assignment. Casualties continued to mount at an alarming rate until finally Major General Geiger, commander of the Third Marine Amphibious Corps, visited Colonel Puller near the front lines and observed for himself the depleted and completely exhausted condition of the First Marine Regiment. Soon thereafter, General Geiger overruled General Rupertus' objections of bringing in the 321st Regimental Combat team of the Eighty-first Army Infantry Division from nearby Anguar.

Finally, on November 24, two and a half months after the Marines had landed on Peleliu, the island was declared secure. Colonel Nagagawa sent his final message to headquarters on the Palau island of Babelthoup stating he had burned his regimental colors, and his remaining force of sixty men had split into two infiltration parties to continue the fight. As for Willie he said, "I was terrified and confused the entire time I was on Peleliu, but like my Marine buddies I somehow continued to function as a proud Marine."

The battle of Peleliu cost the Navy, Marines and Army 6,526 casualties, including 1,252 killed in action. The Japanese suffered near total destruction of their garrison with 10,900 killed. Only 202 prisoners of war were captured and most of those were conscripted laborers. In the meantime, General MacArthur's forces had already landed on Leyte in the Philippines and the invasion of Okinawa was being planned.

Once Peleliu was declared secure the First Marine Division moved directly back to Pavuvu under the new leadership of Major General Pedro del Valle. While the First Marine Division was once again rebuilding, Willie requested permission for temporary duty with the Eleventh Marine Field Artillery Regiment, First Marine Division, to train as a forward observer (F.O.). The request was granted and Willie left the rat and land-crab infested swamps of Pavuvu and returned to Kauai in the Hawaiian Islands for training.

The Eleventh Field Artillery Regiment set up camp near Barking Sands on Kauai and Willie began his training as a forward observer. He also found time to teach swimming once again. Finally his unit embarked for the return to Pavuvu the last week of January 1945.

A forward observer's job is to establish his position as near to the enemy positions as possible and through radio and telephone communications keep his own command post informed of enemy activities. Calling in fire from their own guns onto enemy positions was one of his primary functions. This was a very dangerous and lonely job for any young man to perform.

The First Marine Division's next destination was Okinawa in the Ryuku Islands chain. Okinawa is located strategically between Kyushu, the southernmost island of Japan, and Formosa. The US Military wanted Okinawa for two reasons. It had several air bases the US needed to carry out concentrated air raids on Japanese cities and Japan's war industries. It was also needed as a staging area for the impending invasion of Japan as it was only 350 miles distant from the Japanese home islands.

By mid March of 1945, the US had assembled the greatest armada of ships ever assembled against an enemy in preparation for the landing on Okinawa, scheduled for Easter Sunday, April 1, 1945. Admiral Spruance's fleet included forty aircraft carriers, eighteen battleships, 200 destroyers and hundreds of support vessels. By mid March, 1945, 1,300 U.S. vessels had gathered off Okinawa and over 182,000 American Army and Marine assault troops were a part of this force. The ferocity of the Japanese Kamikaze attacks against the US fleet was unparalleled in modern military history. The US Navy bore the initial brunt of the Japanese will to defend their country from an enemy invasion. Waves of Kamikaze aircraft pounded away at the US fleet but they were unsuccessful in stopping the invasion of Okinawa in spite of the losses they inflicted on US forces.

The US Navy lost nearly 5,000 sailors killed and 4,800 wounded before a single Marine or Soldier had set foot on Japanese soil. The US Navy also lost thirteen destroyers and one destroyer escort. Ten U.S. battleships, aircraft carriers and dozens of other surface ships were heavily damaged and put out of action. The total US Naval losses were thirty-six ships sunk and 368 damaged. The Navy also lost 763 aircraft to Japanese defensive actions but inflicted a staggering loss of 7,800 Japanese planes destroyed. The US Navy sunk sixteen Japanese ships during this engagement and damaged several others.

Willie and the First Battalion, arrived at Okinawa aboard an LST (Landing Ship Tank). Willie said, "There were about 2,000 Marines on board the LST as well as dozens of jeeps, trucks and heavy artillery pieces. We were heading for our assigned landing beach at 8:30 A.M. on April 1, 1945, but when we were about 2000 yards from shore we were struck midship by a Kamikaze plane. Many Marines were killed outright and some drowned after abandoning the ship which sank shortly after being hit."

Willie gathered together some of his personal gear, jumped overboard and started swimming toward shore. He said, "Hal, the reason I managed to get ashore was because I learned to swim in the Glenwood Pool when I was a boy."

In spite of the heavy losses suffered by the Navy, Army and Marine personnel they met very light resistance as they landed on their assigned positions. By evening 60,000 men had reached the beach and established a beachhead eight miles wide and several miles deep. The Army and Marine combat troops were beginning to wonder, "Where are all the Japs". Not one shot had yet been fired by the Japanese but on the second day all hell broke lose. Once the Japanese fired their first shot, every single one of the 180,000 Americans who had come ashore by then would be desperately needed.

Army Lt. General Simon Boliver Buckner was the commander of the US Tenth Army and the Marines were commanded by Marine Major General Roy S. Geiger. Before the last shot was fired on Okinawa, Lt. General Buckner had been killed in action. All of the American forces landed on the west coast of Southern Okinawa at "Hegushi beaches", near the village of Tosuchi located at the mouth of the Bishigawa River. The river was the boundary established between the Marine and the Army sectors.

US forces offshore had no idea the beaches had been intentionally undefended. The 100,000 Japanese troops were well dug into cement tombs, caves and other fortifications and were waiting for the order to open fire. When the Japanese finally engaged the American forces it was devastating. The battle for Okinawa raged on for two months. The entire terrain was a sea of mud caused by continuous rain. The mud stuck to the American's boots, stalled their vehicles and made it difficult to re-locate their artillery pieces. The Japanese were well established in defensive positions on all of the hills and high ground. From these positions they were at liberty to pour down a constant barrage of artillery and mortar shells onto the Marine's positions. The violent fury of the Japanese killed or wounded hundreds of young Army and Marine personnel, but they continued to apply pressure on the Japanese in spite of such losses.

As a FO (Forward Observer) Willie and the three other FO's began to function as a team. They were sent out to locate Japanese guns or troop positions and report their locations via radio or field telephone back to their own gun emplacements. From their secured positions, Willie and his fellow Marines were then able to direct fire from their own guns. Sometimes it was necessary to call in fire almost on top of their positions. It was during one of these occasions when Willie was hit by shrapnel from a Japanese mortar round. He was patched up at an aid station and returned to combat within a matter of hours. Willie's Forward Observation assignments earned him the nickname, "Mad Mack, The Colorado Crevice Crawler". Once while on assignment, Willie found a Baka Rocket in a cave. A Baka Rocket is a bomb piloted to its target by a Kamikaze pilot. Time Magazine took pictures of Willie and the Baka Rocket that was later featured in one of the Time Magazine editions.

For the next two and one half months the First Marine Division was engaged in constant combat with the determined Japanese. Some of the most difficult engagements Willie and his First Battalion Marines buddies faced were Daheshi Ridge, Wana Ridge, Wana Draw and Sugar Loaf. These Japanese emplacements had to be taken before an attack could be launched against Shuri Heights and Shuri Castle. During these battles Willie was shocked at the sight of the bodies of his fallen Marines and the Japanese dead. American and Japanese bodies were frequently left where they had fallen as any efforts to retrieve them only further exposed more Marines to Japanese artillery and mortar fire. Willie recalled all of the decaying bodies, teeming with maggots and slowly rotting in the muck. He said, "It was a sickening sight and I can still see and smell those rotting bodies as if it were only yesterday." On a more pleasant note, Willie recalled meeting Bill Crutcher on Okinawa. Crutcher was another young man from Glenwood Springs who was a Marine Pilot based at Kadena Airfield. The Marines had captured Kadena Airfield from the Japanese just two weeks before their meeting.

Okinawa ultimately became the bloodiest battle of the Pacific War. More than 100,000 Japanese died defending Okinawa. Unfortunately almost 100,000 civilians also became casualties before the carnage on Okinawa ceased. The US Army ground forces lost 4,600 men killed in action and 18,000 more were wounded. The US Marines lost 3,200 killed and an additional 13,700 wounded. Even though Okinawa was a victory for the United States, the military brass and civilians alike were shocked to learn of the heavy losses these young boys had paid for the victory. However, such a terrible loss of American lives on Okinawa gave the US Military and its Allies a bitter forecast of what to expect if they ever had to land on the Japanese home islands. But, above all else, it proved that nothing could stop the Allies in the Pacific or in Europe from moving where they wanted to go. In the end, Japanese General Ushijima himself paid tribute to US forces. In his last message to Tokyo he stated, "Our strategy, tactics, and techniques were used to the utmost and we fought valiantly, but it was nothing before the material strength of the enemy."

Japanese organized resistance on Okinawa ended on June 20, 1945. The First Marine Division moved to a bivouac area at the north end of the island to regroup and receive replacements. Spit and polish followed. Then came more training and re-supply for the eventual Japanese home island's amphibious assault. Around the first of August the First Marine Division embarked on landing ships, L.S.T.'s and L.S.I.'s, and set sail for their rendezvous point to meet up with the main strike force. On their way to participate in the impending invasion of the Japanese home islands, Willie said, "We were well at sea when we received the news that the US had dropped two atom bombs on two Japanese cities and the Japanese had surrendered unconditionally to Allied forces. This was great news to all of the Marines! "

But instead of heading for home as everyone had hoped, the entire First Marine Division was sent to China. One week later Willie and the First Marine Division disembarked at the port city of Tientsin, China. The First Division was assigned the job of repatriating Japanese soldiers back to Japan. Willie said, "This was some switch, instead of fighting the Japanese we are now protecting them and assisting them to get back to their homes." Willie spent nine months in China rounding up Japanese soldiers and escorting them via the Chinese rail system to Chinese ports for transportation back to Japan. He said, "We had to furnish armed guards on all Japanese prisoner trains to prevent Chinese Communists from exacting revenge upon the Japanese soldiers." This was quite an experience for Willie as he felt very strongly that this was unfair after fighting the Japanese and losing so many buddies at Peleliu and Okinawa. He traveled all over China, Mongolia, Manchuria, the Gobi Desert, Peking, and he even made a trip to Vladivostok, Russia. He said the Chinese trains were not very comfortable but he and his buddies were young and tough so they didn't mind the discomfort they had to endure. It was an interesting and educational experience for him and gave him the opportunity to see first hand how fortunate he was to be an American.

When not traveling Willie and his look-alike pal, Andy Anderson, lived in their own house in Tientsin. They even had a houseboy who did everything for them including laundry, cooking and cleaning. Willie said, "Our

182

houseboy was very bright...in addition to Chinese he could speak English and French. We called him Frenchy. We even had our own rickshaw available at all times so we were living the good life when we were in Tientsin." Willie and Andy owned the three-bedroom house they lived in. When they returned to the United States they gave the house to Frenchy along with all of the Chinese money they had. No doubt Frenchy was delighted!

All good things eventually come to an end so nine months after arriving in China, Willie and Andy headed for home. Willie received his release from the Marine Corps on May 6, 1945 and by May 10, 1945 he was back in his hometown of Glenwood Springs. Willie said, "During my time in the Marine Corps I had many experiences, some good and some bad, but I am proud to have served my country."

One week after arriving back in Glenwood Springs, Willie enrolled at Colorado School of Mines where he took summer courses in engineering. That fall he enrolled at Mesa Junior College in Grand Junction, Colorado through the GI Bill. He was also recruited to play football for Mesa Junior College. Being a member of the football team he ate his meals at the "training table" and was also given a room of his own. With these benefits, along with the money he received from the GI Bill, he lived quite comfortably while at Mesa Junior College. In 1947 Willie moved to Denver, Colorado and found a job working as a draftsman for a structural engineering company. While holding down this job he took night classes at Denver University studying to become a civil engineer. Just as he was ready to receive his degree he was re-called back into the Marine Corps and was immediately sent to Korea where he spent the next thirteen months fighting in that war.

It was Sunday, June 25, 1950 in Tokyo when General MacArthur received the news from South Korean President Rhee that North Korea had attacked South Korea. North Korean troops were racing south toward Seoul, the capital of South Korea. The US Army stationed in Korea was not prepared for another war. They were primarily engaged in training the Republic of Korea Army so the North Korean Army met little resistance during their initial engagements against US and ROK (Republic of Korean) troops. Consequently, the North Korean Army initially made great strides and captured all but the southern part of South Korea. The US immediately began sending Army and Marine personnel to South Korea in hopes they could stem the tide and push the North Koreans back north above the 38th parallel.

The US Military began calling up US reserve military personnel and Willie received his orders to report for active duty on September 8, 1950. Two weeks later he and some of the other Marines who had received orders to report for active duty found themselves on an airplane heading for Korea. They made three fuel stops along the way at Hawaii, Midway Island and Japan. On October 1st, Willie found himself deplaning at Kimpo airfield just a few miles from Seoul and about the same distance from Inchon. He and his fellow retreads were loaded into a six by six truck sent from Headquarters and driven to Inchon.

As if the last four plus years were but a brief vacation, Willie was returned to the exact same unit he had served with at Peleliu and Okinawa, the First Battallion, Seventh Regiment, First Marine Division. The Division was engaged in loading ships in preparation for another landing, this time on the east coast of North Korea. The First Marine Division was under the command of Major General Oliver P. Smith and the Seventh Marine Regiment's leader was Colonel Litzenberg.

They boarded ship October 16th and sailed for the port city of Wonson, North Korea. After landing at Wonson on October 26, Willie and his First Marine Division buddies began their march northwest to Sundong. On November 3rd the Marines ran into heavy resistance from the 124th Chinese Communist Division. The First Marine Division only managed to gain Fourteen miles between November 4th and November 7th before the Chinese broke off the engagement. As an FO (forward observer) Willie was busy calling in fire from his own heavy guns. The Chinese were so close to Willie's position a thirteen-ounce shell fragment from one of his own artillery pieces struck him in the arm and shoulder. Fortunately, the force of the shell fragment was almost spent when it hit him so no permanent damage occurred. Willie still has this jagged piece of shell fragment as a reminder of his days fighting at Sundong. It was at Sundong when Willie first heard the Chinese blowing their bugles. He was to hear the bugles once again during the fighting at the Chosin Reservoir. Willie said, " If the Chinese blew their bugles to scare us, it worked."

After the Chinese broke off the engagement at Sundong, Willie's group turned north towards Hagaru-ri where the First Marine Division established their headquarters. From Hagaru-ri, Willie's unit, the Seventh Marines and the Fifth Marines, continued north until they reached Yudam-ni located on the west bank of the Chosin Reservoir. Shortly after reaching Yudam-ni the entire Chinese army struck with full force. At the same time the First Marine Division was also struck with full force by severe winter weather. Temperatures dropped well below zero, their equipment wouldn't operate and many men suffered from frostbite. Willie thought that after Peleliu and Okinawa he could take anything Korea had to offer. But he was soon to learn fighting in Korea was completely different than combat on Peleliu or Okinawa. During the fighting on Peleliu and Okinawa the First Marine

Division engaged only one enemy but in Korea they fought the North Korean Army, the Communist Chinese Army, the mud and snow and the debilitating cold, the worst enemy of all.   Willie said, "In many ways Korea was far more difficult than had been the fighting on Peleliu and Okinawa."

After digging in at Yudam-ni Willie once again took up his position as FO (forward observer). Every time he located a target, Marine Corsairs would attack or US Army or Marine heavy artillery poured down hell upon the Communists, but US troops received their own share of hell from the North Koreans and Chinese troops as well. It became an all-out race to reach the Yalu River, the northern frontier between North Korea, China, Manchuria, and Russia. The situation at Yudam-ni became so tentative, General Smith ordered a full withdrawl of all troops in the Chosin Reservoir area. Later the order to withdraw became known by US military personnel as 'the big bug-out" or as General Smith said, "Retreat hell, we're just fighting in another direction."

Both US Army and Marine troops fought bravely but on December 1st they began   withdrawing their forces as ordered. The First Marine Division reached Hagaru-ri on December 3rd but before they could set up a line of defense they received orders to withdraw to Hungnam as quickly as possible. For nine unbelievable days and nights the first Marine Division fought until it seemed impossible they could survive. Two thousand of Willie's buddies were dead, either killed by enemy action or frozen to death. But, they continued to fight and die during this action.

Before retracing their steps back south the Marines destroyed every piece of equipment and all the supplies they couldn't carry or take with them. They took their dead and wounded and headed for Hagaru-ri where the US Army Air Corps had just established an airbase. Once Willie and his unit reached Hagaru-ri they received medical attention, winter clothing and food

186

supplies. Their wounded and dead were loaded on aircraft and evacuated, leaving the rest of the First Marine Division to continue fighting the Chinese and North Koreans as they battled their way to Hungnam. Shortly after pulling out of Hagaru-ri the Chinese occupied the city. This effectively eliminated any further evacuation activities by the US Army Air Corps.

By December 12th the Marines staggered into the port city of Hungnam where they were once again loaded onto ships to be transported to Pusan, South Korea. The dock area, warehouses and rail center at Hungnam were all pre-primed with explosives and were detonated as the last ships were leaving port. Then the naval guns and air strikes began. The city was completely destroyed and was useless to the North Koreans for several years after the war had ended.

Once the First Marine Division reached Pusan, they immediately set about training new replacements, sending out patrols and rebuilding to full combat strength. After reaching Pusan, Willie was selected for a field commission and sent to Japan for indoctrination. After completing the indoctrination he was told he would be returned to Korea as a platoon leader of a rifle platoon to start his tour all over again. He was also offered the option of receiving a raise in rank and returning to the US. He opted to receive the raise in rank as he didn't want to remain in Korea for another tour. The First Division started their push north once again. By the time they had pushed the North Korean and Chinese Army back to the thirty-eighth parallel, Willie was eligible to rotate back to the United States. Once he arrived at the Marine base in California he was placed on Inactive Reserve and didn't actually receive his discharge from the Marine Corps for another ten years.

The fighting continued until July, 1953 when opposing sides signed the Korean Armistice. The thirty-eighth parallel was once again established as the boundary line between North and South Korea. This caused many people to ask, "What did we gain out of all of this?" The cost was high as US forces suffered 142,000 casualties with 33,000 young men killed in action. Before leaving the Marine base in California, Willie was awarded two Purple Hearts, three Battle Ribbons, and two Presidential Citations. Willie said, "I sure learned that freedom isn't free."

After receiving his release from the Marine Corps on October 11, 1951, he immediately headed for home. Back in Glenwood Springs, Willie saw his firstborn son for the first time. The baby had been born after Willie had been called back into active duty with the Marine Corps. Willie and his wife had two more sons before they eventually divorced. In 1976 Willie married Doris Cadwallader, from Rocky Ford , Colorado and they have been happily married for twenty-seven years.

After arriving back in Glenwood Springs, Willie worked at several odd jobs before being hired by the Bureau of Mines. He continued to live in Glenwood Springs and drove the twenty-seven miles to his job site each day. Three years later the Bureau of Mines closed their Oil Shale Plant at Anvil Point, leaving Willie to look for another job. He was hired by Grand Junction Steel Company as a design engineer and he remained with this firm for the next thirty years. He continued to study for his Engineering Degree until he obtained his license a few years later. Willie worked on projects throughout all of the western states designing bridges, ore-bins, conveyor systems, mining equipment, and tools. He retired at the age of seventy, but kept busy working part time as a consultant for different firms in the area. Willie's honesty and loyalty to his employers and his country has been a measure of his goodness. Willie is a true warrior, experienced in warfare and in overcoming life's adversities.

A WARRIOR'S PRAYER

"Plead my case O Lord, with them that strive with me. Fight against them that fight against me. Take hold of shield and buckler and stand up for mine help. Draw out also the spear, and stop the way against them that persecute me. Say unto my soul, I am thy salvation." Psalm 35:1-3.

My friend and schoolmate, William (Willie) McDonald, passed away on March 8, 2003. The only battle he ever lost was his battle against cancer. Even though he did not receive a medal for this battle, he won my complete admiration and respect for the way he fought it. He was one of the best!

CHOSIN

John Kent. 1st Marine Division

How deep the cold that takes us down
Into the searing frost of Hell,
Where mountain snows,
Unyielding winds, strip our flesh,
Bare our bones.

The trembling of uncertain hearts,
Scream out to echoes not impressed,
As swirling mists of laughing death,
Reach out their fingers to compress.

How white the withered skin exposed,
Turns into black and brittle flesh
And limbs cast out from conscious thought
Still stagger on the artic frost.

Immobile does the breath extend
As crystal on the mountain wind,
And eyes now fixed in layers of ice,
See nothing through the dawning light.

This road that leads down to the sea,
Twists and turns at every bend
And Chosin's ice that molds like steel,
Rains the fire that seeks our end.

The trucks cry out a dirge refrain,
Their brittle gears roll on in pain,
Upon their beds, the silent dead,
In grateful and serene repose.

Still the mind resists the call,
To lie and die in final pose,
As blood in stillness warms the soul,
And renders nil the will to rise.

The battle carries through the night,
Gives witness to the dead betrayed,
When frozen weapons fail to fire,
Their metal stressed by winter's might.

Still we fight to reach Hungnam,
In solemn oath and brotherhood,
As every able-bodied man
Will bring our dead and wounded home

Uphold traditions earned in blood,
Break through the hordes that press us in,
Depress their numbers to the place,
Where waves of dead deny their quest.

And on to the sea.

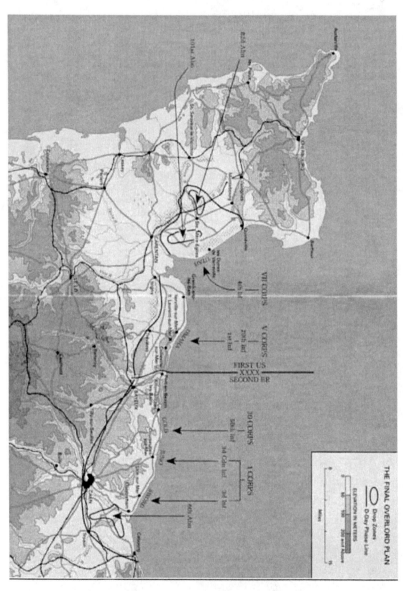

D-Day Landing Beaches
Normandy, France, June 6th 1944

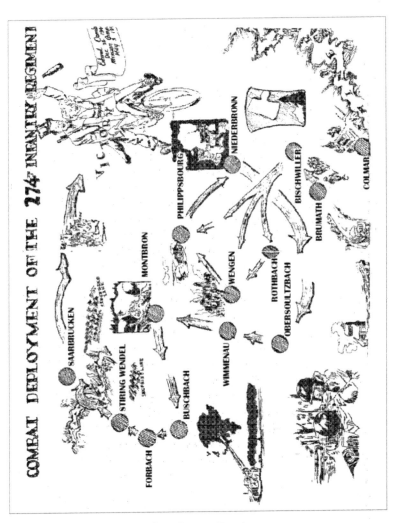

274th Infantry Regiment
France 1944

193

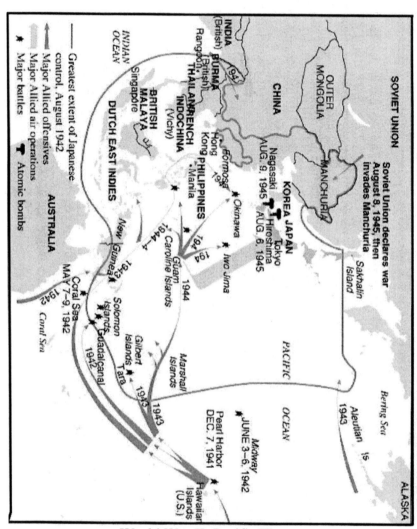

World War II: Pacific Theater

Marine/Seabee Cemetary Iwo Jima

195

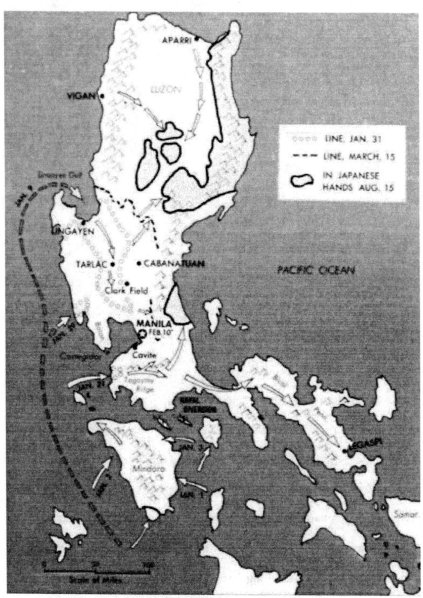

Island of Luzon
Philippines

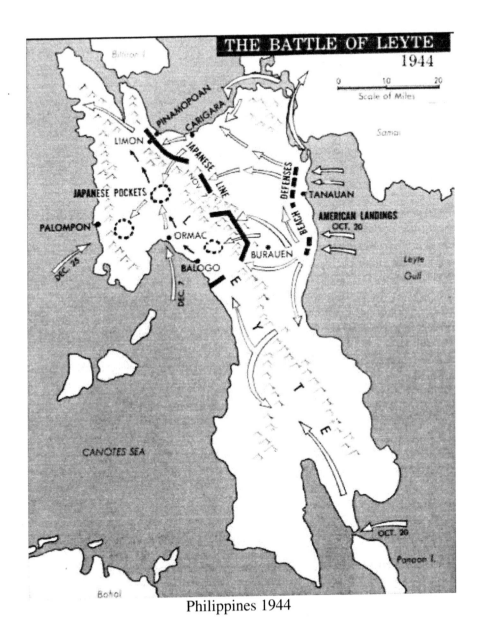

Philippines 1944

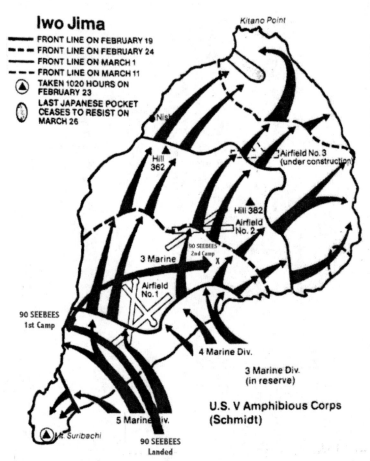

Iwo Jima

- ▬▬▬ FRONT LINE ON FEBRUARY 19
- ▬ ▬ ▬ FRONT LINE ON FEBRUARY 24
- ──── FRONT LINE ON MARCH 1
- ─ ─ ─ FRONT LINE ON MARCH 11
- ▲ TAKEN 1020 HOURS ON FEBRUARY 23
- LAST JAPANESE POCKET CEASES TO RESIST ON MARCH 26

Kitano Point

Nish

Hill 362

Airfield No. 3 (under construction)

Hill 382
Airfield No. 2

90 SEEBEES 2nd Camp

3 Marine

Airfield No. 1

90 SEEBEES 1st Camp

4 Marine Div.

3 Marine Div. (in reserve)

U.S. V Amphibious Corps (Schmidt)

5 Marine Div.

Mt. Suribachi

90 SEEBEES Landed

Iwo Jima 1945
Pacific

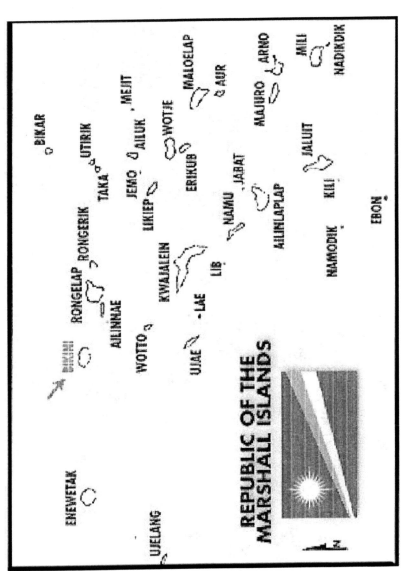

Bikini Atoll Location
Marshall Islands

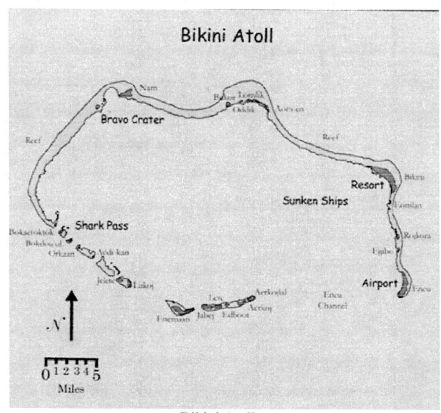

Bikini Atoll

101st Airborne Boarding a C-47
England 1944

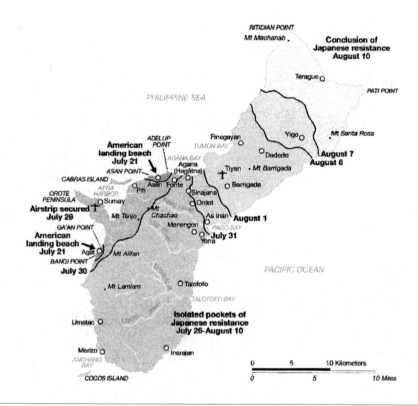

RITIDIAN POINT
Mt Machanao .

**Conclusion of
Japanese resistance
August 10**

Tarague O

PATI POINT

PHILIPPINE SEA

ADELUP
POINT

Finegayan

Yigo O

. Mt Santa Rosa

**American
landing beach
July 21**

TUMON BAY

O Dededo

**August 7
August 6**

AGANA BAY

Agana
(Hagåtna)

Tiyan • Mt Barrigada

ASAN POINT

CABRAS ISLAND

Asan Fonte

O Barrigada

*APRA
HARBOR*

Piti

Sinajana

*OROTE
PENINSULA*

O Sumay

O Ordot

**Airstrip secured
July 29**

Mt
Chachao

As Inan **August 1**

Mt Tenjo

Manengon

GA'AN POINT

O
Yona

PAGO BAY
July 31

**American
landing beach
July 21**

Agat O

Mt Alifan

BANGI POINT

July 30

. Mt Lamlam

O Talofofo

PACIFIC OCEAN

TALOFOFO BAY

**Isolated pockets of
Japanese resistance
July 26–August 10**

Umatac O

Merizo O

O Inarajan

*ANCHANG
BAY*

COCOS ISLAND

0	5	10 Kilometers
0	5	10 Miles

Island of Guam
Marianas Islands

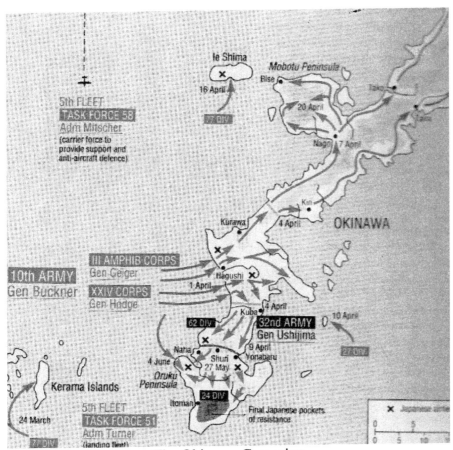

The Okinawa Campaign
April 1-June 14, 1945

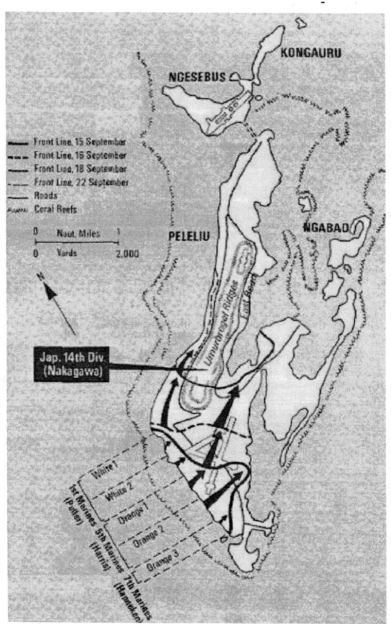

Peleliu, Pacific 1945

204

USN Submarine "Rasher" (the Red Scorpion)
Pacific Theater

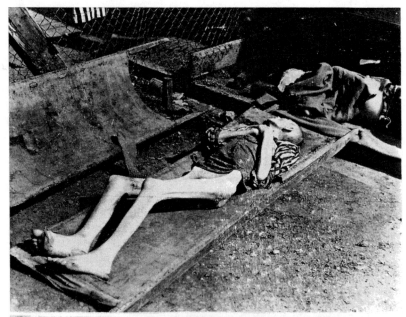

German Death Camp
Austria 1945

German Death Camp
Austria 1945

207

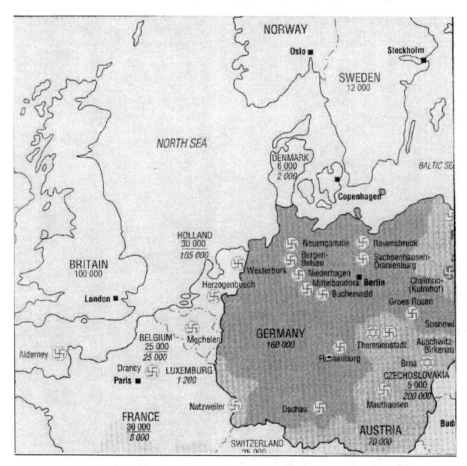

German Concentration Camps

Top Photo: Crash of B-25 at Istres, France
Bottom Photo: Crash of C-47 at Bovingdon, England

Terrell's Aircrew Europe

Herb Osburn 1943
Deceased

HERB OSBURN

A B-17 Crew Chief in Europe

Herb saw his first light of day on August 2, 1925. He was born in Grand Junction, Colorado in an upstairs bedroom of his grandparents home, as was his brother Bob. Herb was christened, Herbert Arthur Nichols, Jr.

Sometime after Herb's brother, Bob, was born just over a year after Herb's birth, the family moved to Albuquerque, New Mexico. The family only stayed in Albuquerque a short time before moving back to Grand Junction where Herb's brother, Bill, was born in 1929. After Bill's birth, Herb's father abandoned the family and Herb said, "We never saw him again for fifty years."

Although Herb's mother was a registered nurse she couldn't find a job after moving back to Grand Junction, so she took a position working in a restaurant in order to support her children. While working at the restaurant she met Herb's stepfather, who was also employed at the same restaurant. After a short courtship they were married in 1933. Herb's sister, Jaymie, was born in 1935 and his sister, Sandra, was born in 1937.

Two years after Sandra was born the family moved to Glenwood Springs, where Herb's stepfather worked as a chef at the Glenwood Café. By the time Herb was fourteen years old he was able to find work at various jobs in order to help support the family. He mowed lawns, did yard work, cleaned garages and even helped a neighbor build some storage shelves. Herb also built storage shelves for Ms. Mabel Peteriens before he knew she was a teacher at Garfield County High School in Glenwood Springs. Herb said, "Ms. Peteriens gave me an old humpback Philco radio as payment for my labor,

212

but the radio didn't work. I replaced one tube in the radio and like magic we had a working radio that the family enjoyed for several years."

The Great Depression had left the country in a difficult economic stress and as a result, any kind of a job was welcome. One place where young boys could usually find work was at the local bowling alley. The bowling pins had to be set by hand as there were no automatic pin-setters at that time. The work was very demanding, not to mention the possibility of injury from the flying pins. Most of the young boys only resorted to working at the bowling alley when they were destitute and in need of a few dollars to help support their families.

When Herb started school in Glenwood Springs in the seventh grade he and his new pal, Rex Sidener, were automatically placed in the "B" class. They both decided they should be in the "A" class, so they didn't fool around in school that year. They diligently applied themselves to their studies and sure enough, they were both promoted to the "A" class the following year.

One day while setting pins at the bowling alley, Herb met Mr. M. J. Mayes, a local attorney in Glenwood Springs. Herb and his brothers, Bob and Bill, were considering changing their last name from Nichols to Osburn, their stepfather's name. Mr. Mayes offered to draw up the papers of adoption and shortly thereafter the three Nichols brothers became the three Osburn brothers. Herb said, "Mr. Mayes only charged us $50.00 for all the legal work involved." Herb's brother, Bob, was working at the local movie theater so with their combined earnings they were able to eventually pay Mr. Mayes in full for his legal services. Herb said, "I'm sure Mr. Mayes' normal fee was much higher than what he charged us, but he understood our financial situation so he gave us a break."

Herb's next job was working at the Glenwood Café as a dishwasher. After school started, Herb worked evenings and nights but going to school during the day proved to be very demanding on Herb's time as well as his health. Nevertheless, Herb managed to keep this job until the summer of 1942 when school let out for the summer vacation. Immediately after school had closed for the summer vacation, Herb stayed on at the Glenwood Café working nights as a cook. Herb said, "There wasn't a lot of business at night, so we made all our own pastries and dinner rolls for the next day." When school started again that fall Herb kept his job working the night shift. This created a problem for Herb as he wasn't able to get any rest and very little sleep. However, Herb partially resolved this problem as he found a way to catch a few winks. Mr. Latson, the shop teacher at the high school, came into the Glenwood Café every morning at 6:00 A.M. for his morning coffee and to pick up his sack lunch that was prepared for him each day. Herb finished his night shift at about the same time Mr. Latson finished his coffee, so Herb rode to school every morning with Mr. Latson. Upon arriving at school, Mr. Latson graciously unlocked the door to the shop so Herb could catch a couple of hours of sleep before his first class at 9:00 A.M. I have often wondered how the youth of today would manage if they were suddenly subjected to the same conditions that existed when Herb and his classmates were fourteen or fifteen years old. I like to believe they would come through just as we did during our youth.

Herb was only five feet three inches tall but he was very muscular and his body was very solid and well proportioned. He looked like he had been lifting weights for years and he was very athletic. During Herb's junior year of high school he organized a gymnastic tumbling team. Participants in this activity included Herb, Charles and Bill Jackson, Hal Terrell, James Abshire and Willie McDonald. Even though the high school staff couldn't provide an instructor, they did support the activity by locating two tumbling mats for our use. Herb was a natural gymnast—he could do handsprings from one end of the gym to the other, even though he had never received any instructions. Herb said, "We all had a lot of fun learning gymnastics the wrong way."

In August of 1943 Herb decided it was time for him to change his life style so he enlisted in the US Army Air Corps Cadet Program. He was called to active duty in September, just two weeks later. His first assignment was at Sheppard Field, Texas for basic training. After completing basic training Herb was transferred to Enid, Oklahoma where he was assigned to a CTD (college training detachment) group, a requirement of the cadet program. After several weeks in this program the entire group was "washed-out" at the convenience of the government. Herb was then sent to Amarillo, Texas to Aircraft Mechanics School.

After graduation from Aircraft Mechanics School, Herb was sent to gunnery school at Las Vegas, Nevada. He was trained as the top turret gunner on B-17 bombers. He completed this assignment in six weeks and was immediately sent to Rapid City Air Force Base, South Dakota for crew assembly. Herb was assigned as Flight Engineer and top turret gunner on the crew of Lt. Herbert L. Osborne. Herb thought this was a good omen to have two crewmembers with the same name. After the crew assignments were completed, Herb's crew was sent to Camp Kilmer, New Jersey where they boarded a liberty ship for a miserable two-week trip to England.

When Herb's ship docked in England, he and his crew were sent to Rougham Field near Bury St. Edmunds, about ninety miles north east of London. The crew was assigned to the eighth Air Force, Ninety-fourth Bomb Group, 410th squadron. Shortly after arriving at Rougham Field, Herb's crew flew their first combat mission against the submarine pens on the French coast. Their first mission was an eye-opener for the ten young men on Herb's crew.

The Ninety-fourth Bomb Group was first formed on January 28, 1942 at McDill Field, Florida, seventeen months before Herb joined the group. Shortly thereafter, the Ninety-fourth group moved to Biggs Field, El Paso, Texas, where they began training in B-17 heavy bombers. After the B-17 entered combat over Europe it was lovingly named the "Flying Fortress", but was sometimes referred to as the "Flack-trap". On January 2, 1943, the Ninety-fourth Bomb Group moved their full complement of aircrews, ground crews, and aircraft to Pueblo, Colorado where the group of airmen, along with their ground crews, completed their final training. In late March of 1943 overseas deployment of the aircrews and ground support personnel began, transferring them to England. Upon arrival in England the Ninety-fourth Bomb Group was split into two groups. One group was assigned to an air base at Bassingbot and the other group was sent to Thurleigh for combat indoctrination. They flew their first mission on the 13th of May 1943 over St. Amer, France, where the German submarine pens were located. After they had completed their first mission both groups were reunited and assigned to Rougham Field permanently. They remained at this airfield until the war ended and the crews were sent home.

Losses were high throughout 1943 and the first few months of 1944. The Ninety-fourth Bomb Group participated in all of the Eighth Air Force missions during this period. After Herb and his crew arrived in England heavy losses had begun to subside. Right after arriving at their new base in England, Herb's crew was assigned targets that included the German aircraft industry, submarine pens, ball bearing factories, synthetic rubber facilities, military transport of all kinds and other targets of growing importance. By the time Herb flew his first mission allied fighter planes were escorting the heavy bombers on most raids. Consequently, allied losses began to dwindle as German aircraft losses began to mount. Even though enemy fighter

216

activity had declined, flack remained a serious problem for the American and British aircrews. Fortunately for the bomber crews, the B-17 heavy bomber proved to be very durable during the daylight raids. The B-17 could take a great deal of punishment and still manage to make it back to their bases in England. The B-17 carried a crew of ten men and the aircraft was armed with ten heavy fifty caliber machine guns. During raids on enemy targets the B-17's flew in tight formation for protection from enemy fighters. This allowed the bomber formations to maximize their firepower against enemy fighters. The Army Air Corps planners thought their heavy armament and tight formations were sufficient to ward off German fighters and still successfully conduct precision daylight raids over Germany. However, when operational bombing missions commenced, the air groups were severely mauled by the Luftwaffe fighters. It was not until the introduction of the P-51 Mustang, which had sufficient range to accompany the bomber groups to their targets, that the bomber groups finally enjoyed a measure of protection from enemy interceptors. The B-17 crews of the Eighth Air Force flew a total of 291,508 sorties over enemy territory and dropped a total of 640,306 tons of bombs on enemy targets. In the process the Eighth Air Force lost a total of 6,000 aircraft but the havoc they rained down on Germany, and the total annihilation they imposed upon the Luftwaffe was just compensation. Before the war ended the Eighth Air Force earned the reputation as the greatest air arm ever used by any country as it eventually reached a total strength of 350,000 personnel by mid-1944. For this reason the Eighth Air Force became known as the "Mighty Eighth". Half of the United States Army Air Corps casualties, worldwide during WWII were suffered by the Eighth Air Force during its strategic bombing campaigns over Europe. More than 26,000 airmen were killed in action during WWII. This represents over one-tenth of all Americans killed during the war. Thousands more young men were wounded and a total of 28,000 were taken prisoner during the daylight raids over Germany. Airmen of the Eighth Air Force were awarded seventeen Congressional Medals of Honor, 220 Distinguished Service Crosses, thousands of Purple Hearts and hundreds of Distinguished Flying Crosses and Air Medals.

The Ninety-fourth Bomb Group flew their last mission on April 21, 1945. They flew 324 missions for a total of 8,884 sorties and dropped a total of 18,924 tons of bombs on enemy targets. By the time the war ended the Ninety-fourth Bomb Group had suffered the loss of 153 B-17's and hundreds of crewmembers had been either killed or were missing in action.

Shortly after Herb's arrival in England he flew a mission to Berlin, Germany. Six hundred and sixty Eighth Air Force B-17's took part in this raid. The raid was escorted by P-51 Mustangs and it was hoped that enemy fighters would engage them. The Luftwaffe fighters were no match for the P-51 Mustangs during such mission so the Germans lost eighty fighter planes and heavy damage was inflicted on Berlin. This raid was considered very successful even though the Eighth Air Force lost sixty-nine bombers. Once the bombers had released their bombs, the P-51 Mustangs were free to leave the Bomber formations during their return trip to their home bases. Thus they ranged far and wide strafing railroads, highways, motorized equipment, enemy troops, and other targets of opportunity. This action was a constant threat to enemy troops and cost Germany the lives of hundreds of soldiers.

In July of 1944 British and American bombers attacked Hamburg, Germany. Herb's group participated in this bombing raid during daylight hours. The British bombed Hamburg at night and these raids produced a "fire-storm" that completely devastated the city. Smoke columns of super-heated air rose over two miles high with winds up to thirty-five miles per hour on the ground. It was estimated that 100,000 Germans were killed as a result of these raids and 300,000 buildings were burned to the ground, leaving 750,000 people homeless.

On February 13 and again on February 14, the Eighth Air Force, which included the Ninety-fourth Bomb Group as well as British heavy bombers, concentrated on Dresden, German as their target. Saturation bombing was employed during these raids and once again a devastating "fire-storm" resulted. Dresden was the cultural center of Germany and the city burned for more than a week. Thirty-five thousand people lost their lives in this raid and 1,600 acres of the city burned to the ground. By the time the war finally ended twenty percent of the total residential areas of Germany were destroyed and hundreds of thousands of people had lost their lives. Over 780,000 people were injured and the war left almost eight million people homeless.

Herb was scheduled to fly a combat mission on May 5, 1945, against U-boat pens located on the North Sea. But this mission was canceled because the Russian Army had already captured this area before the mission could get off the ground. Herb never flew another combat mission after this date as Germany capitulated on May 8, 1945. Herb flew a total of sixteen combat missions by the time the war had ended.

May 8, 1945, was designated as VE Day (Victory in Europe) and there was great excitement throughout England and the world, but for the men of the Ninety-fourth their response was calm. Most of these young men lived with the memories of the devastation they had brought upon Germany and the German people. They couldn't help but wonder how many deaths their actions had brought upon innocent women, children and old people. No doubt keeping such thoughts to themselves is one of the primary reasons most WWII veterans have been so hesitant to talk about their war experiences. They simply wanted to forget!

After the war, Herb's group was scheduled to move to Germany as part of the occupational forces but seven crews, including Herb's crew, were transferred to Marseilles, France. After settling down in their new location they removed the top and belly turrets from their planes and installed cameras that were synchronized with the planes automatic pilots. They also removed the bomb racks and installed extra fuel tanks in the bomb bays. Upon completion of these changes to their aircraft they transferred to Oran, North Africa where they started flying photo missions over North Africa. Several weeks later they moved to Dakar, French West Africa, where they continued map-making photo flights. Herb said, "We would pick up two box lunches during breakfast, then fly for twelve or thirteen hours each day. After returning to our base we had to perform maintenance on our own planes." Ground crews normally performed maintenance duties, but when the point system was initiated the ground crews who had been overseas for two years had the most points so they were sent home first. Consequently, the maintenance of all aircraft fell to the aircrews to perform. Herb said, "Even the engineering officer, a major, was in the grease up to his elbows most of the time."

Herb's group did enjoy a few days off now and then. They usually spent their free time at the beach or on occasion they would fly to Marrakech just to wander around through the markets in the Arab part of the city. Finally Herb's crew left Dakar in mid-February of 1946 and reported to a staging area in Goebstadt, Germany where they were processed for return to the United States. Herb said, "We were sent in a truck convoy to LeHavre, France where we boarded another liberty ship bound for Camp Kilmer, New Jersey." After an uneventful voyage Herb landed at Camp Kilmer where he remained overnight before boarding a train bound for the separation center at Fort Bliss, Texas. Herb was released from active duty on March 23, 1946.

Once Herb had his discharge papers in hand he managed to hitch a ride to Denver, Colorado on an Army Air Corps C-47. From Denver he took a bus to Glenwood Springs where he spent a short visit before going to Grand Junction to visit his aunt and grandmother. From Grand Junction he flew on a commercial flight to Los Angeles and then managed to hitch a ride with a good Samaritan to Hemet, California where his folks resided. He arrived at his mother's home on Mother's Day. It was a wonderful 'home-coming' for both Herb and his mother.

Herb took a well-deserved rest before going to work in his step-father's restaurant in Hemet, but he soon decided he didn't care for the restaurant business. He found a job working for Cyclone Fence Company, a firm specializing in installing chain link fences. Most jobs were fencing horse ranches in the Hemet area.

Herb was considering going to college on the G.I. Bill when he met and married his wife, Pauline. It wasn't long before long Herb found another job working for a local electrical contractor. He liked this kind of work and before long he had formed his own company. He operated Osburn Electrical Company for the next thirty years and he and Pauline raised three children in the meantime. Herb eventually sold his business in 1991, and after forty-two years of marriage he and Pauline separated. For the past few years Herb lived with his daughter and grandson in the San Bernardino Mountains in California.

In September of 2001 a class reunion was held in Glenwood Springs, and many of Herb's grade school and high school classmates attended the affair. Herb also attended along with his daughter and grandson. This was the second time I had seen Herb since our high school days so many years ago.

It was a wonderful and joyful occasion to see Herb once again and he was the same nice, sweet person I had known when we were boys. I enjoyed the all too short time we had together.

General MacArthur was wrong when he said, "Old soldiers never die, they just fade away." A few days after Herb had returned home from the class reunion he went to bed one evening and didn't wake up. So, old soldiers do die, just as Herb died, but he will never fade away. His passing has left an ache in my heart and I will miss him. So to Herb I say, "Aloha, old friend, rest in peace…you have earned it!"

THE UNKNOWN SOLDIER

By Billy Rose

There's a graveyard near the White House
Where the Unknown Soldier lies,
And the flowers there are sprinkled
With the tears from
Mother's eyes.

I stood there not so long ago
With roses for the brave,
And suddenly I heard a voice
Speaking from the grave.

"I am the Unknown Soldier,"
The spirit voice began,
"And I think I have the right to ask
Some questions man to man.

"Are my buddies taken care of?
Was their victory so sweet?
Is that big reward you offered
Selling pencils on the street?

"Did they really win the freedom
They battled to achieve?
Do you still respect the Croix de Guerre
Above that empty sleeve?

"Does a Gold Star in the window
Now mean anything at all?
I wonder how my old girl feels
When she hears the bugle call?

"And that baby who sang 'Hello, Central,
Give me No Man's Land,'
Can they replace her daddy
With a military band?

"I wonder if the profiteers
Have sacrificed their greed?
I wonder if a soldier's mother
Ever is in need?

"I wonder if the kings who planned it all
Are really satisfied?
They played their game of checkers
And eleven million died.

"I am the Unknown Soldier,
And maybe died in vain,
But if I were alive and my country called,
I'd do it all over again."

Ralph Rakich 1943

2001

RALPH RAKICH

The Red Scorpion

Ralph was born July 2, 1925 in a farmhouse in Gentry, Arkansas. His parents, Tony and Hazel Rakich produced a second son, Roy, who was two years younger than Ralph. Ralph's mother was a local girl from Gentry, Arkansas and his father was born in Germany.

The Rakich family moved to Colorado when Ralph was in the fourth grade. They moved back and forth from Arkansas to Colorado nine times before finally settling down permanently in Colorado. They first lived for a short time in Carbondale, Colorado before moving to a small ranch located on Cattle Creek, a few miles from Carbondale. "I really started to enjoy life after we moved to Cattle Creek", Ralph said.

After Ralph completed the fifth grade at the Cattle Creek School, the family moved to Glenwood Springs. Ralph said he had to take the fifth grade over after moving to Glenwood. About the same time as Ralph entered the fifth grade in Glenwood, his mother moved back to Arkansas. Ralph and his brother, Roy, were given the choice of staying in Glenwood with their father or moving back to Arkansas with their mother. Ralph said, "There was no way I was going back to Arkansas because I remembered working at the Allen Canning Factory when I was seven or eight years old, and I certainly didn't want to have anything more to do with that place." His job at the canning factory was nailing crates together for which he received a few cents per crate. Ralph said, "The boss would come by and if the crate was not perfect, he kicked it apart and demanded that I start all over again." Ralph's mother also worked at the canning factory peeling tomatoes. "It was not the most enjoyable part of my life", Ralph said.

Ralph started high school at Garfield County High School in 1941 at the age of fifteen. His father built a new log house not far from school so Ralph, along with his brother and father, settled down to a fairly stable and organized life style. Ralph's father owned two trucks and he delivered coal around town, as almost everyone heated their homes and cooked their meals on coal-burning stoves. Both Ralph and his brother, Roy, were required to help their father deliver coal and Ralph said, "I have shoveled enough coal to last me a lifetime." Two or three times a week Ralph drove one of the coal trucks to the Streitter Coal Mine to get a load of coal. The Streitter Mine was located about seventy-five miles from Glenwood Springs. Ralph's pal, John Artaz, went with Ralph occasionally, to help him load the truck and drive home. Sometimes Ralph didn't get back to Glenwood Springs before one or two o'clock in the morning, then he had to clean up and go to school. If children in today's society had to work in a canning factory nailing crates together when they were seven or eight years old, or had to drive a truck seventy-five miles to get a load of coal when they were fifteen or sixteen years old, such activities would be labeled "child abuse."

During one of Ralph's return trips from the Streitter Mine, State Patrol Officer, Oran Doolan, stopped Ralph in Silt, Colorado. It was 2:00 A.M. in the morning and Ralph said, "Officer Doolan asked me if I remembered driving over a flower garden one day while delivering coal to his house. I told him that I did remember the occasion, but I also told him the garden was planted partially in the alley." Patrolman Doolan then told Ralph he had promised his wife he would issue the perpetrator a ticket when the opportunity presented itself. Ralph wasn't old enough at the time to be driving a truck, and he didn't have a driver's license. Ralph said, "Patrolman Doolan was a very nice man and he didn't give me a ticket." The Colorado State Patrol at that time was called, "Courtesy Patrol", so Ralph concluded that Officer Doolan had extended him a measure of courtesy. No doubt Officer Doolan was aware of Ralph's family financial situation, so he chose to ignore the entire matter.

In June of 1943 a recruiter from the Military Arsenal in Ogden, Utah came to Glenwood Springs to recruit people to work at the Arsenal. Ralph thought it would be a great adventure so he signed up. The pay was good and Ralph said, "It was the first time I ever received a paycheck that I could call my own." Ralph worked at the Arsenal all that summer and fall as a truck driver, bus driver, and as the personal chauffeur for the Arsenal Commander. Ralph was the youngest licensed truck driver employed at the Arsenal and he hauled everything from trash to live ammunition, in addition to driving the school bus.

Ralph said, "The Arsenal Commander had little or no mercy as he kept me busy day and night. He thought speeding up and down country roads at night with the siren blaring and the red light flashing would keep sheep, cattle, people and other cars off the road. I never worked so many hours in all my life. He was far worse than my father. I told him he was going to get us killed and if I was going to die, I wanted to do it in the war." The Arsenal Commander informed Ralph that he wouldn't release him from his job so he could join the service. He told Ralph he was married to his job for the duration.

Ralph had just turned eighteen and he was as cocky as most other eighteen year olds, so he challenged the Arsenal Commander's authority, packed his bag and caught a bus to Glenwood Springs. When Ralph arrived in Glenwood Springs, he found his draft notice waiting for him. Ralph said, "I guess the Arsenal Commander had some authority after all as I have always believed he had something to do with me being drafted so soon after turning eighteen." Ralph reported to Fort Logan in Denver, Colorado on

December 12, 1943 for his physical examination and induction into the armed services. Much to Ralph's amazement, he was asked which branch of the service he preferred to join. Ralph had already determined he didn't want to be in the Army or the Marine Corps so he chose the Navy. Ralph said, "My father was in the Army during WWI and was left on the battlefield for dead. He survived but was partially disabled for life, so I didn't want to be in that branch of the service. I didn't want to be in the Marine Corps either because I thought it was too dangerous and I might get killed. So I chose the Navy, believing the Navy was the safest branch of the service to be in." Ralph went on to say, "I sure had this all wrong because I ended up serving aboard a submarine, which was probably far more life threatening than either the Army or the Marine Corps."

Ralph was sent to Farragut, Idaho for boot camp training. After sixteen weeks of boot camp, Ralph reported to the San Diego Naval Base where he was trained in the operation of stern torpedoes and high-pressure hydraulics. Upon completing these training schools, he was asked if he intended to spend his entire Navy career in school, or if he thought it was time to go to war. Ralph replied, "I would prefer to go to another school." He was told to wait while a search could be made where there might be an opening in some other school the Navy could offer him. After ten or fifteen minutes wait, Ralph was informed he could indeed go to another school, but this one would be submarine school in New London, Connecticut. "Not exactly what I had in mind", Ralph replied."

After graduating from sub-school Ralph was shipped back to California by train. The train made a stop in Glenwood Springs where Ralph was met by his father and brother for a short visit. Upon arrival in San Francisco at 3:00 A.M., Ralph was met at the depot and taken directly to Hunters Point where he was assigned as a crew member on the submarine, Rasher-SS-269.

Ralph, and other crewmembers spent the next six weeks re-fitting the Rasher and getting her ready for her next patrol. They made several sea-trials out of Hunters Point to check all of the equipment in order to insure the Rasher was completely sea-worthy and ready for combat. During sea trials no one was able to get much sleep, as crewmembers and technicians were busy going over every detail checking and rechecking equipment.

The Rasher's overhaul and sea-trials were finally completed, so Captain Adams backed the Rasher away from her berth and sailed under the Golden Gate Bridge on December 20, 1944. A band played, "Anchors Aweigh" as the Rasher pulled away from the pier and she looked brand new in her fresh coat of paint. She proudly displayed her potent five-inch aft gun, a forty-millimeter gun on her deck and a forest of new antennas sprouting from her conning tower. The crew was made up of both veterans from previous patrols as well as new crewmembers fresh from sub-school in New London, CT.

Upon departing from Hunters Point the Rasher made for Hawaii. Rough weather accompanied her all the way from California to Hawaii, so the crew was relieved when they finally passed Diamond Head and sailed into Pearl Harbor. She tied up alongside a finger pier and immediately began taking on 38,000 gallons of fuel. She also topped off her water tanks and loaded many other supplies aboard before getting underway, headed for Midway Island.

On January 2, 1945, the Rasher arrived at Midway after once again encountering very rough weather the entire way. Ralph said, "By this time I was ready to join the Army or the Marines." The Rasher had once again survived the bad weather and the crew had survived sixteen days of intense wolf-pack training along with two other submarines. The Rasher made a stop at Midway Island before entering Tanapag Harbor on the island of Saipan in the Marianas Islands. After arriving at Saipan the Rasher once again took on supplies and fuel. The Rasher, along with the Fishback and the Pilotfish then proceeded to their assigned areas in the China Sea.

Orders called for this trio of submarines to form a coordinated attack group to patrol the southern part of the East China Sea from Hangchow Bay, China to the Formosa Straits. This patrol was to be terminated on March 8, 1945, making for a forty-five-day run. The East China Sea presented many hazards. The waters in this area were only 100-fathoms deep, which was much too shallow for safe submarine activities. Mines were also a constant threat, especially at night when it was impossible to locate "floaters", or mines that had broken loose from their anchor chains. Ralph said, "We lost several subs to floating mines. On clear days we tried to shoot them whenever we sighted them, but this was very tricky because wave action hid the mines." Ralph also said, "We were depth-charged several times. Sometimes these enemy attacks lasted for hours. One time the air got real bad before we could surface to get fresh air. Many times we were down for as long as eighteen hours. Even though no man on the crew outwardly showed any fear, we were all terrified. I didn't know if my next breath would be my last one or not. It was very stressful and almost debilitating at times. A person doesn't realize how precious life is until he is faced with the possibility of losing it any moment." Ralph went on to say, "One night we saw a Jap ship with Red Cross markings that indicated it was a hospital ship. It was sitting too low in the water to be a hospital ship. It was probably loaded with war materials. We let it go, but another sub sank it. It was an ammunition ship, as it kept exploding for six hours. The captain of the sub that sank this ship received a court marshal as it did have a few wounded Japanese on board. Sometimes I don't know which is worse, war or politics. Not much difference, I guess."

After Japan lost the Marianas Islands, their vital convoy routes into the South Pacific and the East China Seas were severely compressed. The US brought a large submarine force to Guam and Saipan, just 1,500 miles from these sea-lanes. Admiral Lockwood organized his submarine wolf packs into groups of three to five boats. Their mission was to sever the flow of raw materials, Japanese troops and munitions to and from Japan. A new group of boats (submarines) showed up on station each week or two thereafter. The Japanese responded with larger convoys, more destroyers, and land-based air cover from Formosa. The Japanese also unleashed four escort carriers in support of their coverage, but the entire Japanese flotilla was under constant submarine attacks. The USS Rasher was one of these boats assigned to this operation. Collectively, Admiral Lockwood's wolf packs sank 201 Japanese war ships totaling 540,192 tons. Among these 201 Japanese war ships were four large carriers, one battleship, four small carriers, three heavy cruisers, eight light cruisers, forty-three destroyers and twenty-three submarines. Additionally, and of great importance, the submarines operating in the Pacific sent 1,213 Japanese merchant ships to the bottom for a total tonnage of 4,779,902 tons, which was only one million tons less than the entire pre-war Japanese merchant fleet.

US submarines operating in the Pacific accounted for fifty-five percent of all Japanese losses in the war. This was more tonnage sunk than by all the other U.S. surface ships, carrier planes and the US Air Corps combined. These statistics read more like a fiction novel than a historical narrative.

On March 8, 1945, the Rasher and her crew docked at Apra Harbor in Guam. Crewmembers reported to Camp Dealy for rest, and the Rasher went into dry-dock for repairs. Ralph said, "There were still quite a few Jap stragglers roaming around in the hills on Guam and their favorite pastime was sniping at U.S. military personnel. Every time we had to go to the toilet we had to be escorted by a Marine guard."

After repairs were completed, which took about two weeks, the Rasher and her new captain, Commander Nance and his crew, participated in two or three sea-trials before heading for their next patrol a few miles off-shore of the Japanese home islands. During this patrol they searched for floating mines, sank or damaged a few small ships, stood on assigned stations to pick up downed B-29 air crews returning from raids on Japan, and kept an eye out for Japanese subs operating in the same area.

Finally Ralph's luck ran out. The Rasher was operating on the surface a few miles off the coast of Japan when she was attacked by a large Japanese aircraft. As the Rasher dived two bombs exploded on either side of the submarine causing minor damage and a few water leaks. Ralph and one of his mates were resting in their bunks at the time. Ralph said, "My bunk and the one next to me ended up in the torpedo pit, bunk frames and all. It beat the hell out of both of us. My back has never been the same."

At the conclusion of this patrol, Ralph was put aboard the sub tender, Griffin, and sent to Midway Island to wait for a hospital ship to take him back to the United States. All hospital ships were already overcrowded so Ralph remained on Midway Island for several weeks until the Griffin sailed for San Francisco with Ralph on board. Once the Griffin reached San Francisco, Ralph was transferred to the Naval Hospital on Treasure Island where he remained for the next three months.

Ralph was very proud to have been a crewmember aboard the Rasher, as she was one of the most famous boats in the Navy. Under previous Captains, the Rasher had achieved an enviable record. She was commissioned on June 8, 1943 in Manitowoc, Wisconsin and by the war's end she had participated in eight action-packed war patrols. Ralph was a crewmember on two of these combat patrols. The Rasher's combat record earned her the nickname, "The Red Scorpion". Her actions against the Japanese were the stuff legends are made of. The Red Scorpion sank eighteen Japanese naval and merchant vessels, including the Japanese aircraft carrier, Taiyo. By August 15, 1945, when the war officially ended, the Rasher had sent a total of 99,901 tons of Japanese shipping to "Davy Jones's Locker". This represented the second highest tonnage sank by any submarine operating in the Pacific or the Atlantic. She was carrying out offensive sweeps west of the Philippines and attacking enemy shipping near Formosa when she received the famous radio message from Admiral Chester Nimitz, "Cease offensive operations against Japanese forces." The war had finally ended, but the road to victory had been a long and difficult journey. The Japanese had felt the sting of the Red Scorpion.

By the time the Rasher was decommissioned on June 26, 1946, she had been in combat a total of 401 days. In addition to the 99,901 tons of Japanese shipping sunk, the Rasher had steamed a total of 122,655 nautical miles, made 861 dives and fired 165 torpedoes. At war's end the Rasher's crew had been awarded four Presidential Citations, seven Battle Stars, four Navy Crosses, twelve Silver Stars, sixteen Bronze Stars, six Letters of Commendations, one Legion of Merit---and one eighteen year old young man from Glenwood Springs, Colorado had been a part of this action.

With his discharge papers in his pocket, Ralph headed for Glenwood Springs, to visit his brother, Roy, before returning to New London, CT. Ralph said, "Being sent to sub school in New London was the best thing that ever happened to me. While going to sub school I met a young lady and fell in love. Her name was Doris Rubano and we have now been married for over 50 years. Her family came to the United States from Italy just before the Great Depression hit America in 1929. At that time her family, like every other family in the United States, worked twelve to sixteen hours a day just to survive.

Ralph and Doris started their married life in Colorado, but after the war good jobs in Glenwood Springs were hard to come by, so Ralph and Doris moved back to Connecticut. Ralph worked at several jobs, all related to the trucking industry. In the meantime Ralph and Doris had four children and were enjoying life to the fullest. Ralph finally formed a partnership with a friend and they owned and operated a truck-garage for the next twenty years. Ralph said, "We kept the garage open seven days a week, twenty-four hours a day." Eventually, Ralph and his partner dissolved the partnership and Ralph purchased his own trucks and became a very successful trucker, operating throughout the United States. Ralph recalled one occasion when he was driving one of his tank trailers through Glenwood Springs. He stopped to see his brother, Roy, and left the following morning at 4:00 A.M. While driving through the Glenwood Canyon he was involved in a serious accident. The accident occurred when an elderly lady failed to negotiate a sharp curve in the canyon. Ralph's tanker truck and two other large trucks were involved in the accident and three people lost their lives. Ralph said, "My rig rolled over on its side which caused considerable damage to my new Peterbilt cab unit." Fortunately the tank didn't suffer much damage, which was of great concern to Ralph, as he was hauling a tank full of 140-proof brandy (un-cut). Ralph wasn't seriously hurt having suffered a few cuts and bruises. Ralph said, "My greatest concern had to do with fire which would have made matters even worse than they already were. I guess the devil didn't want me that day and neither did the Good Lord. Three months and $36,000 later I was back on the road again. I ended up hauling bagels and I made more money then than I ever had before. The best part was, I got paid every week." All good things eventually come to an end so Ralph sold his trucking business and moved to Florida in 1987.

While Ralph and Doris were living in Florida they lost their oldest son to cancer and their oldest daughter contracted MS. Upon receiving this bad news they decided to "go home". They moved back to Connecticut, purchased a new home and settled down to enjoy the rest of their lives as best they could under the circumstances. Ralph said, "We are in good health for our age and we hope the downhill slide will be a long one. I still drive an eighteen-wheeler one or two days a week…just enough to keep me active."

Ralph is truly a unique individual and is a typical WWII veteran!

SUBMARINERS POEM

Anonymous

There are stories told about knights of old and the shooting of Dan McGrew
And the classic tale of the great white whale still thrills us through and
through.
There's Farragut and John Paul but the saltiest of them all
Were the boys in blue from World War II who answered freedom's call.

Now I won't boast so I'll drink a toast to the boys who went down under,
With Navy pride they fought and died when their boats were ripped asunder.
They learned their trade, our debt they paid in the world beneath the sea
And there they sleep in waters deep, a part of history.

Those noble ships with sonar blips once fought their way to Glory
And the men inside, because they died, left none to tell their story.
Proud Argonaut, you had your shot, you and the Amberjack,
"Twas near Rabual you gave your all and never more came back.

Pompano, you and Runner too, were lost in forty-three,
Your gallant crew went down with you, defending liberty.
The Pickerel too, and sleek Wahoo, the Grampus, and the Herring,
The Albacore, all lost in war, have taken their last bearing.

So many more, subs by the score, went to their watery grave,
In silence deep, they lie asleep, the young lads and the brave.
But this I know, somewhere below lay those who paid the price,
Our debt is paid because they made the final sacrifice.

Alex Rule 1943

2001

ALEX RULE

Twenty-five missions over Germany Targets

"Alex Rule became a man before he ever had the chance to be a boy!"

His fractured family life and desperate economic situation were the two contributing circumstances that changed his life. He was born on March 8, 1926, in Santa Barbara, California. There were two other children in the family, an older sister and a younger brother. The family moved to Silt, Colorado in 1931, where Alex attended the first grade. Shortly after entering the first grade his mother passed away, leaving his father with the responsibility of supporting and raising three children. By the time Alex was ready to enter the second grade, his father had moved the family to Glenwood Springs, a distance of 21 miles.

Alex remained in school in Glenwood Springs through the eighth grade, but those ne years were difficult ones for him. His father was not physically capable or inclined to look after Alex, so his care became the responsibility of his older sister, Olive. From age fourteen, Alex managed to survive on his own, even though he lived with his sister or wherever else he could find temporary accommodations. The day Alex turned sixteen he cajoled his sister into signing a document stating that he was eighteen years old. He also managed to have his birth certificate doctored so it showed he was eighteen years old. With these documents in hand he visited the Army Air Corps recruiter on March 11, 1942, and gave himself a birthday present by enlisting in the service of his country. From that moment on, this young boy began his new life as a man and became a true success story to be admired---an inspiration for every young person living in today's society, and absolute proof, "where there is a will, there is a way". Alex's life is one of the most touching chronicles to come out of The Great Depression and the aftermath of World War II.

Alex never got lost in his dreams but lived them to the fullest. He received his basic training at Sheppard Field, Texas. Upon completing basic training, he remained in Texas for the next nine months to attend aircraft mechanics school, a prerequisite to qualifying as a Crew Chief on a B-17 Superfortress. His next assignment was a six-week stint in gunnery school in Las Vegas, Nevada. After completing gunnery school he reported to Gowan Field, near Boise, Idaho for additional flight training. Mastering simulated combat flight training, Alex was assigned to the 8th Air Force, 379th Heavy Bomb Group, 524th Bomb Squadron. He arrived in England in April of 1943 and was stationed at Kimbolton Air Base, approximately sixty miles from London.

In addition to the 524th Bomb Squadron, the 379th Bomb Group was also made up of three other Bomb Squadrons--the 525th, 526th and the 527th Squadrons. All the airmen in these four squadrons were assigned as crewmembers on B-17 Flying Fortresses with each bomber carrying a crew of ten men. Alex and his crew flew their first combat mission against the U-boat pens at St. Nazaire, France on April 29, 1943.

Alex was a diminutive young lad who measured five feet, five inches in height. He served as the tail gunner on his crew but also flew other gun positions as well. The tail gunner position was known as Tail-End-Charlie and was the most vulnerable position on a B-17 bomber. German fighters generally launched their attacks against B-17's from the rear as fewer guns could be brought to bear against them when attacking from this position. Consequently, tail gunners suffered the highest casualty rate of any other crew position on a B-17.

As was the custom, Alex and his crewmembers named their B-17. The name they chose was "Sweater Girl". In spite of suffering damage on almost every raid against German targets, "Sweater Girl" always came through and brought her crew back to England. "Sweater Girl" flew another twenty-two missions after Alex had finished his tour of 25 missions. Alex said, "I later ran into a guy I knew while in England who told me 'Sweater Girl' had been lost over Germany while on her 47th mission. She must have looked like she had smallpox by then because she was full of dozens of holes and covered with as many patches when I left the group. She was a fine aircraft and had earned the respect of every crewmember who ever flew with her on a mission. Losing that plane was just like losing a member of the family...I loved her! No crewmember who flew a mission on "Sweater Girl" was ever injured, but all of us were always scared out of our wits. Anyone who wasn't scared was either numb or nuts. I know I was scared a lot but we never talked about that amongst ourselves. We mostly talked about how heavy the flak was or how many German fighters there were. We didn't see many of our own fighters because our missions were flown before our own escort fighters became available. The British Spitfire was a great short-range fighter but it didn't have the range to escort us to our targets. Once they reached the French coast they headed back to England and we were on our own."

General Eaker, Commander of the 8th Air Force in Europe, identified German aircraft industry as the highest target priorities, especially German fighter assembly plants, engine factories, petroleum targets and transportation systems. Submarine base targets also continued to be top priority as well.

In addition to heavy losses suffered from German flak and fighter action, erratic weather was also a constant enemy. Nevertheless, the 524th Bomb

Squadron continued their operations and mounted major missions deep into Germany against important industrial targets. It was on August 17, 1943, when the Eighth Air Force launched its ill-fated raid against the ball-bearing works at Schweinfurt, Germany. Three-hundred and seventy-six B-17's participated in the Schweinfurt raid, including Alex's crew aboard "Sweater Girl". Sixty bombers were lost to enemy flak and fighter action during the raid. It was one of the most intense air battles of the war against the Luftwaffe. Of the 254 bombers that made it back to England, over half of them suffered severe damage and many crewmembers were either, killed, wounded, or taken prisoner.

This mission was number eleven for Alex--only fourteen more to go until he could rotate back to the United States. However, his prospects of completing twenty-five missions were not very likely as losses continued to mount. It was not a very pleasant thought for the B-17 crews to have to face knowing they would either be shot down or killed in action. During all of 1943 and the first half of 1944, air crews could only expect to survive 13 or 14 missions. One's chances of survival were very bleak indeed.

In spite of such heavy losses against Schweinfurt, the 8th Air Force made another massive raid on September 6, 1943, against Stuttgart, Germany. This was the sixteenth raid for Alex--only nine more to go!

General Eaker sent 262 bombers against Stuttgart, but German fighters and flak shot down forty-five of the B-17's during that raid. Undaunted by such heavy losses, General Eaker organized his bomber force for another maximum effort once again against Schweinfurt, Germany. This raid took place on October 14, 1943, and the group suffered heavy losses as expected. The second Schweinfurt raid became known as "Black Thursday." The 8th Air Force lost sixty-two bombers out of a total of 228 B-17's flown against the target that day. Of the surviving 166 B-17's, 138 suffered heavy damage and a high casualties, leaving only twenty-eight bombers unscathed. But, Alex had only five more missions to go!

Such high attrition rates meant the average bomber crews would not be around to fly their twenty-fifty mission. After "Black Thursday", it became clear to General Eaker that he was faced with a serious dilemma. Daylight bombing raids against Germany had reached a crisis point and drastic measures were called for. British bomber crews had long since given up on daylight raids due to heavy losses and had switched to night-raids. However, General Eaker and the 8th Air Force brass were convinced that daylight raids would bring Germany to her knees, so they picked up where the British had left off. The morale of all bomber crews was at its lowest point and something had to be done to alleviate the situation. At the rate of current bomber losses it became clear that the 8th was flying itself into extinction. Bombers just could not survive beyond the range of fighter escort. Since the Allies did not have fighters with sufficient range to serve as escorts, losses continued to plague the bomber crews.

Major General James H. "Jimmy" Doolittle replaced General Eaker as the 8th Air Force commander on January 6, 1944. Doolittle was convinced fighter escort was the key to successful bombardment of German targets. He immediately began building an air wing of P-38 Lightning and Republic P-47 Thunderbolt fighters to escort the B-17's on future raids against German targets. He also discovered that by adding fuel-drop-wing-tanks and British Rolls Royce Merlin engines to the American P-51 Mustang, he could extend fighter escort all the way to Berlin and back. Unfortunately, these plans were not put into action until Alex had finally flown his twenty-fifty and last mission against Bremen, Germany on December 13, 1943. After fighter escort came into being, the 8th Air Force mounted a third raid against

Schweinfurt, Germany in early February of 1944. Only eleven bombers were lost on this raid out of a total of 231 bombers flown against the target.

The following is a complete list of the twenty-five missions flown by Alex. His crew was the first and only crew of the 524th Bomb Squadron to complete their twenty-five missions.

MISSION NUMBER	TARGET	DATE
1.	St. Nazaire, France	April 29, 1943
2.	Bremen, Germany	June 13, 1943
3.	Hamburg, Germany	June 25, 1943
4.	Lemans, France	July 4, 1943
5.	Villa Coublay, France	July 14, 1943
6.	Zuider Zee, Holland	July 17, 1943
7.	Heroya, Norway	July 24, 1943
8.	Kassell, Germany	July 30, 1943
9.	Amiens, France	August 15, 1943
10.	Le Bourget, France	August 16, 1943
11.	Schweinfurt, Germany	August 17, 1943
12.	Villa Coublay, France	August 24, 1943
13.	Wattan, France	August 27, 1943
14.	Amiens, France	August 31, 1943
15.	Romilly, France	September 3, 1943
16.	Stuttgart, Germany	September 6, 1943
17.	Brussels, Belgium	September 7, 1943
18.	Rennes, France	September 9, 1943
19.	Emden, Germany	October 2, 1943

20.	Schweinfurt, Germany	October 14, 1943
21.	Gelsenkinden, Germany	November 5, 1943
22.	Oslo, Norway	November 16, 1943
23.	Bremen, Germany	December 5, 1943
24.	Emden, Germany	December 11, 1943
25.	Bremen, Germany	December 13, 1943

Even though Alex had put a lot of his worst moments out of his mind, he did finally share some of his bad experiences with me. "It really doesn't bother me to talk about my experiences," he said, "It's just that I sort of pushed them back out of the way and started to live in the present. There were some things I saw that were not pleasant to witness, just as it probably was for a lot of other men. I will never forget the worst mission I ever flew. It was, without question, the first raid on Schweinfurt, Germany where the ball-bearing works was our target."

The Stars and Stripes reported a loss of sixty planes that day, but Alex thinks he himself watched close to that many go down even though he had a lot more to do than count planes. He said, "I never saw anything like that raid. I swear, I saw parts and pieces of planes falling out of the sky and parachutes just about everywhere I looked. I remember seeing more than one plane pull away from the group and then seeing parachutes blossom. It was hard to accept when a plane went down and only two or three chutes opened. Often, those who didn't make it back to England were friends and guys I bunked with and lived with. This was hard to deal with but was a regular occurrence and happened on every mission."

The first Schweinfurt mission was especially costly because the group missed the target approach on their first pass so the entire bomb group had to go around again in order to line up on the target. This gave the Germans two chances to put up an intense flak screen, and it also gave the German fighters time to land, refuel, and launch a second attack on the group. Some of the planes lost that day had run out of fuel on their way back to England. By the time the group had turned around for the second approach to the target, every fighter in Germany had jumped them. Alex saw B-17's shot down by flak or brought down by German fighters. He also witnessed crippled B-17 stragglers being shot down by German fighter planes. It wasn't a pretty sight to see a B-17 lose a wing and start to spin towards earth. The possibility of being shot down was devastating to all crewmembers. Such thoughts were constantly on every crewmember's mind as it might be his turn next time. Every mission was a bad experience, but the first Schweinfurt raid still weighs heavily in Alex's memory and on his mind.

Alex recalled, "One time we came back from a raid, I don't remember the target, but I do remember we lost an engine over France and carried a cannon shell home in the oil cooler. All crews were de-briefed after each mission in order to assess the damage to the target and also to report on the aircraft that had been shot down. Sometimes it might be a B-17 right off our wing and I knew the name of the airplane and the name of every man in that crew. I would pray that the men would be able to bail out, as did every other crewmember. It was heart rending when only two or three chutes opened. This always brought tears to my eyes and an ache in my heart. It was constantly on my mind if it would be my turn the next time. Living in fear every time I flew a mission was difficult to accept but I just had to learn to deal with that possibility. I had no control of my destiny under such conditions. Each and every man on every crew had to deal with these same thoughts in his own way. I also remember the relief I felt the day I completed my twenty-fifth mission." Between April 29, 1943 and December 13, 1943, Alex survived his twenty-five missions over enemy territory. Eventually mission requirements were raised to thirty-five, but not before fighter escort became available in 1944.

By the time the war had ended in Europe, the 8th Air Force had a total of 350,000 men and women stationed in England. Of this number, 200,000 were combat crew personnel. The 8th Air Force lost 26,000 men killed in action and 28,000 became prisoners of war. Nine thousand bombers were shot down by enemy flak and enemy fighter action and untold numbers of American aircraft had suffered damage. The British aircrews also suffered extensive losses. In addition to the 8th Air Force and the British Air Groups, the 9th, 12th and 15th Air Forces were also present in Europe. Before the war ended, the 9th Air Force was almost as big as the 8th and all of these combat groups had also suffered extensive losses over enemy targets.

In May of 1944, it was announced that the 379th Bomb Group had made an unprecedented "Operational Grand Slam" during the preceding months. The 379th was first in every phase of bombing. Bomb Groups were graded in several categories, and the 8th Air Force Grand Slam was a very unique honor that included achievements and recognition in:

1. Best bombing results (greatest percent of bombs on target).

2. Greatest tonnage of bombs dropped on target.

3. Largest number of aircraft attacking targets.

4. Lowest losses of aircraft.

5. Lowest abortive rate of aircraft dispatched.

On January 6, 1944, a US Army Press Censor in Europe released a news article to the Glenwood Post in Glenwood Springs, Colorado. The article read:

"The Glenwood Post received early this week a news story concerning a Glenwood Springs youth, who is now stationed somewhere in England. 'Tail-End-Charlie" finished up his tour of operations on a recent Fortress mission over Bremen, Germany. He has accounted for three enemy aircraft destroyed, and two damaged with two probables, fitting testimony to the accuracy of his guns and his own ability as a gunner.

"Tiny's full name is Staff Sergeant Alex S. Rule and he is from Glenwood Springs, Colorado. Only seventeen years old, the youthful gunner has been on such missions as Schweinfurt, Hamburg and Bremen. On a Schweinfurt mission a few weeks ago, he scored twice, sending two enemy aircraft down in flames, one of them exploding in mid-air."

Alex left the Army Air Force on a medical discharge on April 6, 1944 with the rank of Staff Sergeant. For his actions in combat, he was awarded the Distinguished Flying Cross, the Air Medal with three Oak Leaf Clusters, and two Presidential Citations.

Distinguished Flying Cross:

Criteria: Heroism or extraordinary achievement while participating in aerial flight.

Air Medal:

Criteria: Heroic actions or meritorious service while participating in aerial flight

Devices: Silver oak leaf cluster.

Presidential Unit Citation:

Criteria: Extraordinary heroism in action against an armed enemy.

After completing his twenty-fifth mission on December 13, 1943, Alex was sent back to the United States. He enjoyed a thirty-day furlough in Glenwood Springs, Colorado, before reporting to Santa Monica, California Air Base where he received a thorough physical examination. A spot was discovered on one of his lungs that, unfortunately, turned out to be tuberculosis. Alex was immediately admitted to the Army Air Force hospital in Santa Ana, California where he was confined for the next two months. He was next sent to the VA hospital in Walla Walla, Washington where he spent the next nine months in treatment. After his release from the hospital in Walla Walla, he went back to Colorado and found a job working for the Grand Junction Sentinel as a night watchman and Cub Reporter. However, this job was short-lived as Alex was once again admitted to the VA hospital in Van Nuys, California where he spent the next year. After leaving the hospital in Van Nuys, he spent an additional fifteen months in the hospital at Kerrville, Texas where he received additional treatment. Alex finally won his battle against TB just as he had won his battle against the Germans. He was released from the hospital in Kerrville, Texas in May of 1950.

During the months Alex had been confined in the various hospitals he studied for and was awarded his high school equivalency certificate. He enrolled at Mesa Junior College in Grand Junction, Colorado, for the fall term in 1951. He spent the next two years at Mesa Junior College before transferring to Colorado State College, Greeley, Colorado in 1953. Alex maintained an "A-minus" average and was a popular figure around campus, having been elected Student Body President during his second year.

Alex graduated from Colorado State College with a BA degree in 1955. He enrolled directly into the Master's program and received his Master's Degree in Education in 1957, once again maintaining an "A-minus" grade average. Even though Alex never spent one single day in high school, he had the determination and the intestinal fortitude to better himself. His achievement is one of which he can be very proud!

Alex taught school at Compton High School in Lompoc, California for four years before accepting a teaching position at Rangely High School in Colorado. Alex taught for one year at Rangely High School before he and his wife, the former Helen Lake, whom he had married on January 11, 1951, moved to Seward, Alaska where he retired in 1986.

Alex never lost his interest for flying after the war and he eventually turned this interest into a business. He obtained his Private Pilot's License in 1966, his Commercial License in 1970, his Instrument Rating and his Seaplane Rating, also in 1970. In 1971, he earned his Flight Instructor's Rating and went on to acquire his Multi-Engine Rating in 1975. From 1971 through 1976, he flew part time as a Bush Pilot for an Air Taxi Service known as Harbor Air, which he purchased in late 1970 and eventually sold in early 1976.

Alex continues to own and fly his own plane but is somewhat concerned that he may have to sell it soon as he may not be able to pass his next FAA physical.

"I'll keep flying as long as I feel I am not jeopardizing anyone else and the FAA approves my medical," he said. "There is no other thrill on earth like piloting your own plane, especially in this part of the world where God created so much beauty."

It might be said that Alex Rule started life "on the wrong side of the tracks." It might also be said he had "three strikes on him" the day he took his first breath. However, it can definitely be said, "he left a big foot-print" with every step he took throughout his entire life. He distinguished himself during WWII, in college, in graduate school, in his teaching profession, and in the business world. Without a doubt he is an inspiration to all who know him and to those who will get to know him through his story in this book. This man is a true American icon!

HIGH FLIGHT

John Gillespie Magee, Jr.

Oh! I have slipped the surly bonds of Earth
And danced the skies on laughter-silvered wings;
Sunward I've climbed, and joined the tumbling mirth
Of sun-split clouds,--and done a hundred things
You have not dreamed of—wheeled and soar
And swung
High in the sunlit silence. Hov'ring there,
I've chased the shouting wind along, and flung
My eager craft through footless halls of air...
Up, up and long, delirious, burning blue
I've topped the wind-swept heights with easy
Grace
Where never lark nor ever eagle flew—
And, while with silent lifting mind I've trod
The high untrespassed sanctity of space,
Put out my hand, and touched the face of God.

Rex Sidener 1943

2001

REX SIDENER

A Marine at Iwo Jima

Rex and his family moved to Glenwood Springs from Minturn, Colorado during the summer of 1936. He entered the sixth grade that fall and his first teacher was Mrs. Quail. She was a dear lady who was loved and respected by all of her students. There was a boy in Rex's class by the name of Louie Columbo. One day Louie came to school with a play about Snow White and the Seven Dwarfs. The class decided to put the play on for the rest of the grade school classes and Rex played the part of the Huntsman who protected Snow White. The play was such a success the class put it on for the High School classes. Little did Rex realize at that time that he would once again play the part of the Huntsman, but this time he would protect his own country rather than Snow White.

High School didn't hold much interest for Rex but he did have an interest that he pursued. To this day Rex says that pursuing this particular interest was the best decision he ever made. He started dating Helen Comrie, whom he later married. Helen has been his wife and best friend for the past fifty-seven years and it is very touching to hear Rex speak so lovingly about Helen and what she has meant to him. In our society today approximately fifty percent of all marriages end up in divorce, so it is truly refreshing to hear Rex speak with pride and conviction about those fifty-seven years he and Helen have shared.

At the beginning of Rex's junior year in High School, the United States had already entered WWII. Rex decided to quit school and enlist in the U.S. Marine Corps. He enlisted on November 9, 1942 and was immediately sent to the Marine Recruit Depot in San Diego, California. Rex had just turned seventeen when he enlisted but he was full of enthusiasm and looking forward to the excitement of a new adventure. He was like all of the other young teen-age boys at that time, but it didn't take very long until reality set in. Within a few months Rex lost his teen-age dreams. Literally overnight he became a man faced with the impact of what his immediate future held for him. After a short stay at the Marine Corps Recruit Depot he was assigned to the Marine Training Base as Camp Pendleton, California. Upon completing training as a combat Marine Rifleman his group was sent to Camp Tarawa on the Big Island of Hawaii for further training. He was assigned to the Fifth Marine Division while stationed in Hawaii and his division was trained in tactics that would later be essential to their survival during their assault on the Japanese Island of Iwo Jima. The Fifth Marine Division had just recently been formed and was made up of a high percentage of seasoned combat veterans as well as the new recruits.

Before the outbreak of WWII, Iwo Jima was inhabited by 1,100 permanent Japanese residents. Most of them worked at mining and processing sulfur that was shipped to the home islands of Japan. Before WWII Iwo Jima was a fairly attractive place for the permanent Japanese to live. It was green in the spring of the year and the local Japanese raised sugar cane, pineapples, papaya, bananas and beans. Nevertheless, it must have been difficult for these locals to get accustomed to the "rotten-egg" smell of the sulfur fumes that permeated every square foot of the island. Even though the clouds of sulfur smell hung heavy in the air, life for these 1,100 Japanese citizens went on quite comfortably for the most part. There were two schools on the island staffed by two teachers as well as comfortable housing, small markets and the Taihei-ken Inn that was the social center of the island. Supply ships arrived at Iwo Jima and the other volcanic islands in the area at regular scheduled intervals. The Bonin Islands, Chichi Jima, Nanpo Shoto and other small islets belonging to Japan stretched like a string of pearls all the way from Tokyo to the Marianas Islands, a distance of some

1,100 miles. The Mayor of Tokyo made a stop at Iwo Jima in 1887 and declared that Iwo Jima would henceforth be incorporated into the prefecture of Tokyo. Thus, when WWII broke out Iwo Jima and all of the islets between Tokyo and Saipan were considered to be a part of Japan itself. This declaration made Iwo Jima a part of the sacred Japanese homeland.

By 1937 the Japanese military had already started making preparations to fortify Iwo Jima. In December of 1941, a Japanese naval detachment of 900 men arrived and the evacuation of all the civilian population began. An airstrip was built on the narrow stretch of land joining Mount Suribachi to the broader part of the island. The Japanese had also started construction on two more airstrips in the meantime.

By February of 1944 Iwo Jima took on a greater strategic role for the Japanese high command. In March of 1944 the Japanese military had established a naval garrison of 5,000 troops on Iwo Jima and early in 1945 the Japanese had 23,000 troops entrenched in an underground network of defensive installations. There were scores of pillboxes, blockhouses with five-foot concrete walls, over 750 large gun emplacements and miles of tunnels connecting each of these defensive positions. The Japanese had a complete 300 bed hospital dug deep beneath Mount Suribachi and a seven-story gallery for storage of food, water and war materials. They had also dug 1,500 rooms into the rock and connected them with sixteen miles of tunnels. General Kuribayashi's command post was dug seventy-five feet below ground with five-foot walls and a ten-foot thick ceiling made from concrete. Mount Suribachi itself bristled with over 1,000 pillboxes and heavy gun emplacements.

Every single gun on the island was zeroed in on the landing beaches and this would later prove to be very costly and devastating for the US Marines and Sea-Bees. General Kuribayashi was the architect of this build-up on Iwo

Jima. He possessed a strong fighting spirit and he was as tough as nails. He knew what he would soon be facing and he and his troops were prepared to fight to the last man. General Kuribayashi knew the Marines would soon invade Iwo Jima and he had prepared his men well. He told his troops the US Marines weren't ordinary soldiers. They were told the Americans were lunatics, felons and murderers and most had recently been released from prisons and institutions on condition they would fight the Japanese. Japanese soldier were charged with a goal to kill at least ten Americans each before they themselves were annihilated.

By summer of 1944 the Americans had begun daily air raids on Iwo Jima. All of the above ground structures were totally destroyed but by then the Japanese had completed their under-ground fortifications and were living like moles in the labyrinth of tunnels and rooms. The U.S. Navy had begun their daily bombardment with their heavy guns and the Marine and Navy Carrier Pilots routinely carried out bombing raids, as did the Twentieth and Seventh Air Force's heavy bombers from Guam, Saipan and Tinian. These constant attacks on the island may have had some psychological effect on the Japanese soldiers but they were still prepared to fight to the last man. Rex can testify to this fact without any reservation whatsoever.

The results of the constant pounding turned Iwo Jima into a desolate moonscape scene. General Kuribayashi, in one of his communications to the Japanese Military Headquarters in Tokyo, stated there were no birds left on the island and the fish had left the area. General Kuribayashi never doubted an invasion was imminent, he just didn't know when it would come. He had prepared for the inevitable as best he could and had taken measures to get his personal affairs in order, as he knew he wouldn't be going home for a very long time, if ever.

By mid-1944 American forces had forced the Japanese out of the Gilberts, Marshals and the Marianas. US forces had recaptured Guam, Tinian and Saipan which brought Japan within reach of the newly developed B-29 Superfortresses of the Twentieth Army Air Corps. By late 1944 the Twemtieth Air Force had mounted daily strikes against the home islands of Japan itself. Due to the long distance to reach their targets, fighter escort was not possible so the B-29 crews had to go it alone. They were forced to fly at extreme altitudes in order to partially avoid Japanese fighter attacks and concentrated flak from Japanese anti-aircraft guns. This reduced bombing accuracy and burned fuel at an excessive rate as they faced fierce headwinds on their return to their home bases. Planes damaged over Japan had little hope of making it back to their own airfields. Morale was very low and casualties were appalling. Iwo Jima was the obvious solution to these problems. Iwo Jima was the only island flat enough to accommodate a runway where crippled B-29s could land during their return trips from Japan. Consequently, the United States Military had no other choice but to invade and capture the island. The existing airstrip the Japanese had constructed, as well as the two airstrips under construction, could also serve as bases for the P-51 fighters. With the recently development of the wing drop-tanks, Japan was well within range of the P-51 fighters, so they could escort the B-29s to their targets. But first, Iwo Jima had to be taken. It became obvious, not only to the Americans but to the Japanese, that an invasion of Iwo Jima was imminent. General Kuribayashi expected the invasion would be made in the very near future, but he could only guess at the date it might occur.

The Seventh Air Force continued daily raids on Iwo Jima with their B-24 heavy bombers. During the six weeks prior to the invasion of the island they had flown 2,700 missions against Iwo Jima and had dropped 5,800 tons of bombs on the island. On October 3, 1944, the Joint Chiefs of Staff ordered

Admiral Chester Nimitz to prepare a plan for the invasion and seizure of Iwo Jima. Admiral Spruance assigned Task Force Fifty-one and Task Force Fifty-three, which included 500 ships, to support the Third, Fourth and Fifth Marine Divisions for the coming actions against Iwo Jima.

The assault on Iwo Jima began on February 16, 1945 with a three-day barrage laid down by U.S. Naval ships. The preliminary bombardment expended 6,800 bombs and 22,000 naval shells. However, this heavy bombardment had little effect on Kuribayashi's troops as their gun positions were artfully camouflaged. D-day for the Third, Fourth and Fifth Marine Divisions was February 19, 1945. Sixty-eight LVT (landing vehicles, tracked) amphibians led the way. Hundreds of LVT-4s and LVT-2s also carried the Marines ashore in six different waves. Eight thousand Marines stormed ashore on their assigned beaches within the first few hours. Initially little resistance was offered by the Japanese. However, when the fourth, fifth and sixth waves came ashore all hell broke loose. It was at that moment when an eighteen-year-old boy from Glenwood Springs, became a man. The landing beach itself was the first opponent Rex met. It was almost impossible to walk, let alone run, in the black volcanic sand. It was impossible to dig a fox- hole because the loose sand kept sifting right back into the excavated area. It was suicide to try to advance inland, even for a few yards. Tanks, jeeps, wheel-mounted guns and landing vehicles littered the beach or were stuck in the sand. Hundreds of Marines were killed by well-placed fire from Japanese mortars, artillery batteries, sniper fire and a rolling barrage that was masterfully executed. The Americans expected General Kuribayashi would launch a major banzai attack the first night after the Marines landed, but this did not happen. General Kuribayashi rejected any banzai attacks as he opted to hold his well-designed and camouflaged positions and let the Marines subject themselves to his well-hidden positions.

The Fifty Marine Division was assigned to land on "Red-Beach", which was the closest beach to Mount Suribachi. Rex and his Fifth Marine buddies were to cross the narrow neck of land separating Mount Suribachi from the rest of the island. They were then to pivot north and assault Mount Suribachi head on. Shortly after Rex hit the beach he was wounded, but his injury wasn't serious enough to earn him a reprieve from the action that was to follow. Rex managed to survive the next thirty-one days of fighting before he was evacuated from the island. Intensive fire from the Japanese occupying Mount Suribachi continued to rain down on every landing area and the casualties continued to mount. At 11:30 AM on the first day of the landing, AP Photographer, Joe Rosenthal, was in a landing craft making its way to the beach. Rosenthal later reported that the entire water's edge was littered with wreckage, boats, vehicles and bodies of dead Marines. Rosenthal kept thinking, "Here are young men who haven't lived yet." The odds that any Marine would survive the initial assault were very poor as it was estimated that one out of every three men would either be killed or wounded during the first few hours of action. This turned out to be quite accurate as the final count of Marines who were either killed or wounded was thirty percent. No man who survived that first day on that beach can tell you to this day how he did it. It has been said moving inland from the beach was like walking through a rainstorm without getting wet.

Rex did survive and he saw the American flag raised on top of Mount Suribachi on the fifth day after the invasion. By nightfall of the fourth day the Fifth Marine Division had lost 2,057 men. Total casualties for all of the invading forces during the first four days was 4,575 killed or wounded. The carnage and unrelenting hell went on for another twenty-eight days before the island was finally declared secure. The battle for Iwo Jima was the only major battle in the Pacific campaign in which the US military forces suffered greater casualties than were inflicted on the Japanese defenders. By the time the island was declared secure the US forces has suffered 28,686 casualties, either killed or wounded. This figure includes Navy, Medical Corpsmen, Seabees, Doctors & Dentists, Army personnel, Air Corps crewmen and US Marines. The Japanese lost 20,000 men killed and only 1,083 prisoners were captured and most of them were conscripted Korean workers or severely wounded Japanese military personnel.

On March 4, two weeks after the Marines had landed, the first crippled B-29 made an emergency landing on the captured air strip while the fighting raged on. Thirty-five more crippled Superfortresses made emergency landings during the battle as well. C-47 transport planes began landing on the airfield within hours after the Marines had landed. They evacuated the seriously wounded to Saipan and Guam. They also started flying in ammunition and other supplies while the Japanese were still fighting and firing upon any aircraft making a landing or taking off. The first B-29 to make a landing on Iwo Jima was named the Dinah Might. By the time the war had ended only Sergeant Robert W. Braskett of Dallas, Texas was still alive out of a crew of eleven airmen who were crewmembers on this airplane.

Within days after the airfield on Iwo Jima was captured, the Twentieth Army Air Corps mounted a raid on Japan with 334 B-29's from the Marianas. P-51 fighter escorts from Iwo Jima joined the B-29s during this raid. They dropped 1,665 tons of fire bombs on Tokyo which killed 84,000 people, destroyed 265,000 buildings and the resulting fires left over one million people homeless. The total damage of this raid exceeded any conflagration in history, including the burning of Rome in sixty-four A.D., the London fire in 1666, the earthquake that destroyed San Francisco or the Chicago fire. On the return from this raid two damaged B-29s landed on Iwo

Jima and fourteen others went down at sea but the crews were rescued. By the time the war had ended, thirty thousand airmen were saved because of the sacrifice made by the Marines and other US forces that participated in the capture of Iwo Jima. The horror these young men experienced is almost incomprehensible to understand when one considers that the average age of these warriors was not quite nineteen.

One of the pilots who made a forced landing on Iwo Jima was quoted as saying, "When I landed on this island, I gave thanks to God and the men who fought for it." Rex also gave thanks to God for his life and he has been forever grateful to President Truman for having had the courage and foresight to use the atomic bomb, which finally brought Japan to her knees.

After the surrender of Japan, Rex returned to Hawaii for a rest before being sent to Sasebo, Japan as part of the occupation forces. He served in this capacity in Japan for six months before being returned to Camp Pendleton, California and then to Mare Island, California for discharge from the service.

Helen was waiting for Rex after he was discharged from the service. They were married in August of 1946 and from that union two children were born. Rex found a job as a body and fender repairman and he held that job until he moved to Fairbanks, Alaska. Rex and his family resided in Fairbanks until 1953 before moving to California. In 1959 they moved once again and have made their home in Grand Junction, Colorado ever since.

Rex worked as a body and fender repairman until 1967 before starting his own business as a Snap-On-Tool dealer. Two years later Rex accepted a position at Mesa Junior College in Grand Junction, Colorado as an instructor in their new vocational education program. He retained this position for six years before retiring after having two coronary bypass surgeries. Since his retirement he has gotten involved in lapidary work as a hobby and has polished many rocks and made lots of jewelry. Rex said, "Life has been good to us and God was more than gracious when He gave me Helen to walk with me and be my mate. Without her, this old man would be nothing."

AMERICA
Samuel Francis Smith

My country, 'tis of Thee,
Sweet land of liberty,
Of Thee I sing.
Land where my fathers died,
Land of the pilgrims' pride,
From every mountain-side
Let freedom ring.

My native country, Thee,
Land of the noble free—
Thy name I love.
I love Thy rocks and rills,
Thy woods and templed hills;
My heart with rapture thrills
Like that above.

Let music swell the breeze,
And ring from all the trees
Sweet Freedom's song.
Let mortal tongues awake,
Let all that breathe partake,
Let rocks their silence break,
The sound prolong.

Our fathers' God, to Thee,
Author of liberty,
To Thee we sing;
Long may our land be bright
With Freedom's holy light;
Protect us by Thy might,
Great God, our King.

Don Sillivan 1943

2002

DON SILLIVAN

Escape From a Japanese Submarine

One of my very best boyhood friends joined the human race on November 7, 1924. Even though Don and I only managed to get together on three different occasions during the past sixth-three years, our friendship has endured and is as steadfast as ever. We still share many of the same memories and those memories are just as vivid today as they were when we were young boys. Don will always be with me in my mind and in my heart as long as the Good Lord allows me to hang around. I'll bet "all my marbles" Don feels the same way!

Don's mother came to Colorado by way of Iowa and Minnesota around the turn of the century. Don said, "My mother arrived in Colorado with her family in a covered wagon when she was a small girl. The family later moved to Nebraska where she married my father, Floyd Sillivan." Don and his four sisters were born in Nebraska. When Don was quite small his family moved to Wyoming where they lived but for a short time before moving to Craig, Colorado.

Don's father found work in an oil refinery in Craig. He worked at the refinery until he was killed in an explosion in 1927. Don was only three years old at the time of his father's death. His youngest sister, Floy, was born three months after the death of her father. Don said, "The next few years were hard times for my mother but she somehow managed to keep the family together, clothes on our backs and food on the table." Eventually, Mrs. Sillivan filed on, and obtained homestead rights on a piece of land approximately ten miles northwest of Craig. She had a difficult struggle maintaining this property until she finally met and married Vernard Waters. The family continued to live on the homestead property for several years and life was not so difficult after Don's stepfather joined the family. Don said, "I tell my friends, if they ever saw 'Little House on the Prairie', that is pretty much how we lived." Don and his sisters went to school in a one-room schoolhouse about two miles from their home. They walked both to and from school every day except when there was a bad storm. On such occasions Don and his sisters would stay with their teacher, who lived in a small house located next to the schoolhouse. Don said, "The years on the homestead bound my sisters and myself together and even though we now live quite a distance apart we are still very close."

Eventually, Mrs. Waters' mother and father, and her brother and sisters, moved to the Craig area where they also took up homestead property. Don said, "I never could figure out why anyone would want to live on such land, as it certainly was not good land for farming. It was hard trying to make a living there, but somehow we managed and never went hungry. I remember the time we tried to raise turkeys. The coyotes killed more of them than we ever ate. Sometimes during the winter months my sisters and I would hide on top of our haystacks to chase the jackrabbits away so they wouldn't eat the hay we were saving for our horses and cows."

The Watson family, relatives of Don's father, also lived in the Craig area. Don's idol was his cousin, Bob, who was three years older than Don. Don said, "Bob taught me to ride a bucking calf. He would hold the calf until I was securely mounted before letting go of the calf. I could only manage to stay on for two or three jumps but I was determined, so I would jump up and get right back on--always with the same results."

In the early thirties Don's family left the homestead and moved into Craig where his stepfather operated a creamery. The family remained in Craig until 1934, at which time California started to beckon. Once the family arrived in California they settled in Stockton, where Don's younger brother,

Ray, was born. Don's stepfather found a job working on a dairy farm that was located approximately twenty miles from their house. Consequently, the family only saw Mr. Waters occasionally on weekends. By then, two of Don's sisters, Helen and Eileen, were no longer living at home as they worked for room and board while attending school in Stockton.

Everything was going along quite well for Don and his family and they would probably have remained in Stockton if one of his uncles hadn't appeared upon the scene and moved in with the family. He was a brother to Don's mother and he didn't have a job, so the family graciously took him in. Don said, "It wasn't long before my uncle convinced my parents to move to Healdsburg in northern California. Everyone living in that part of California burned wood in their stoves so my uncle was certain we would all get rich cutting and selling firewood I spent every week-end and after-school hours stacking and cording wood." Don entered the fourth grade in Healdsburg, but by spring his uncle had become disenchanted with cutting firewood and had decided to move to Washington State. Don said, "We were more than happy to part company with that big blow-hard." So, his uncle moved to Washington and Don's family moved back to Colorado and found a small farm to operate near Grand Valley. Don's grandparents, Mr. and Mrs. Jones, lived in Grand Valley, two miles from where Don and his family settled down. Don's grandparents were getting along in years by then so they were happy to have family as neighbors. Don loved to visit his Grandpa Jones and he was fascinated with the stories his Grandpa shared with him. Grandpa Jones was one of Don's favorite people in his life and he left a wonderful impression on Don's young mind. Don recalled one of the many stories Grandpa Jones told him. He said, "When Grandpa Jones lived in the Nebraska territory he became friends with some of the local Indians. One time Grandpa Jones was invited to eat with an Indian friend and as they sat in the teepee around a fire, Grandpa Jones started to ladle some stew from a large pot. The Indian friend said, "Dig deep, Mr. Jones, the puppy is in the bottom." Don is quick to say his Grandpa Jones had a lot to do with molding his mind and his thinking by giving him sound advice, not only by word but by action as well. Don said, "Grandpa always said, don't say anything about someone unless you have something good to say-- or, no job is worth doing unless it is done well."

Don's family remained in Grand Valley, (now known as Parachute), for the next two years before moving to Glenwood Springs. His sister, Helen, was married by then and his sister, Eileen, found a job working at the Redstone Inn, twenty-two miles from Glenwood. Don said, "Living in Glenwood was the happiest time of my life. That was when I met Hal Terrell and we became great friends. That was also the time we enjoyed our many exploits together. I recently spent a few days visiting with Hal and we reminisced about the wonderful days of our youth. We talked about many things, such as going through the railroad tunnel hoping a train didn't come along, exploring the Fairy Caves with only a couple of candles for light, sleigh riding, playing marbles, ice skating on the duck pond, sneaking into the Hot Springs Pool (naked) after dark, camping, fishing and the time we both got mad at the maitre de at the Colorado Hotel and walked out on our jobs right then and there. Such wonderful memories brought tears to our eyes as we remembered those glorious days. It was proof positive that one could be poor in worldly goods but rich in one's heart, mind and soul in the company of a dear friend."

Don's family was on the move once again two years after moving to Glenwood Springs. Their next move was to Palisade, Colorado where they remained for two years. By that time Don and his younger brother, Ray, were the only children still living with their parents. From Palisade the family moved to Hotchkiss, Colorado but only stayed there for a few months before moving to a small farm on the Redlands near Grand Junction. Don and Ray attended a country school on the Redlands and Don said, "I enjoyed it there and found some good buddies, but I believe most of them have since left the area or have passed away."

In the meantime, Don's sister, Eileen, had married a sheep rancher who lived on Piceance Creek in the Rio Blanco area of western Colorado. Don enjoyed spending the summer months living with his sister and helping his brother-in-law manage four herds of sheep. Don loved taking the sheep to the "high-country" in the summer where they could find good grazing. He also found it interesting to bring the sheep down to the lower elevations in the fall to be shipped to Utah for winter grazing. Don said, "I remember one year when I got to help herd the sheep down the cliffs above Parachute. It was quite an experience to get the sheep to go down the cliffs on narrow paths, but once we got them started it was OK. We had goats to lead and the sheep would just follow the goats." At the end of the summer, Don returned to his home on the Redlands and once again attended school.

When Don was ready to enter high school he ran into a problem. The nearest high school was in Grand Junction and since that school wasn't a community school the family was required to pay $8.00 per month tuition. They couldn't afford to pay the tuition so Don moved back to Glenwood on his own so he could go to high school. He worked for Mrs. Mayes for his room and for Mrs. Llewellyn for his board. Don said, "It was fine doing this, but it was demanding trying to take care of two jobs before and after school. There was no time for me to play football or participate in any other after school activities. What little free time I did find I spent in the company of my pal, Hal Terrell". On weekends Don spent time at the local golf course in hopes of finding a job caddying. Don said, "The older boys usually got most

271

of the jobs. Anyway, to become a caddie you had to swim the Roaring Fork River naked. Of course you would end up far down river on the opposite bank, then you had to walk twice the distance back up river for the return trip in order to land on the bank back where you started. I guess every boy who ever caddied at the local golf course had to swim the river, which in retrospect, was quite dangerous. Unfortunately, we didn't have any female caddies hanging around."

Don recalled the mischief we occasionally got into with my father, who was the Sheriff of Garfield County, and with Mom Terrell who was the Matron of the Jail. He remembered the times Mom Terrell locked us in one of the jail cells as punishment for some minor trouble we caused. She did this mostly as a joke, so we never had to remain incarcerated more than ten or fifteen minutes. Don also recalled the time we were painting something and managed to get paint on Mr. Terrell's car. Don laughed about the time we were riding my bike down a hill much too fast and failed to negotiate a turn. Don said, "A tree acted as our brake--neither one of us was badly hurt but your bike didn't fare all that well. I have always remembered something Mr. Terrell said to me one time. He asked me if I was a Democrat or a Republican. I said I didn't know but guessed I was whatever my parents were. Mr. Terrell then asked, if your father is a damn fool should you also be a damn fool? He was telling me to be my own person, and ever since that day I have tried my best to be just that."

Even though Don believed his years in Glenwood were the happiest time of his life, he was still plagued with struggles he had to overcome. He had to be at Mrs. Llewellyn's on a regular schedule, as he had to help serve meals to the boarders, who were mostly schoolteachers. After everyone had eaten, Don and Mrs. Llewellyn sat together at a small table by the kitchen door and ate their meals. Don said, "I was not expected to be heard from, but one day a man, one of the boarders, was complaining about the possibility of the government initiating a draft system in order to fill their military requirements. Everyone at the table was having fits over the injustice of it all, so I piped up and said I couldn't understand why everyone was complaining, as I thought it was our duty. To say the least, I was really taken to task, so right then and there I made up my mind I had had enough. I decided to go home, but when I told Mrs. Mayes of my decision, she tried to smooth things over, but to no avail. Anyway, my stepfather was ill and my mother needed me at home. A few days later I said goodbye to my pal, Hal Terrell, and my other friends. It would be twenty-five years before I would see my good pal, Hal Terrell again."

Don's parents were pleased to have him home and he managed to enter high school in Grand Junction. Don said, "One day I got on the school bus to go home. It was the day after Pearl Harbor and I had just turned seventeen. When the bus stopped at a light, I got off and went directly to the recruiting office and enlisted in the Navy. I then walked the eight miles home and told my mother what I had just done. All she said was, 'I guess you had to do what you had to do'. It must have been a difficult moment for my mother as I don't believe I handled the situation very well."

A few days later Don was on a train heading for Denver where he joined several dozen other Navy recruits. Don and his fellow recruits were duly inducted into the US Navy on December 19, 1941, and immediately departed by train for the Navy Base at San Diego, California. Right after completing boot camp, Don was sent to a destroyer base where he was assigned to the Navy Armed Guard. Nobody knew what the Armed Guard was all about but they soon learned. This group of sailors would be trained and assigned as gun crews on merchant ships. The Armed Guard grew to a total of 144,900 men during WWII. These men sailed on 6,236 merchant ships of which 710 were sunk by enemy action and as many more were greatly damaged. The casualty rate in the Armed Guard was second only to the US Marine Corps. Hundreds of Armed Guard sailors were either killed outright or died from exposure in lifeboats in the blistering sun or died in freezing water. Oddly enough, most of the Armed Guard sailors had never seen the ocean before the war. The men who became members of the Armed Guard had to be in excellent health as none of the merchant ships carried a doctor on board. They had to have perfect eyesight as they stood watch four hours on and four hours off around the clock. When they did have time off they were kept busy maintaining their weapons and painting or cleaning.

Don's cousin, Bob Watson, was also in the Armed Guard. He was assigned to a merchant ship as one of the twelve members of a gun crew. His ship joined the ill-fated MURMANSK CONVOY sailing to Russia. In June 1942. The Murmansk Convoys lost 115 ships sunk by German U-boats. Don said, "My cousin, Bob, was on one of the ships sunk on the Murmansk run. He survived but was badly wounded."

During Don's training period he learned to fire machine guns, and three and five inch deck guns. After Don's group completed training most were shipped to the east coast for assignment. Don remained on the west coast and was soon assigned to his first ship that sailed on Friday, the thirteenth of March 1942. Don said, "We had thirteen men in our gun crew and we were thirteen days at sea. I have always considered thirteen as my lucky number."

Don's first trip was a great experience. His ship sailed to Honolulu, Hawaii and returned to San Francisco. He stood his four-hour watch on and four-hours off, even though he was seasick most of the time. Other members in Don's gun crew also suffered from seasickness but they soon learned to hang their hammocks under the gun mounts. Even though it was sometimes wet and cold the fresh air helped to relieve their seasickness. Each trip thereafter was to a different port, but the cargo was always much the same. Every trip was treacherous and dangerous as the ships were loaded with explosives, munitions, machinery, guns, oil, planes, vehicles, parts, wood products and food of all sorts. Don said, "I never sailed on any trip with the same buddies. I guess this was good in a way because losing a good friend would have been more devastating than losing a shipmate whom you had only recently met." Each trip the crews were assigned to newer vessels with better equipment and guns, but these ships were "sitting ducks' just waiting for an enemy torpedo. None of the ships were equipped with range finders, radar or sonar, so the crews had to rely on their eyes. After hours and hours, and days and days of watching and praying that each little white cap wasn't a periscope, it became hard for the gun crews to maintain their concentration. They all realized if they did encounter a Japanese submarine, there was little or no hope of escaping. At least they might have a slim chance to survive if the enemy subs would surface, but Japanese subs always made their attacks from below the surface.

Don recalled one trip where he said, "We went to Noumea, New Caledonia and sat there for sixty eight days with temperatures of 120 degrees in the shade. Of course, iron ships were even hotter and though we would have liked to go swimming, we weren't allowed to do so as there were lots of barracuda and sea snakes in the water. One day all of the fleet ships in the harbor left about four in the afternoon. I think they were going to join the battle of the Coral Sea." The following morning Don's ship prepared to leave as well. "We didn't know where we were going, but this was standard procedure because we were seldom privy to such information. Anyway, we ended up at Guadalcanal where we delivered a ship-load of supplies to the Marines who were occupying that island." Once Don's ship had finished unloading their cargo they spent the next thirty-eight days at sea without seeing land. This trip was a very rough one as the ship was empty and riding high in the water, so we were at the mercy of rough seas. Eventually Don's ship arrived in Chile where they took on a cargo of nitrate of soda used to make explosives. From Chile they sailed through the Panama Canal and up the east coast to Brooklyn. Don said, "That was my only trip on the Atlantic Ocean and I was glad, as many ships were sunk all along the east coast."

After discharging their cargo at the Brooklyn Ship Yards, they went back to New Caledonia where they spent more time at anchor before going to Bougainville to unload supplies at the newly established Navy base there. The next port of call was Wellington, New Zealand where they picked up the remnants of the First Marine Division that had been sent there for rest and recuperation. They were assigned to transport the Marines to Australia to re-form the First Division. However, after leaving the Cooks Strait, they turned south as two ships had recently been sunk right after departing from New Zealand. Don said, "We went south of Tasmania where we hit very bad storms and very cold weather. I thought we would see icebergs at any time. Shortly after departing from New Zealand we sighted a Japanese periscope. The Japanese submarine was obviously trying to get into position to fire a torpedo but the foul weather helped us avoid a serious situation. The submarine followed us for several hours before we finally lost it. It was a nerve-racking experience as we expected to be hit at any moment. We were fourteen days at sea, and after such a long time, the Navy thought we had been sunk. But, we finally made it to Sydney and then to Brisbane, Australia without further incident. From Brisbane we headed north with short stops at some of the Solomon Islands before returning to San Francisco."

Don had this to say about his experiences at sea, "I remember always being afraid, and I often wondered what I would miss in life if I didn't make it back home. All of us had many moments that were scary, but fortunately, we never got sunk."

Back in San Francisco, Don became a gunnery instructor for a while. He was entertaining the idea of applying for submarine service, but changed his mind when he got the chance to go to Washington, D.C. to electro-hydraulics school. Electro-hydraulics were the mechanism that operate the large naval guns. He did quite well at this school and was fortunate to be selected to take advanced courses that kept him in Washington, D.C. for the winter.

While stationed in Washington, D.C., Don was proud and honored to have been chosen to stand Honor Guard on Pennsylvania Avenue for Franklin D. Roosevelt's funeral. That was also the same day Don met Janice Conrad, who was to become his wife. Don's next duty station was Newport, RI where he was assigned as a crewmember on the new cruiser, Fargo. He attended a gunnery range while waiting for the ship's company to be finalized. Fortunately, before the Fargo was ready to sail, the war ended. After serving in the Navy for four years Don decided to get out of the Navy. He was sent to Boston, MA where he received his discharge.

Don's wife, Janice, was from Bethlehem, PA so the couple made their home there. Don said, "After I got out of the navy I had no education or trade to fall back on, so I looked for work right away. I got a job as an apprentice carpenter. I loved my work and within two years I was promoted to the position of foreman." Don's employer had a good reputation as a builder of fine homes and he operated his company with the idea that honesty and hard work would pay dividends. Don has followed this ideal all of his life. Eventually Don started his own construction company and it has been very successful. Everything was going along as well as could be expected until Don's wife, Janice, suddenly passed away. Don said, "It was a difficult time for me and the children but life had to go on." In 1971 Don met and married Joanne Hunter Little. Jo had two children, Susan and Jeffery, so the six of them became a loving family.

Don's firm specialized in building custom built homes, hospitals, schools, churches and industrial buildings. Don was proud to tell me that his firm had been nominated and had won the "Contractor of the Year" award of eastern Pennsylvania. He said, "I have always put my customers first and my own children who now operate the company subscribe to these same ideals".

Joanne and Don bought a seashore home in Avalon, New Jersey several years ago. They spent twenty-two summers there enjoying their boat and fishing. Jo didn't care much for the ocean but Don had a fishing buddy who often joined him for an outing. Don said, "I lost my fishing buddy to cancer a few years ago, so I soon lost interest in fishing and sold my boat." Don went on to say, "It seemed as if we had enough things to do at home, so we decided taking care of two homes was pretty much out of the question for folks our age. Last year, we sold the seashore house--we miss it but we stay busy without it."

Over the years Don served as a deacon of his church for nine years. He also served three years on the board of directors of the Associated Builders and Contractors Association. He also served on the board of directors of the National Board of Builders and Contractors Association.

As we have all experienced, life goes on! Don's mother and stepfather are gone now, along with his sisters' husbands. Even though his children now operate the business, Don still gets involved and helps solve problems when he is needed. He also spends a lot of time in his garden and plays golf several times a week. Don said, "All in all I am quite busy and very happy with my life."

It is a joyous feeling for me to be able to say, "Don Sillivan is a dear friend to me and I value my relationship with him." Eleanor Roosevelt once wrote, "Many people will walk in and out of your life, but only true friends will leave footprints in your heart." Don has left those footprints in my heart!

A FRIEND OR TWO
Wilbur D. Nesbit

There's all of pleasure and all of peace
In a friend or two.
And all your troubles may find release
Within a friend or two.
It's in the grip of the sleeping hand
On native soil or in alien land,
But the world is made—do you understand-
Of a friend or two.

A song to sing, and a crust to share
With a friend or two;
A smile to give and a grief to bear
With a friend or two.
A road to walk and a goal to win,
An inglenook to find comfort in,
The gladdest hours that we know begin
With a friend or two.

A little laughter, perhaps some tears
With a friend or two;
The days, the weeks, and the months and years
With a friend or two;
A vale to cross and a hill to climb,
A mock at age and a jeer at time--
The prose of life takes the lilt of rhyme
With a friend or two.

The brother-soul and the brother-heart
Of a friend or two,
Make us drift on from the crowd apart,
With a friend or two;
For count no hours but the ones made glad
By the hale good times we have ever had
With a friend or two.

Then brim the goblet and quaff the toast
To a friend or two,
For glad the man who can always boast
Of a friend or two.
But fairest sight is a friendly face,
The blithest tread is a friendly pace,
And heaven will be a better place
For a friend or two.

Bob Simillion 1944   Bob Simillion 2001

Paul Simillion 1943
Deceased (Died in the service of his country)

BOB SIMILLION

The Ultimate Survivor

Of all the boys in the class of 1944, Bob probably had the hardest time growing up due to his family circumstances. At times he and his family were desperately poor, but his dear mother did her best, as a single parent, to support her seven children. Bob never allowed these circumstances to drag him down. He never once let go of his "boot-straps" but rather used them to pull himself out of the abject poverty life had dealt him. His determination to rise above his poverty is a wonderful success story, as he eventually became a very well known and respected business executive in Western Colorado.

Bob was born in Morton, Utah on February 16, 1927. He was the second oldest, his brother, Paul, being the oldest. Bob's mother married Rocco Simillion in Helper, Utah in 1924 where he was working in the coalmines at the time. In 1930 Bob's parents moved the family to a rural area just a few miles south of Glenwood Springs, Colorado to an area named Four Mile Creek. By then another brother, Kenneth, had been born. Bob's grandparents, Joe and Elizabeth Simillion, had previously homesteaded a small farm/ranch on Four Mile Creek. Bob's grandparents had three sons, Albert, Rocco (Bob's father), Louie and a daughter, Laura.

Grandfather Simillion worked at the Sunlight Coal Mine located on Four Mile Creek and he supplemented his meager pay by growing alfalfa and vegetables. He also kept chickens, rabbits, pigs and a couple of beef steers. Bob remembers his grandfather had a very nice house with a large kitchen, living room and three or four bedrooms. Bob and his family lived with his grandparents for four or five years before moving into a two room cabin with a dirt floor. This cabin was also located on Four Mile Creek but was a few miles closer to Glenwood Springs. The family lived in this cabin for about one year before moving once again.

While living on Four Mile Creek four more children were born. These new family members included Bob's brothers, Norman and Ronald and sisters, Josephine and Pamela. Their food consisted mostly of wild game and vegetables from their own garden. Occasionally their grandparents, or Uncle Albert would stop for a visit and present the family with a deer or a few rabbits to help supplement their larder.

Bob and his brother, Paul, went to school in a one-room schoolhouse. The schoolhouse was two miles from their home so the two boys would ride a horse to school bareback. After arriving at school they would turn the horse loose and it would go home. The horse they rode to school was part of a team that was needed to pull the farm machinery and the wagon. The two boys would walk home after school, quite often stopping along the way to visit an old bachelor, Jim Burnsides. Mr. Burnsides was kind to Bob and Paul and on occasion he would feed the boys a meal of homemade biscuits, groundhog stew and polenta. This meal was always a welcome respite for the boys because food was in short supply at home. There was no "hot-lunch" program offered at the Four Mile School so their lunch usually consisted of bread and jam sandwiches they brought from home. Occasionally, Grandma Simillion would send a cookie in their lunch.

Bob remembers the schoolhouse had wooden floors and the desks were separated according to grades. The teacher's desk and a coal/wood-burning stove were located at the front of the room and a blackboard was attached to the wall. A pail of spring water was always available so the children could quench their thirst as there was no such thing as a water fountain in the school building. There was an outside toilet located just behind the schoolhouse. It was a "two-hole" facility and was used by both the boys and the girls. Some of the students who attended the Four Mile Creek School eventually graduated from Garfield County High School in Glenwood Springs, including both Bob and his brother, Paul. Most of the boys who went to school at the Four Mile Creek School also served in the military service during World War II.

Bob's father and one of his friends used to make "moonshine" (whiskey) in his mother's kitchen. This operation was always carried out during the night and the still was set up on the kitchen stove. These two entrepreneurs also made homemade beer that they bottled. Bob recalls that some of the bottles would explode and sound like a gunshot. On Strawberry Day (an annual celebration in Glenwood Springs) everyone would load into an old touring car and drive the twelve=miles 12 miles into Glenwood Springs to join in the festivities. Bob said, "I can remember during the trip, either to town or back home, having to stop and repair a flat tire or two". They always took along several blankets as the entire family would sleep out for a night or two. The blankets also protected the bottles of "moonshine" from breaking that his Dad sold in Glenwood Springs.

Bob helped during the haying season, driving a team of horses that raised the hay stacker which in turn deposited the load of hay on top of the haystack. Bob was seven or eight years old at the time but in spite of his young age he was expected to help with the work. Other chores assigned to Bob and his brother Paul included milking the cows, keeping the kitchen stove wood-boxes full of wood, feeding the pigs and chickens and doing other chores around the house.

For entertainment, Bob's parents took the entire family to a neighbor's house on Saturday night. Other neighbors would join in as well and everyone enjoyed the "barn dances" held in Mr. Perko's large barn. Bob's father played the guitar, another neighbor played the accordion, and other neighbors played the piano, mandolin, and drums. An old Negro gentleman who often came to the "barn dances" was an excellent banjo player. Each family brought food for the midnight supper that was a ritual, and all of the children enjoyed these events very much. There was always plenty of homemade beer, wine and moonshine whiskey readily available for the adults to enjoy. The younger children would wrap up in a blanket and go to sleep on a bench or in the corner of the barn on a pile of straw while the adults danced and partied the night away.

Bob and his brother Paul enjoyed fishing on Four Mile Creek. They didn't own any modern fishing equipment so they attached a length of store string to a willow pole, bent a straight pin to form a hook and baited the hook with a worm. Surprisingly, they managed to catch quite a few fish that were plentiful in Four Mile Creek at the time.

Eventually, Bob's father accepted a job in Glenwood Springs and moved his family into town. Shortly after settling in Glenwood Springs, Bob's parents divorced and Bob's father left town leaving Bob's mother as the sole provider of seven children. Bob learned later that his mother was supposed to have received $75.00 per month child support but this money never materialized. From that day on Bob and his brothers and sisters lives took a definite turn for the worse and the family's struggle to survive became a matter of urgency.

Even though neither Bob nor Paul had yet entered high school, they both understood the predicament their mother now faced. Mrs. Simillion was a very proud woman, but her circumstances forced her to put her pride aside and accept assistance from the county. Many neighbors and other good Samaritans also helped her as best their own situations would allow. The Lyke family was one of these good Samaritan families. This family operated a sawmill on upper Four Mile Creek and they generously took Bob into their

285

home during the summer months as a way to help relieve some of the strain facing Bob's mother. Bob shared the work and the chores with the three older Lyke children and even accompanied the men when they went into the woods to harvest trees. Bob said, "One of the benefits of living with the Lyke family was all of the meals were bountiful and delicious".

The Lyke family usually took a trip in the early fall. They loaded one of their trucks with bedding, food, camping equipment and other such supplies and spent a week traveling and exploring, mostly throughout Western Colorado. The entire family left Four Mile Creek and drove through Aspen, over Independence Pass to Buena Vista, Leadville, Minturn, Eagle, Glenwood Springs and back to Four Mile Creek. The entire trip took about a week and covered 250 miles, but Bob thought he had "been-around-the-world". To this day Bob will tell you that living with the Lyke family and being the recipient of the love this family gave to him when he needed it the most, helped him to become the good person he is today. He is still quick to say that the upper Four Mile area is one of the most beautiful places in the world with its streams, meadows, acres of wild flowers, elk, deer and other small animals and birds. The pure joy of riding a horse through this wonderland of beauty that nature provided is indelibly engraved in Bob's mind and will remain there until his last day on this earth. He said, "I can still see the horses flax colored mane flying in the breeze as I roamed the lovely mountain meadows and forests." What a joy for a young man not yet into his teens to have experienced! And how fortunate that Bob was so acutely aware of his surroundings and is now willing to share these special experiences and memories with me! Bob said, "Scenes like these last in one's mind forever."

Bob's mother had a difficult time finding a place to live. Bob remembers living in various houses around town but none of them were large enough to comfortably accommodate a family of one parent and seven children. After living with various families temporarily Mrs. Simillion found a place to live that was located in an area known as Noonan's Grove. The house was a one-room cabin but it put a roof over their heads until Mrs. Simillion found a four-room house to rent. From there they moved to an apartment on the second floor of a building that housed the local mortuary. Eventually, the family settled into an apartment above the Ryan Bakery located on Main Street in Glenwood Springs. Bob slept a lot better above the bakery than when they lived above the local mortuary.

Life at home was sometimes crowded for the Simillion family. Sleeping four in a bed, wearing second-hand clothes, eating "relief food" which consisted mainly of beans, rice, flour, grapefruit, potatoes and canned vegetables was the norm. Nevertheless, Bob's mother always managed to have a large pot of soup or stew on the stove. The butcher at a local market occasionally gave Mrs. Simillion soup bones to add to the stew or soup.

Bob and his brother, Paul, entered elementary school in Glenwood Springs, Colorado in the fourth grade. Both boys enjoyed school and soon made friends with their peers. Bob liked sports and enjoyed playing basketball on Saturday and Sunday mornings during the 7th and 8th grades. He played tackle football with no pads or protective equipment. "This was real blood and guts football," Bob said.

When Bob was in the fifth grade he went to work selling newspapers on the street. He received two cents for every paper he sold, but there was competition from other boys who also tried to earn a few cents by selling newspapers. Bob also worked at the local bowling alley setting pins, as did many of the other boys his age. There weren't many opportunities during those depression years for young boys to earn money so they had to accept whatever was available to them. Bob also worked part time at the local movie theater taking tickets and changing the marquee and advertising posters. When he was about thirteen years old he found a job as a "pearl-diver" at a local restaurant. "Pearl-diver" is a fancy word for dishwasher, but Bob was delighted with this job as it paid $2.50 for a ten-hour shift. This job gave Bob the opportunity to learn short order cooking, frying hamburgers, making sandwiches, cooking breakfast meals, baking pies, preparing desserts and other basic cooking skills. During his shift as dishwasher, he was also required to clean the grills, steam tables and the kitchen floor. With his newfound skills, Bob worked at various other local restaurants. He honed his skills by working with some outstanding chefs. They taught Bob a great deal about food preparation and food service. For the next three or four summers Bob continued to work in these establishments. When not working in one of the local restaurants, Bob supplemented his income by delivering the Rocky Mountain News and the Denver Post. These jobs were usually winter jobs that required Bob to get up before daylight as the newspapers were always delivered in the A.M. before school.

One of Bob's favorite jobs was working at the Glenwood Golf Course. While waiting for a caddie job the boys played "Tippi" (a game similar to the English game of Cricket). They also went swimming in the Roaring Fork River and roasted ears of corn appropriated from Mr. Donegan's field. Occasionally someone would manage to capture a stray chicken that they also roasted. Life was great!

The summer approaching Bob's senior year in high school, he found a job working for Mr. Ray Houghton who owned and operated Houghton Tire Shop. Bob's buddy Bob Osburn, also worked for Mr. Houghton that summer. Both boys became tire re-cappers and salesmen while Mr. Houghton spent his afternoons at Louie's Pool Hall playing cards. They both kept their jobs until school started in September of 1943.

Immediately after graduating from high school, Bob joined the Navy along with his good pal, Bob Osburn. They had to get their parents to testify they were seventeen-years old at the time. They traveled together to Denver where they took their physical examinations. They received their orders to report to the Naval Training Center in San Diego, California. Bob's first homesickness came when he was subjected to the harassing by the 'old-salts' who had arrived two or three days earlier. They would chant, "You'll be sorry", as the two Colorado boys marched past.

Boot camp life passed quickly for Bob and he soon got into the routine of washing his own clothes, making his bed and doing all of the chores required by Navy regulations. Shortly after arriving at the Naval Training Center in San Diego, the two Bobs met up with several other Colorado boys. They formed a basketball team that defeated all of the competition offered by other Naval units. Bob won most of the swimming events and they also had a very good boxing team made up of boys from Glenwood Springs, Grand Junction, Pueblo and Cortez, Colorado. Bob Osburn was the outstanding boxer on their team and won all of his bouts.

The two Bobs got their first liberty and couldn't wait to visit San Diego. They went to the San Diego Zoo, saw the Marine football team beat the Navy team and stopped at the YMCA for refreshments. While at the YMCA they were invited to attend a party at a private home. They jumped at the invitation with expectations there would be plenty of food, girls and booze available. When a private vehicle picked them up they were certain that "the old blind sow had found an acorn". Upon arrival at the party they were served sandwiches, punch and cookies and given a sermon from the Bible. Both boys had a good laugh over this experience for many years thereafter. Bob said, "Sometimes one can become very gullible when an invitation sounds so good." This was the only liberty the boys were given during boot camp and the results of this liberty were not what they had envisioned.

After completing boot camp, Bob was given a fifteen-day leave. He returned home to Glenwood Springs and was surprised to discover the town had changed so much in such a short time. The military camp at Pando had been completed and 10th Mountain Division soldiers stationed at Camp Hale loved to hang around Glenwood Springs. Also, the Navy had taken over the Colorado Hotel and the Hot Mineral Pool as a convalescent facility for treatment of Naval and Marine personnel, so the town was full of service men.

Before going on with Bob's story, I need to devote the next three paragraphs to Bob's brother, Paul. On October 20, 1943, Bob's brother, Paul, enlisted in the US Navy and was sent to boot camp in Farragut, Idaho before being stationed at the Naval Air Station in Florida. Paul was learning to be an Air Radio Gunner on a TBF Navy combat aircraft. A TBF plane crew consisted of a pilot and a radio gunner. On Paul's final training flight on October 24, 1944 the plane crashed on landing, killing both Paul and the pilot. Paul had already purchased his ticket to fly to Denver so the news of Paul's death was devastating to his family and friends. Bob had just finished Navy boot camp and was home on leave at the time of the accident. He was able to extend his leave in order to be with his mother and attend the funeral services for Paul in Glenwood Springs. Paul's remains arrived in Glenwood Springs via rail accompanied by a Navy escort. Unfortunately, the escort proved to be very unworthy. He swindled Bob's mother out of several hundred dollars while he was in Glenwood Springs. Shortly thereafter this unsavory individual scammed Bob's mother out of some additional money through the US mail. Bob said, "I have often wondered how many mothers who lost a husband or a son were victimized by such unscrupulous individuals;" I am sure there were many excellent service related escorts but as the saying goes, "there are always a few bad apples in the barrel".

Paul was an excellent student and was consistently on the Honor Roll. Paul never participated in sports other than the physical education classes required by the school. In these classes Paul proved to be very athletic and was an outstanding softball pitcher. It was during Paul's senior year in high school that the coach talked him into trying out for the football team. He proved to be a very good halfback and was an asset to the team.

Paul, being the oldest, was the overseer of the other children while their mother was working. Naturally, there were quite a few scuffles and fights between the brothers and sisters but Paul made sure that everyone finished their assigned chores. During the summer season, Paul worked part time at a local café. He also worked part time at a beauty shop located in the famous Hotel Colorado. It was there where Paul set up his own shoe-shining business and did quite well at that endeavor. Bob said, "I can't help but think of the waste of my brother Paul's life. It seemed so useless for a young man to have lost his life in an accident at his own airbase. The only positive thought I have of the incident is at least his body was not lost at sea or in some far away foreign country. I can still visit his gravesite and keep our spirits together."

After attending his brother's funeral services, Bob reported to the Mission Beach Navy Training Pool. He remained there for the next two months before being sent to the San Diego Gunnery School where he learned to operate anti-aircraft guns as well as 20mm and fifty caliber machine guns. He also had some instructions in loading and firing five and three inch deck guns. This training lasted for approximately two months after which he was sent to Treasure Island, near San Francisco, where he was assigned to his first ship. The USS Freemont Older was a merchant vessel and carried a crew of twelve naval personnel in addition to a complement of Merchant Marines who operated the ship. Prior to sailing on Christmas day, Bob was given liberty and he visited San Francisco for the first time in his life. During his short visit to San Francisco an unusual incident occurred. Bob was in the YMCA making a phone call home. When he finished his call he stepped out of the phone booth and found himself looking directly into the face of his high school pal, Bob Osburn. They spent Christmas Eve together riding around the city with a taxi cab driver who had been celebrating the holiday. He apparently felt sorry for the two boys so he took them to all of the interesting and exciting places in town. Bob said, "We sure did have a great time", but he refused to elaborate any further. Early the next morning, Christmas Day, both boys reported back to their respective ships and they never saw one another again until after the war had ended.

On Christmas Day, the USS Freemont Older sailed under the Golden Gate Bridge headed for the Pacific and unknown destinations. During this entire voyage each man took his turn standing watch, participating in gunnery practice and doing all of the other chores required to keep the ship in "ship-shape" condition. Since the Freemont Older was a merchant ship, the Merchant Marines were responsible for the operation of the ship while the regular twelve man Navy personnel were responsible for manning and operating the guns. Bob's crew was made up of a few "Old-Salts" and the rest were newly trained sailors like Bob. Some of the "Old-Salts" were full of stories about German submarines they had encountered, when they were sailing in the Atlantic. There were others who had sailed in the Pacific and they had stories about the Japanese attacks and how ruthless the Japs were to prisoners. For a seventeen-year old boy with limited travel experience, this was cause for him to wonder about the eventual outcome of the war and what might happen to him and the Freemont Older.

In addition to gunnery practice, there were other daily routine chores to perform. They had to keep their guns and equipment clean and properly maintained, keep their living quarters neat and organized, and they had to spend hours with a chipping hammer chipping away rusty paint from their gun-tubs. They were also required to participate in daily physical conditioning, thus leaving them with little time for personal matters. The Freemont Older sailed on for twenty-four days, moving further west each day. Precautions were taken by sailing in a zigzag maneuver while the watch was constantly vigilant for any aircraft that might approach the ship. Their course took them all the way northwest to the Aleutian Islands where they took on fuel and sailed southwest to the Marshall Islands. They dropped anchor at Anewetak Island after having been at sea for over thirty- days. At Anewetak Island the crew was allowed to go ashore, a special treat for everyone. They drank beer in the Navy Beer Garden, ate potato chips, played baseball, received mail from home and posted the letters they had written while at sea. After a short stay at Anewetak Island the Freemont Older joined up with several other ships to form a convoy before continuing their voyage to other unknown destinations.

Their next stop was New Guinea, where they unloaded their cargo onto barges and immediately departed from New Guinea on their return voyage to the United States. When they crossed the Equator the crewmembers making their first crossing were subjected to the ritual given to all sailors. This ceremony originated with the first sailing ship following Columbus' discovery of America. Once Bob had received the "Domain of Neptunus Rex" he was thereafter considered to be an "Old-Salt".

Their return voyage from New Guinea took them to the Solomon Islands, the Marshall Islands, Hawaii, then directly to San Francisco. Upon reporting to the Treasure Island Receiving Center in California, Bob was assigned to his next ship. He boarded the USS Edmond G. Ross and seven days later, with an entirely new crew, they headed for Midway Island, the Marshall Islands, Guam and eventually to the Philippines where they anchored along with other ships in a bay between Mindanao and Leyte. General MacArthur was in the process of recapturing the Philippines, so the cargo the USS Edmond G. Ross had aboard was vital to this effort. Nevertheless, they remained at anchor in the bay between Mindanao and Leyte for three weeks before joining up with several other ships and sailed into Manila Bay where they unloaded their cargo. During the three weeks at anchor between Mindanao and Leyte, Bob and the crew spent a lot of time swimming and diving off the ship. Once, during Bob's turn to stand lifeguard duty he spotted a man in serious trouble. He immediately grabbed a life jacket, jumped into the water and swam out to help his crewmate reach safety. Some months later Bob received the Gold Lifesaving Medal from President Truman for his brave action.

After unloading their cargo they headed back to the United States. Just off the Island of Palawan, in the Philippines, the USS Edmond G. Ross was attacked by Japanese planes. The attack lasted for about two hours before US fighter planes drove off the attackers. Their main concern was Kamikaze planes, but their luck held and they managed to escape with but little damage to the ship or crew.

After arriving back in the United States, Bob was once again sent to Treasure Island where he learned all Merchant Ship gun crews would be transferred back to the fleet. He was given a thirty-day leave and immediately headed for Glenwood Springs. It was at this point Bob heard the news that America had dropped the atomic bomb on Japan and Japan had capitulated and the war was over. After enjoying his leave, Bob returned to Treasure Island where he received his new assignment. Bob and twelve other sailors were flown to Shanghai, China where they were billeted in the Yangtze Hotel in downtown Shanghai. For the next thirty- days all they did was report for roll call and enjoy liberty every night. Bob did a lot of exploring in Shanghai, spent time at the enlisted men's club, danced, played pool and enjoyed life in general. Somehow Bob and the other twelve men got lost in the shuffle and confusion, but eventually this leisure life came to an end when Bob and his mates were ordered to travel to Tangshah and Tianjin, China to assist in the evacuation of a Navy hospital. When they arrived at their destination, they discovered the hospital had already been evacuated. They returned to Shanghai where Bob was assigned to the USS Prairie, a large Destroyer Tender. This ship was being used as the Flag Ship for the China area, so Bob was happy to find himself doing something useful once again. He was assigned to the ship's printing shop and was promoted to 3/class Printer. Four months later, the USS Prairie anchored in Hawaii at which time Bob was transferred to a Destroyer Escort and they sailed for San Francisco. Once they reached San Francisco, Bob was sent to Shoemaker Receiving Base for separation. He received his honorable discharge from the US Navy on June 8, 1946. Bob said, "My tour in the Navy was very interesting and educational in many ways. It was breaking away from home and learning to survive by myself. I learned to get along with people and work together for a common cause. I observed people living in other cultures where they do not have any of the conveniences that I had even though our family was quite poor and we received assistance from the County Welfare. We were lucky in many ways as my mother always seemed to make sure we had something to eat, something clean to wear and a place to live."

Once Bob received his discharge, he returned to Glenwood Springs, After arriving in Glenwood Springs he had a difficult time trying to decide what he should do with his life. He gave up the idea of going to school on the GI Bill as he thought he just wasn't college material. Bob's uncle had purchased the Glenwood Cafe so Bob took a job with him as a cook. He also started dating Patricia Ament and they were married on June 6, 1947. Bob and Pat's first child, Paul Alan was born in 1949 and later joined by a girl, Gerri Lynn, who died shortly after birth. A year and a half later another girl, Kendra Lynn, joined the family.

Bob was then offered his old job at Ray Houghton's Tire Shop. After accepting Mr. Houghton's offer Bob and Pat's lives began to settle down. Eventually Mr. Houghton decided to open another tire shop in Fruita, Colorado. He took Bob in as a partner, so Bob and Pat moved to Fruita. However, business was not what Bob had expected as a small tire shop just could not compete with the larger establishments. Bob finally had to close the doors and once again he began a search for a new job. He and Pat moved back to Glenwood and Bob once again went to work at the Glenwood Café.

Bob applied to the Colorado State Patrol and was delighted when he received a call from the Deputy Chief offering him a position as a State Patrol Officer. Bob jumped at this opportunity, and after completing the required Cadet-Training Academy he was stationed at Lafayette, Colorado. Bob now had his teeth into a job that he felt held a future for him.

On September 28, 1953, Bob's wife Pat, passed away from polio. Bob's son also contracted polio and was admitted to Children's Hospital in Denver. He spent one month in Children's Hospital for special treatment for polio but completely recovered showing few effects of the disease. With two small children to care for and the responsibility of a new job, Bob arranged for his children to live with his mother and his sister, Pam, in Glenwood Springs. In the meantime, Bob continued to work out of Lafayette, Colorado while he waited for approval of his request to be transferred to the Western Slope of

Colorado. Shortly thereafter, Bob's request for a transfer was approved so he moved to Meeker, Colorado, sixty miles from Glenwood Springs.

In January of 1954, Bob married Dannette Arnold of Meeker and brought his children to live with them in Meeker. In August of 1955 a son, Patrick Cole, was born. Bob's transfer proved to be very beneficial and he loved the area. He became involved in community services. He formed a parent's group that used a school bus to transport young people in the area to the swimming pool in Glenwood Springs where Bob taught a swimming program. This program created enough interest with the County Recreation District to inspire them to build their own pool in Meeker. Bob also served on the Ute Indian Meeker Massacre Reenactment Uprising that is performed on the Fourth of July every year. He also worked with local schools, was an active member of the volunteer fire department and became a Thirty-second Degree Mason in the Masonic Lodge.

After ten years of living and working out of Meeker, Bob was disappointed to receive news of his transfer to Steamboat Springs, Colorado. He moved his family to Steamboat in March of 1962 and began the process of re-adjusting to a new environment. Life as a patrolman created conflicts with the activities of his wife and children and working in the high mountain passes in the winter was no picnic. One year after his transfer he resigned his position as a Colorado State Patrol Officer and took a job with the local rural electric company as their Public Relations and Marketing Manager. He became a member on the board of directors of Club Twenty which consists of twenty counties in Western Colorado. The main thrust of this group is to promote business throughout these twenty counties. Consequently, Bob spent a lot of time in Denver and Washington, D.C. lobbying for Western Colorado's interests. Bob also served as President and District Governor of the Steamboat Springs, Colorado Chamber of Commerce.

Tragedy reared its ugly head once again on September 28, 1983. Bob's wife, Dannette passed away after a lengthy illness. Her passing created a significant void in Bob's life. Ten months later, his son, Patrick, was tragically killed in an accident at the Colorado Ute Power Plant.

On November 10, 1990, Bob married his present wife, Carol. But, bad luck struck again when Bob suffered a heart attack that required bypass surgery. In August of 1991, Bob was admitted to the hospital for an emergency gallbladder operation. A few weeks later it was discovered he had a tumor at the base of his tongue that turned out to be malignant. He received radiation treatment later followed by surgery.

I never cease to admire the courage, the stamina and the ability Bob has demonstrated over the years with his will to overcome one adversity after another. What he has experienced in his lifetime would have broken the average man years ago. How many people do you know who would be able to look at life in such a positive way as Bob does? I am very proud to be able to count Bob as one of my very best friends. This man is a true Work of Art!

MY FINAL RESTING PLACE

(Author unknown)

It's just next door to heaven,
This place I love to go.
It's high up in the Rockies,
Where alpine flowers grow.

There's deep lakes and babbling brooks,
There's wild-life great and small.
Humming birds and eagles too,
In love God made them all.

Lifting branches to the sun,
Are spruce and aspen tall.
Breezes whispering through their tops,
Suggests God's love for all.

Mountain peaks reach to the sky,
And heaven's just next door.
I'm at peace with God and man,
I wish for nothing more.

EARL SOUTHARD

Escape from a German Prison Camp

Earl Southard and his family moved to Glenwood Springs from Arkansas around 1936. Even though Earl was a year older than most of the boys in our grade school class, he was also one of the smallest boys. I never learned much about Earl and his life before he moved to Glenwood Springs, and for that matter, I never learned much about him after he started school when he entered the third grade in Glenwood Springs. He was a quiet lad and never had a lot to say. He never displayed emotions but he certainly wasn't timid. All of the boys in the class soon learned that Earl was unique in as much as he never expressed emotions or showed fear in any way whatsoever. Simply stated, Earl was a fearless and courageous boy and no one had any doubt that these attributes would carry over into his later years.

In May of 1943, Earl left school and enlisted in the U.S. Army Paratroops. Seven months after his enlistment, the following article appeared in the Glenwood Post newspaper on December 30, 1943:

"Pvt. Earl Southard, son of Mrs. James Black, Jr., of 1010 Bennett Avenue, Glenwood Springs, Colorado, has won the right to wear the world-famous wings and boots of the U.S. Army Volunteer Paratroopers, the most feared warriors of World War II. He made his fifth and qualifying jump on December 17, 1943. His fifth jump was a tactical leap made at night while in training at the Parachute School at Ft. Benning, Georgia. This qualifying leap completed his four weeks of jump training followed by twenty-six weeks of infantry training. Jumping at the Parachute Training School had been steadily developed to a recognized war science. There was but one percent chance of suffering injury while jumping during jump school at that time. In addition to producing jumpers for combat, parachute specialist training was given to qualified men in the art of camouflage, communications, demolition and parachute rigging, vital skills for the new and better infantry soldiers."

Earl's mother, Mrs. James H. Black, received a letter from Earl dated July 27, 1944, which read:

"Dear Mother:

I know how you have been worrying about me, but I could not write before. The first mail that I got from you since D-Day was dated the eleventh of July. I wish I could tell you why, but I can't. I jumped in France shortly after mid-night on D-Day and the Jerries, or Germans, were on hand with a warm reception. I never saw so damn many Jerries in my life. I don't know how many I got altogether, but you can bet that I got my share. Here is some real good news. I am back in England, safe and sound. Those Jerries are poor shots.

"No, Mother, I don't think I will be able to come home until it is all over. I get a six-day furlough starting Tuesday and two months pay, or about $150.00. If you think that I am not going to have fun, think again.

"The French people were sure glad to see us boys over there. If the French people had not been on our side, I would not be here to tell about it. We are having a Regimental party tonight in town. Don't expect me to write until I get back from my furlough. I don't know just where I'll go. Your loving son, Earl."

Within two to three weeks all of the paratroopers who had jumped into Normandy on D-Day, and who were still alive, had returned to England to begin training for their next combat assignment. It was several weeks after D-Day before Earl finally got back to England as he had been detained by the Germans. The following letter was received by Earl's mother on September 14, 1944 and it is one of the most outstanding and interesting stories to reach

Glenwood Springs relatives and friends. In this instance it relates the story of a local boy and his escapes from the Germans in France after being captured. The youth is Earl Southard, a member of the world-famous United States Army Volunteer Paratroopers. In his letter, Pfc. Southard wrote:

"Dear Mother: How is everything at home? Fine I hope. I am well and enjoying life. That is as much as could be expected. I do have a lot of fun to be so far away from home, or I did until we moved." (It is unclear where Earl moved to but no doubt it was a training camp in England or Scotland).

"I can't tell you where or how far we moved, but it was too far from home. There isn't much of anything to do around here. In fact, we have been here some time and I haven't been out of camp. I have been too busy to do much of anything. I start to radio school next week."

Continuing in his letter, Earl recounted roughly his experience with the Germans. He explained, "I was captured by the Jerries two different times while I was in France. I got away both times by the skin of my teeth. No, Mother, they weren't firing at me when I got away, but they sure fired at me plenty afterward." (This probably alludes to his next jump into Holland in September of 1944). "I escaped on the 27th of June but was re-captured and detained once again. Then I escaped again on the 30th of July and managed to get back through the German lines after my second escape. Two medics escaped with me the second time and we had to get through the German lines after dark.

"We still weren't sure that we were through the German lines and behind our own lines, so we hid in a barn one night and waited until morning. As it turned out there were two of our men in the barn next to the one we slept in, not more than twenty-five feet away. I can't ever remember being as happy as I was to see anyone as I was to see those two boys that day." A couple of days later Earl was back in England. Another interesting detail was that Earl's second escape was made on his 19th birthday.

In September 1944, Earl made his second combat jump at Einhoven, Holland. This was an ill-fated attempt to stop the Germans as they tried to advance to the port of Amsterdam, Holland in order to cut off the Allied supplies arriving through that port. The airborne troops who participated in this action suffered heavy casualties as they tried to stem the German advance. This was the beginning of the Battle of the Bulge that eventually drove Earl's unit into Bastogne, Belgium where they made their famous stand and earned the name of, "The Battered Bastards of Bastogne." Earl remained in Europe after Bastogne was relieved and participated in further action in the Rhineland and along the Rhine River. He was finally sent home for discharge two or three months after the end of the war in Europe.

Earl's activities after the war are very sketchy and I wasn't able to learn much about him, other than he ended up living in Coos Bay, Oregon for many years. He was a union representative and organizer for many years before his death in 1995. I regret that I didn't try to obtain more details about Earl and his life before he passed away. I am also sorry I didn't have the chance to personally interview many of these special friends while they were alive, because it is now too late in many instances.

THE KID HAS GONE TO THE COLORS

W. M. Herschell

The Kid has gone to the Colors
And we don't know what to say;
The Kid we have loved and cuddled
Stepped out for the Flag to-day.
We thought him a child, a baby
With never a care at all,
But his country called him man-size
And the Kid has heard the call.

He paused to watch the recruiting,
Where, fired by the fife and drum,
He bowed his head to Old Glory
And thought that it whispered: "Come!"
The Kid, not being a slacker,
Stood forth with patriot-joy
To add his name to the roster,
And God, we're proud of the boy!

The Kid has gone to the Colors
It seems but a little while
Since he drilled a school-boy army
In a truly martial style.
But now he's a man, a soldier,
And we lend him a listening ear,
For his heart is a heart all loyal,
Encouraged by the curse of fear.

His dad, when he told him, shuddered,
His mother—God bless her!—Cried;
Yet, blest with a mother's-nature,
She wept with a mother's-pride.
But he whose old shoulders straightened
Was Granddad—for a memory ran
To years when he, too, a youngster,
Was changed by the Flag to a man!

Bobby Tate 1943

Deceased 1983

BOOOY TATE

From D-Day to Mauthausen Death Camp

Robert Glenn Tate, or just plain "Bobby" to his classmates and friends, was born November 1, 1925 in Glenwood Springs.. Small in stature, Bobby was a giant in every other way. He was raised in a family of nine children, he being the sixth oldest. Bobby was six years old when he entered the first grade in Glenwood Springs. He remained with the same group of schoolmates until the summer of 1942, at which time he enlisted in the U.S. Army. The exact date of his enlistment is not known as his service records have long since disappeared, but he was seventeen years old at the time of his enlistment. All that follows are the memories his younger sister, Bette Black, which she shared with me.

After completing his basic training, Bobby, along with his unit, was shipped to England where he received additional amphibious training for the impending invasion of the European continent. The invasion began on June 6, 1944, generally known as D-Day. Bobby was right in the thick of the action. Even though his unit suffered heavy casualties, Bobby came through those first few days without injury. After weeks of heavy fighting through the hedgerows in Normandy, the US forces finally broke out and began their push across France and into Germany. Herb Osburn, one of Bobby's schoolmates, recalled a feature article about Bobby, that appeared in the Stars and Stripes newspaper after D-Day. Herb, who also has a chapter in this book, was stationed in England with the 8th Army Air Corps at the time, and he recalled that the article praised Bobby for his ability to hold up his end of the fighting, even though he was quite small. Herb said, "The article was titled something like Dynamite Comes in Small Packages."

Bobby's sister, Bette, said, "I remember Bobby talked about his part in the liberation of some of the German Concentration Camps. Bobby didn't like talking very much about it, but he had the courage to remember and share these experiences with me as well as with some of my other family members." Bobby and his unit ended up in Austria just as the war ended. He loved Austria and thought it was the most beautiful place he had ever seen. He always wanted to return to Austria, but the years passed him by, and he never did satisfy his longing desire.

Even though Bobby thought Austria was beautiful, it also had its ugly side, which Bobby remembered until the day he passed away. Most Americans had no idea the Germans had established concentration camps and death camps throughout most of Europe. It is also quite likely that a large percentage of the German population were not aware of the existence of these camps either. Bobby didn't know November 8, 1944 was the beginning of a "death march" for 40,000 Jews from Budapest, Hungary, to the concentration camp at Mauthausen, Austria. Consequently, Bobby was shocked into disbelief when his unit entered the Mauthausen Camp and witnessed the horrors that confronted him and his fellow soldiers.

Mauthausen was a concentration camp primarily for men. It was located near Lintz, Austria and was classified by the SS as a camp of the utmost severity. Conditions there were horribly brutal, even by SS standards. One hundred thousand prisoners of various nationalities were either tortured to death or worked to death at this camp before the Americans arrived in May of 1945. It was shortly after Bobby entered this camp that he learned the full meaning of bitterness and hope, which was the legacy of the Holocaust.

Bobby saw men emerge from this camp that had been robbed, stripped, abused, tortured and disoriented. Even though the Americans had liberated Mauthausen, it didn't necessarily mean that those people who had been

307

confined there were truly liberated. Most had nothing left to return to--no homes, no friends, and no community--so they continued to experience intense anti-Semitism and persecution. How could these liberated people, or Bobby and his fellow soldiers ever forget the smell of death, or what they saw and felt as they entered this camp? Thousands of naked, emaciated bodies were laying in the streets where they had fallen or where they had been thrown into shallow graves. There were lice and other vermin and insects crawling over the bony frames of the dead. It was like stepping back into the dark ages for Bobby and the other liberators of Mauthausen. Tragically, by war's end, over sixty-million people had died, and more than half of them were civilians. One out of every twenty-two Russians was killed, one out of every twenty-five Germans died; one out of every 150 Italians and one out of every 200 Frenchmen lost their lives during WWII. But, during the Nazi's war against the Jews, two thirds of the Jews living in Germany and Europe had been murdered. "Take heed...lest you forget the things which your eyes have seen, and teach them to your children and to your children's children." **Deuteronomy 4:9.**

It must have taken a great deal of courage for Bobby to remember what he saw at Mauthausen, but I'm certain Bobby faced such evil images just as he faced the rest of his life...head-on. The way Bobby lived his life after the war was his testimony against the twisted, vicious inventiveness of some human minds. He realized that those millions of lost lives must have an enduring meaning. He knew that all of us must remember to be vigilant so the ashes and the unmarked graves of all of those victims can, and will, become sanctified and provide human hope for all who understand the meaning of love.

After being discharged from the Army, Bobby returned to Colorado and made his home in Denver. Bobby's sister, Bette said, "Bobby formed a wonderful friendship with a gentleman named Paul Campbell. Mr. Campbell was like a father to Bobby and they adored one another."

She added, "Bobby was an amazing person and he could do anything with little effort. He could put a roomful of people in stitches the minute he entered a room. To know him was to love him!" The following is how Mr. Paul Campbell eulogized Bobby:

"I first met Bob Tate forty years ago, and we developed a wonderful and lasting friendship. In comparison, many men of greater size and stature fell short of standards set by Bob, when it came to determination and desire. As I think about it, I guess you could say that the monuments he built at the sixteenth Street Mall in Denver and the mansions he constructed in Vail and Aspen can attest to the fine craftsmanship he displayed.

"The gift of a craftsman, which the Lord had granted him, was an art which Bob used to perfection. When he worked it was almost as if each finger knew its duty and carried it out with unquestioning ease. This did not go unnoticed, as he was honored with not only the admiration of his co-workers and peers, but with being named Colorado Carpenter of the Year in 1971.

"Probably the greatest testament to Bob's goodness came during his final months of life. He was a man who was always full of life and I watched helplessly as his strength drifted away. Even when it would have been so easy to give up, he found courage to carry on with dignity. Even when his body was no longer willing, Bob still found a way to touch everyone's heart with a twinkling eye and a knowing grin.

"Now that we have gathered to honor Bob, I ask that you remember not the pain that he bore but how he faced it. I ask that you pray with me...

"Dear Lord...I ask that you grant us the strength and wisdom to continue our lives in such a way that we may honor Bob. We thank you, Lord, knowing that the pain and suffering are over for Bob, and that he now may know the pleasure and comfort of being home...Truly home. In Jesus' name, Amen".

Robert Glenn Tate: November 1, 1925 - April 24, 1987

He served in the Armed Forces during World War II. He was a superb craftsman, a skilled carpenter and a loyal construction worker. He was involved in the construction of buildings from Fort Collins to Pueblo, Colorado. Some of the buildings he worked on included Villa Italia, Cinderella City shopping center and the Bronco's Mile High Stadium in Denver, Colorado. He was also involved in the erection of multi-million dollar condominiums and homes in Vail, Aspen, Breckenridge, Boulder and the Denver area. Bob was an avid fisherman and rock hunter.

Bobby's sister, Bette, left me with the following comment, "This has made me realize that all of us should keep a journal of our lives. I was at an unimpressionable age when my brothers were away fighting. I can remember my mother being so unhappy and worried during those times, and so glad when they both came home."

As for me, Bobby shall never grow old as we who are left grow old. Age shall not weary him or the years condemn him at the going down of the sun. So every morning for the rest of my life I will remember my little friend and classmate with all my heart.

THERE IS NO DEATH

Gordon Johnstone

I tell you they have not died,
They live and breathe with you;
They walk here at your side,
They tell you things are true.
Why dream of poppied sod
When you can feel their breath,
When flow'r and soul and God
Knows there is no death.

Death's but an open door,
We move from room to room.
There is one life, no more;
No dying and no tomb.
Why seek ye them above,
Those that ye love dear?
The All of God is Love,
The All of God is Here.

I tell you they have not died,
Their hands clasp yours and mine;
They are but glorified,
They have become divine.
They live! They know! They see!
They shout with every breath;
"Life is eternity!
There is no death!"

Hal Terrell 1944

2005

HAL TERRELL

Lucky Me

I was born in New Castle, Colorado on March 19, 1926. My mother, Martha Terrell delivered my sister and me at home as there was no hospital in New Castle. My father, Roy Terrell, was the Marshall of New Castle and his salary was $75.00 per month. We survived on his salary better than some families, but we certainly didn't have any of the conveniences that we are accustomed to today. Even though we didn't have much, my parents shared what we did have with those less fortunate. Such memories have remained with me all of my life and I have tried to emulate the kindness and generosity my parents bestowed upon those who needed a helping hand. In our busy society of today I believe we have lost some of these virtues and values.

In 1933 my father was hired as the Undersheriff of Garfield County so we moved to Glenwood Springs, Colorado, which was and still is, the County seat. My folks found a house right away and the rent was $15.00 a month. Since my father's salary as Undersheriff was $125 per month we were able to enjoy a few extra privileges. The house we lived in was a two-bedroom house with a coal burning stove set in the middle of the living room floor. On cold nights we gathered around the stove for warmth, as this was the only way we had of heating the house. My mother cooked on an old iron stove that burned wood or coal. My responsibility was keeping the coal buckets full and the kindling box full of kindling that was used for starting the kitchen stove fire.

Shortly after moving from New Castle to Glenwood Springs, I started school. Approximately forty other children were in my second grade class and many of us remained together through grade school and high school. For the past sixty-seven years most of us have stayed in touch with one another.

314

People today find it hard to believe the wonderful relationships we formed in our youth are still alive and vibrant.

It never occurred to me to ask my folks for money because I learned at an early age whatever money my father earned went to feed and support our family. Consequently, at the ripe old age of eight, I found a job working for a wonderful neighbor lady. Every day I filled her coal hopper, removed the clinkers that built up in the furnace and split kindling so she could start a fire in her "monkey-stove". A monkey stove is a small stove used to heat water and can be used independently from the main furnace unit. These chores were my responsibility seven days a week, and I kept this job for the next four years. I was paid the grand sum of $5.00 a month and with this money I purchased my first pair of ice skates. In addition to the skates, I was also able to buy my first bicycle with the money I earned from Mrs. Mangnall and other neighbors.

Mrs. Mangnall liked me a lot because she knew she could depend on me to do my job every single day. She knew my responsibility to her was a matter of honor and pride to me, even though I was only eight years old. She always gave me a big box of caramel suckers at Christmas time. I loved those suckers and so did my dog. It was great fun to watch him try to dislodge the caramel from his teeth, but he couldn't resist taking seconds. I supplemented my income from Mrs. Mangnall by doing other odd jobs wherever I could find them. I sold newspapers for five cents a copy and got to keep two cents for myself. I visited the Goodie Shop on main street and purchased what we called "penny-candy". A jawbreaker cost one penny and it lasted for an hour or two. A candy bar cost five cents so I seldom invested that much money at one time for what I perceived to be a short-lived pleasure. Jawbreakers were clearly a better investment and just as satisfying as a candy bar.

Two years after we moved to Glenwood Springs from New Castle, my father ran for Sheriff of Garfield County and was duly elected. He remained Sheriff of Garfield County until he retired in 1946. My mother was the matron of the county jail, and she took this job quite seriously. Arguing with or resisting my mother was not a wise decision for women prisoners to make as she was six feet tall and weighed 175 pounds. The same held true for my friends and myself. All of us learned early on it was healthier to avoid confrontation with her because to do so was a guarantee you would end up scoring a poor second. She was also the family disciplinarian and didn't hesitate to employ the rod when necessary. My father used a completely different method for meting out punishment. Seldom using force, he instead made an appointment with either my sister or myself to discuss the problem. Usually he let us think upon the matter for a few hours before informing us, "It is time". A lecture from him was enough to make Virginia or me ashamed and regretful. I preferred my mother's more direct method rather than being subjected to my dad's heart rending lectures because he had a way of making us totally ashamed of our behavior.

The one time he used a switch on both my sister and myself was a lesson I still remember. My dad took the family on a short vacation and my sister and I sat in the back seat of the car and fought and argued for two or three hours. Dad warned us several times to cease and desist our fighting and bickering but his warnings fell on deaf ears. Finally, Dad stopped the car near a small stream and had me get out of the car. He took me aside and told me to go down to the little creek and select a switch so he could whip my sister with it. I located the meanest switch I could find as I thought my sister deserved to have her backside attended to in a proper manner. While I was locating my switch, Dad sent my sister to the other side of the road to find a switch he informed her he intended to use on me. I think the switch my sister chose was even bigger and meaner than the one I had chosen for her. After the two of us returned to the car, Dad had us trade switches and we each got it good with the switch we had chosen for the other. Had I known what my Dad had in mind, I would have selected a small clump of dry grass for my sister. I have never forgotten this lesson and I admire the way my Dad settled this matter between my sister and me.

In 1933, I got a big, black dog, but I never got around to giving him a proper name, I just called him Pooch. He and I were inseparable friends for the next six years. I loved him dearly and he returned my love unconditionally with full measure. Sometimes a memory of him brings a big smile to my face and at other times I find myself wiping tears from my eyes. Even though Pooch could not talk he could somehow manage to get his message across to me. With a glance he was able to command my full attention. He was a special, affectionate, and loyal friend. I think Pooch had a "built-in" clock in his head. He followed me to school every single day and at lunchtime he was there to meet me. When school let out at 4:00 P.M., he was there right on time wagging his tail.

Pooch loved to sleigh ride with me. He loved to grab the sled rope in his teeth and race back up the hill as fast as he could go. He sat on the sled in front of me with his big black ears flapping in the breeze as we raced down the hill. He was also quite helpful to my mother. Before there were any supermarkets in Glenwood Springs, everyone shopped at one of the several small grocery markets in town. Occasionally my mother needed something from the market right away so she would give Pooch a large canvas bag with a note in it and Pooch would race off to the market to do the shopping. Amichaux Grocery, where we had an account, cut and sold their own meat, so when Pooch arrived at the front door of the market they retrieved the bag and the note and gave Pooch a bone to chew on while they filled my

317

mother's order. They always put a package of meat scraps in the canvas bag for Pooch as his reward for doing the shopping. After they gave him back the bag he would race for home as fast as he could go. Everyone in town was amazed Pooch could do the shopping for my mother. The local paper even wrote an article about Pooch and his shopping sojourns.

Growing up in Glenwood Springs before WWII was a very special time for all of us who shared this experience. We didn't have any of the modern conveniences young people of today have. We simply found our own ways to entertain ourselves. We went fishing, we explored the Fairy Caves or the Cave of the Chimes and we rode our bicycles up the Glenwood Canyon to camp or picnic at Grizzly Creek. We went sleigh riding and ice-skating in the winter, but best of all, we made life-long friends. The economic circumstances at the time had a lot to do with creating such wonderful and lasting friendships. None of us realized we were poor, at least in a materialistic sense. We didn't miss all of the amenities kids have today because such things did not exist in our society at that time. We were poor by today's standards but I never missed a meal and I always had clean and decent clothes to wear. The closest we ever came to knowing life as it is today was reading about Buck Rogers and his adventures in the Sunday funny paper section of the Denver Post.

I did quite well all through grade school and high school. My grades were well above average and I participated in everything possible. I played the French horn in the school band and orchestra. I had a part in all of the school plays and I respected and admired my teachers. My father taught me three simple rules I have tried to live by. He said, "Don't lie, cheat or steal", and I have tried to live my life accordingly. I have passed this advice along to my two children, I believe with good success.

During my wonderful high school years I always felt as though God was smiling down on me every day. Because of the support of my teammates, I was chosen as an all-conference basketball and football player during my junior and senior years in high school. I was also selected to play on the Colorado All-State Football Team in 1943. During my four years of high school I was elected to various school offices and did my best to represent my school in the most exemplary manner possible.

I continued to find jobs during my high school years in order to earn a bit of money. I still never considered asking my folks for money because I knew it was not available. One summer I got a job picking up and delivering laundry from local motels, hotels and private homes. I took a second job that same summer as a bellboy at the Colorado Hotel. I worked nights at the hotel, so during the late evening and early morning hours I managed to get a little rest so I would be able to report for work at the laundry the following morning. My pay at the laundry was $12.00 per week and I made about $3.00 a night in tips at the hotel. What I managed to save during that summer by working two jobs kept me in spending money most of the following school year. The summer between my junior and senior year of high school I got a job working for Brown Construction Company at Pando, Colorado. The United States Government had just started construction of Camp Hale, an army base where the Tenth Mountain Division received their training. Some of my friends learned it was possible to get a job there, but it was necessary to join the union. I had very little knowledge as to the relationship between unions and contractors. I just assumed they were more or less one and the same. None of us had the $25.00 necessary to join the union but it was rumored if a contractor would agree to hire you the boss-man at the union hall in Leadville, Colorado would allow a person to join provided you agreed to pay the union dues out of your first paycheck. I was delighted when Brown Construction Company agreed to hire me at $1.90 per hour. This was a fortune to me and I was absolutely delighted with the prospect of earning so much money.

After I visited the Brown Construction office in Pando and was offered a job I hitched a ride to Leadville. I located the union hall and entered the office with great expectations. However, the boss-man was not in his office. The only person there was the office assistant. He informed me the boss-man would be back shortly so I found a chair and settled in to wait for his return. Since I had hitched-hiked thirty miles from Pando to Leadville I didn't fancy repeating this scenario the next day. After I had waited for three hours the office assistant finally informed me the boss-man was across the street in the Vendome Hotel partaking of the charms of one of the local ladies who worked the bars in Leadville. I decided it would be a good idea to phone the boss-man's room to let him know I was waiting in his office. This turned out to be a very poor decision on my part. Within a few minutes the boss-man came storming into his office with blood in both eyes. Needless to say, he wasn't in the mood to forego the $25.00 union fee until I had received my first check. Instead, he ordered me to vacate his office immediately or he would personally throw me out. By this time I wasn't in the mood to take any of his abuse so I took him to task and we engaged in some pretty rough conversation that only made matters worse. I was seventeen years old at the time, six feet, two inches tall and weighed about 175 pounds. The boss-man was about my size but probably outweighed me at least thirty pounds. He was about thirty years old but I took a stand and accepted his offer to throw me out of his office. We immediately engaged in some very serious physical activity and I was holding my own when the office assistant decided to enter the fray and lend the boss-man a helping hand. A few minutes later I found myself sitting on the curb in front of the union hall nursing a swollen eye and

320

a few facial abrasions. After getting my second wind I decided to go back into the union hall for seconds. I must admit, I miscalculated the eventual outcome as once again I ended up in the same location on the curb outside the union hall office. I was also nursing a few more lumps to go with the ones I had already acquired. I thought about giving it another try but my better judgment prevailed so I walked to the edge of town and hitched a ride back to Pando.

When I arrived back in Pando, I went immediately to the Brown Construction office to report that I hadn't been successful in my attempts to join the union. I was questioned about how I had gotten the swollen eye and other abrasions on my face, so I explained what had happened during my visit to the union hall in Leadville. This was my very first inkling that a contractor and the union weren't all that friendly. At the conclusion of my explanation, Brown's Personnel Manager took up a collection and sent one of his men back to the union hall with $25.00 with instructions to sign me up in the union. I was then offered a job as a "Bull-Cook," so I told the Personnel Manager I didn't know a thing about cooking. He laughed and explained a "Bull-Cook" was the person in charge of labor crews. Was I ever surprised to learn my pay would be $2.50 per hour rather than $1.90 per hour, the going rate for a laborer. The lumps I received at the union hall were worth it because I worked the entire summer as a "Bull-Cook" and saved what was then a small fortune.

I never ran out of ideas as to how I could earn a few dollars. Every fall it was possible to get excused from school for a few days if one agreed to help the farmers harvest their potato crops. The Italian farmers living and farming in the Roaring Fork Valley grew lots of potatoes. Since the war had already started, it was almost impossible for them to find short-term help. Therefore, they solicited the high schools in our area for help. I always worked for the same Italian farmer and was paid thirty-five cents per hour for my labor. This particular farmer was always the first to get his potatoes picked, sacked and stored in his potato cellar. He came up with a very innovative and clever idea that worked like a charm. The routine was to start down a row of potatoes depositing them into a gunnysack you pulled behind you. The farmer placed a gallon of homemade wine at the end of each row and every time you finished a row you were permitted to partake of the "grape". No doubt the football coach wondered what had happened to his "potato-picking" football players during practice. I personally thought the coach should have figured this out during practice when he saw a swarm of fruit flies buzzing around my head during practice. I still love wine to this day and I must admit, I've probably spilled more wine than most people have ever consumed.

While in high school I always had a job working evenings and weekends, if I wasn't participating in a basketball or football game. One job was working at a Conoco service station and another job was setting duckpins at the local bowling alley. Duck pins and the bowling balls used were much smaller than the regular pins and balls used in bowling alleys today. There were no automatic pinsetters so we had to set the pins by hand. We sat on a board that was elevated about four feet above and to the rear of the pin-pit. When we saw the ball coming it was wise to lean back and raise one's legs as high as possible as the pins flew in every direction. Clearly, it was more conducive to one's health to let the pins hit the back of your legs rather than one's head. We were paid five cents per line but I really didn't like this job even though I could earn as much as fifty cents for an evening's work.

In my early teens I earned a little money boxing in the Battle Royal Fights. These fights preceded the main events. They were held once each month and were called Smokers. Six boys between twelve and fourteen years of age would enter the ring wearing fourteen-ounce gloves. When the bell rang, the fight was on and for a few minutes there would be a lot of leather in the air. There were no scheduled rounds, so the fight lasted until only one boy was standing. There were no set rules, so each boy could hit anyone of the other boys in the ring. When a boy was knocked down he had to exit the ring. At the conclusion of the fight the spectators tossed coins into the ring and the last two participants took off their gloves, spread a towel on the mat and collected the coins. Once back in the dressing room, the two combatants split the money sixty-forty with the winner getting the sixty percent. This usually led to another fight because the combatants couldn't agree on the mathematics of the split.

My high school days were some of the best years of my life. It was a special privilege to have grown up in a small town like Glenwood Springs. But, with the beginning of WWII our lives began to change. The war eliminated the opportunities for boys our age to enjoy our teen-age years. The carefree days of our youth disappeared and we began to experience an entirely new set of circumstances. Rather than waiting to be drafted into the service, most boys enlisted. I enlisted in the Army Air Corps Cadet Program at the age of seventeen on July 7, 1943. I was not called to active duty until after my eighteenth birthday on March 19, 1944.

Our high school Superintendent, Mr. Henry J. Igo, had a profound influence on my life. I admired him and respected him, as did all the other students. He was very strict, but fair, and he always gave us the best advice possible and guided us in the right direction down the path of life. Just prior to enlisting in the Army Air Corps, five of us decided to join the Rangers. When Mr. Igo heard about our plans, he called us to his office and tried to talk us out of this reckless idea. Orville Deckrow was the only one who joined the Rangers and less than a year later he was killed at Anzio, Italy.

Leonard Rule, another one of the five, was in the infantry and shortly after arriving in Europe he was killed in Belgium. Vernon Schleicher was in a tank division and he was killed just before his unit crossed the Rhine River into Germany. Bus Abshire was seriously wounded during the battle to capture the Saar Valley near the little French town of Stiring Wendel. He survived his wounds and returned to Glenwood Springs after the war. Bus passed away in 1997, so I am the only one of the five still alive. Why was I spared and not the others? I am eternally grateful that I survived the war but I will always harbor feelings of guilt…why me and not the others?

My first five days in the service were spent at the Induction Center at Ft. Logan, Colorado. The night I boarded the train in Glenwood Springs I met up with Morris Hoopingarner. He was also from Glenwood Springs, so for the next five days we were constant companions. We were issued a set of WWI leggings but we couldn't figure out the logic as to why we were issued these leggings. We were instructed to wear them at all times. The first time I tried to lace mine on I got them on backwards. Morris just about died laughing and, until he passed away in 2000, he called me "Spats Terrell".

During my short stay at Ft. Logan I was introduced to the wonderful world of GI humor. Some of the "old-timers" who had arrived at the induction center at Ft. Logan two or three days prior to my arrival shouted at the newcomers as we marched past. "Wait until you get that shot in the left testicle with the square needle." The corporal who was in charge of my group shouted such educational slogans as, "We're all in this thing together, so you play ball with me and I'll shove the bat up your @$%. I don't like this any better than you do, and I can stay here all night if I have too, so let's see a-holes and elbows. Pick up everything that doesn't grow and if you can't move it, paint over it. Fall out, I don't want to hear that door slam but once, and when that dust clears away in the company street I want to see

324

three rows of statues standing at attention. Don't tell your troubles to me soldier, go see the Chaplain and get your TS card punched."

On the sixth day after arriving at Ft. Logan, I was sent to Shephard Field, Texas for basic training. I don't know where Morris was sent, but he eventually ended up in the Pacific Theater of Operations. After basic training I was sent to Aircraft Radio Operator's school at Chanute Field, Illinois. I was at Chanute for three months before being sent to McDill Field, Florida where I received additional training in Radio Navigation. My next assignment was Sioux Falls, South Dakota for more training in aircraft radio navigation procedures. This phase of my training lasted three months before being sent to Scott Field, Illinois. At Scott Field I was assigned to an aircrew and started applying what I had learned at Chanute Field and Sioux Falls Air Bases.

During my stay at Sioux Falls Air Base, I wasn't able to enjoy many of life's pleasures as money was in short supply. I received $54.00 a month and out of that I paid $3.20 for laundry, $6.50 for insurance and $18.00 a month for a savings bond. That left me a grand total of $26.30 a month for pocket money. I solved this problem one night while resting on my bunk wishing I had something to eat. Most GIs were always hungry but at night there wasn't any place available to buy a snack. That weekend I got a pass and went into Sioux Falls where I located a little sandwich shop. The owner of the shop agreed to make fifty sandwiches that he promised to deliver to me at the main gate the following Monday evening. He charged me fifteen cents for each sandwich and I sold the entire lot for twenty-cents each in about twenty minutes. This worked so well I gradually increased my sandwich order until I was selling 300 sandwiches every night. I hired two other soldiers to sell the sandwiches for me and I gave them a nickel for every sandwich they sold and kept a nickel for myself. When I left Sioux Falls Air Base, I sold my thriving sandwich business to another soldier for $50.00.

From Scott Field I reported to the Embarkation Center at Greensboro, North Carolina where I was processed for shipment to Europe. There were sixty ships in our convoy and the convoy sailed at the speed of the slowest ship. We zigzagged all over the Atlantic Ocean for fourteen days before landing at LeHavre, France. We probably could have made the crossing in four or five days had we taken a direct route rather than all of the zigzag maneuvers. Contrary to what we were told by the Navy, most of us concluded that all the zigzagging was done to accommodate the enemy and give them more time for their submarines to locate us and pay their respects with a torpedo. After the third day out, it really didn't matter much, as all of us were so seasick we just didn't give a damn what happened. Some of the troops actually prayed we would hit a mine or a submarine would sink us. If you have ever suffered from seasickness you can readily understand why someone would react in such a manner.

After landing at LeHavre, France, we were loaded into trucks for a short ride to the local train depot where we transferred to a train to take us the rest of the way to our assigned replacement depot. The train we boarded was made up of small boxcars the Americans referred to as 40 & 8 trains. The numbers, 40 & 8, was printed on every boxcar indicating each boxcar had the capacity to haul forty men and eight horses. Such an assumption was ridiculous and only the French would come up with such an idea. There were twenty-two men along with our flying gear in my boxcar and we were so crowded we had to take turns just to sit down. The boxcar I was assigned had been strafed and since it had been raining for several days we were thoroughly soaked as was all of our gear. We only traveled at night, so during the day the train idled on a siding. The trip to the replacement depot took three days to complete. During one of our many stops, someone located a pile of straw. We all jumped off the train and grabbed an armload that we placed on the floor of the boxcar so we would have something soft to rest on. Unfortunately, the straw was full of lice and it took me two weeks to get rid of them. This situation didn't do much for morale, but the wonderful and unique sense of humor of the GI took over once again and turned this entire fiasco into a laughable incident. Some of the GI's started singing a song to the tune of "Get out Your Old Blue Bonnet". The words they put to this tune eased the otherwise miserable conditions to which we were subjected. Before long, everyone was singing…

Get out the old blue ointment
The crab's disappointment
And we'll drive those bastards away.
Oh, it stings and it itches
But it kills those sons-of-bitches
In a good old-fashioned way.

Once we reached our destination, a replacement camp near Chateau Thierry, France we were billeted in tents that could accommodate twenty men. We arrived during Thanksgiving season, and because it was still raining, we had to wade through a mire of mud just to get to the field kitchen for our meals. On Thanksgiving, an incident happened that profoundly affected me and I have never forgotten it to this day. It was necessary to get in line in order to be served our food. After finishing a meal you had to get in line once again in order to dispose of any leftover food into a fifty-five gallon drum. Two more fifty-five gallon drums containing hot soapy water and hot rinse water were available for washing and rinsing our mess kits. We were served a substantial meal but turkey and trimmings were not on the menu. A great deal of bitching dominated most conversations and I did my share of bitching right along with the rest of the men. After I had finished my meal and gotten back in line to wash my mess kit, I was suddenly confronted with a situation that has continued to haunt me. As I approached the barrel where we were supposed to deposit the food we hadn't eaten I noticed a line of civilians begging for the leftovers. A little French boy, perhaps twelve years old, was holding out a cup in hopes I had something left for him. He was wearing a pair of shorts and an old sweater and it was obvious to me he was suffering from the cold. He had been injured and only had one eye. He also had an injured leg that caused him to limp. To this day I regret having complained about the meal I had that day. I have since formed a different view of what Thanksgiving really means to me. How does one ever forget such heart rending moments?

One week after arriving at the replacement depot I was assigned to the Ninth Army Air Corps, 324th Troop Carrier Squadron, and was sent to Bovingdon, England, one of the many American air bases in the United Kingdom. After arriving at Bovingdon, aircrews were formed and we were assigned our airplanes. We immediately started flying whenever the weather would permit. My squadron flew almost exclusively the Douglas C-47. This aircraft treated me well and even though it was slow, it was one of the most reliable aircraft ever built. When the C-47 was first manufactured it was known as the DC-3. Between 1936 and 1941 the DC-3 was recognized for its great potential as a passenger plane. When WWII broke out its great potential as a military transport aircraft was recognized. Before WWII had ended, 13,177 of these aircraft were in service and many of them are still flying to this day. The C-47 served in every theater of operations throughout the world during the war. The Japanese manufactured this aircraft under a license agreement with Douglas Aircraft before the Japanese attack on Pearl Harbor. Even the Russians manufactured the C-47 as the Lisunov Li-2 during the war.

The C-47 had several nicknames: Gooney Bird, Skytrooper, Biscuit Bomber, The Placid Plodder, Old Bucket Seats and Vomit Comet, a nickname used by the U.S. Army paratroops during the Normandy invasion. The C-47 had two 1,200 hp Pratt & Whitney engines and weighed 16,865 lbs. Maximum speed was 230 mph but cruising speed was only 207 mph. The range of this aircraft was 2,125 miles and it carried no armament.

As crewmembers on the C-47 we performed many functions. We transported troops, litter patients, VIPs, towed gliders, hauled all sorts of cargo to and from England, Italy, North Africa, France and Germany. On one occasion my crew was assigned a mission to deliver dozens of small drums of DDT to the island of Sardinia. Grasshoppers were eating the crops so the DDT was badly needed to eradicate these pests. Over a period of two weeks we made several trips between England and Sardinia. The Italians never did get around to using the DDT but the grasshoppers did get around to eating everything. I didn't mind these trips to Sardinia as the British had an air base there where I could purchase a bottle of scotch for $4.00. Scotch was in great demand and our ground personnel would gladly pay $20.00 for a bottle. Our missions were referred to as "Milk Runs" by all the bomber crews. But, I didn't mind, because my job was a lot safer than being a crewmember on a bomber. Almost always we flew alone and this caused the crew some concern, especially when flying over water. It was always on our minds that if we ever had to ditch in the water, would we ever be found? Consequently, I made it a practice to take position fixes about every fifteen minutes. This gave us a comfort level of sorts as our position could be radioed to one of the many bases in the area momentarily.

Flying on any military aircraft during the war was risky business. I remember when a group of glider pilots were reassigned to our squadron to be trained as co-pilots on C-47's. Our crew had a close call when one of the glider pilots assigned to our crew "got behind" on takeoff and the plane began skewing down the runway. Fortunately, our pilot was experienced and he saved the day just as we reached the end of the runway. I was relieved to learn that glider pilot was reassigned to another crew.

One day my flying status suddenly took a drastic change. Our commanding officer learned that I could type sixty words per minute and take shorthand at 120 words per minute. He immediately sent for me and installed me in an office right next to his office. I became the Colonel's private secretary, radio operator/navigator and errand boy from that moment on until I was finally sent back to the United States for discharge. He would suddenly inform me to get the aircraft ready for takeoff because we were going to a meeting in Paris, Naples or some other exotic destination. Upon arrival at these destinations, I attended the meetings with him and took shorthand notes on everything that transpired. This was great duty and I was the envy of every aircrew member in our squadron.

There were two types of parachutes worn by aircrew members. One was a seat pack and the other was a chest pack chute. I always wore the chest pack as it could be quickly and easily snapped on or off my parachute harness. It was cumbersome to wear as it hindered my ability to work at my table location on our aircraft. Most of the time I would unsnap the chute and place it under my seat. My mind constantly played tricks on me when I thought I could hear a slightly different sound in one of the engines. When this occurred, which was frequently, it only took me ten seconds to snap my chute back into the harness rings.

When we were scheduled to fly longer than usual flights we picked up sandwiches at the mess hall before taking off. This resolved the matter of hunger but we still had to deal with the matter of relieving ourselves. We kept a small bucket in the back of the aircraft for this purpose but when it was necessary to relieve one's bladder, a relief tube was used. A relief tube was nothing more than a three-foot section of hose with a small funnel stuck in one end. It took only one experience to learn that it was wise to stand to one side while using this wonderful invention. Otherwise, it was quite likely that an airlock would occur and the person using this contraption would be subjected to an unwanted shower. Using the bucket was much simpler. The bucket was lined with a wax-covered paper bag that was simply thrown out the door, always over an enemy town or village.

Part of my squadron was eventually transferred to Nice, France to occupy the airfield there. We took four C-47 aircraft with us along with our ground crews. The French Riviera was a wonderful place to be stationed and every man in our squadron was delighted with this new assignment. We were billeted in one of the major tourist hotels and when we weren't flying, we enjoyed the beach and the girls in their bikinis. Another group of airmen joined us shortly after our arrival in Nice. They had been stationed in North Africa and Italy and they brought four B-25 Mitchell Bombers with them along with their ground crews. Altogether we numbered about 125 aircrew and ground crew personnel. From that point on, all of our flying consisted of transporting combat crews to Nice from various locations throughout Europe for rest and recreation. We were also flying reconnaissance missions, mostly in the Mediterranean and North African area. It was at this point when I first began flying as a crewmember on the B-25 Mitchell.

An incident occurred while we were stationed in Nice, France that caused a lot of controversy. It was discovered that some of the less desirable French citizens were stealing parachutes from our airplanes. The parachutes were made of pure silk and were quite valuable on the black market. We had to post guards twenty-four hours a day in order to prevent any further thievery. Even though we realized the vast majority of the French people were very grateful to have us there, we still resented the idea that a Frenchman would steal our parachutes.

The B-25 Mitchell was made immortal on April 18, 1942. It was the first United States aircraft to bomb Japan. Sixteen B-25 Mitchell bombers, commanded by Jimmy Doolittle, took off from the deck of the USS Hornet and flew 800 miles to attack their assigned targets in Japan. By the end of WWII, 9,889 B25's had been built. Thirty-four of these aircraft are still airworthy today. The B-25 had two 1,700 hp Wright Cyclone radial engines that produced a maximum speed of 272 mph and a range of 1,350 miles. The B-25 was equipped with twelve machine guns and carried a bomb load of 4,000 pounds. It was the most successful light bomber of the war and was used in every combat theater of operations during WWII. It was even flown in combat by the British and the Russian air forces. By the end of the war the B-25 became the most widely used medium bomber flown by the United States and its allies.

One member of our squadron was a little dog by the name of Margie. Margie liked flying and always managed to hitch a ride to the flight line where she would jump aboard one of our planes. She was already a part of my squadron when I arrived and she was still there when I left. I have often wondered what happened to that little dog. One of our crewmembers made a sash for Margie and sewed Master Sergeant's stripes on it. Two holes were cut into the ends of the sash so her front legs could be inserted through the holes, thus keeping the sash in place over her back. She proudly displayed her stripes and our squadron insignia thereafter. It was common knowledge that Margie had more flying time than any other member of our squadron. All members of our squadron thought it unfair that Margie wasn't eligible for flight pay. However, Margie did eat with our squadron in the dining hall. The food we were served was quite good so Margie enjoyed this special privilege in spite of the fact that she didn't draw flight pay. There was a sign just above the door of our dining hall that read, "FOOD WILL WIN THE WAR". The idea was to remind the GI's to conserve food and not take more than one could eat. Once again the humor of the GI took over as some clever soldier had printed his own sign and had attached it to the sign above the dining hall door. This sign read, "YES, BUT HOW IN THE HELL DO WE GET THE ENEMY TO EAT HERE"?

On one of our reconnaissance missions over Germany, we lost an engine. We managed to limp back to Istres Air Base, located in southern France. Shortly after we had made a successful emergency landing, another B-25 attempted to make an emergency landing, but their attempt was unsuccessful and they crashed. The entire crew was killed but the plane didn't burn. Our crew chief, along with myself, found two aircraft mechanics to help us cannibalize the parts we needed from the crashed B-25 so we could make repairs on our own B-25. This incident has been a source of embarrassment and regret to me as I have often felt we had stolen something from those men who had just died. I have never been able to get this incident entirely out of my mind, but I was thankful that I was not a member of that crew. I have often wondered where home was for these young men and what their families were like. I wish I had been thoughtful enough to learn the names of the five men who died in that crash. Perhaps a letter from me might have helped their relatives deal with their devastating loss. I witnessed several crashes after that crash, but none affected me like the one at Istres.

We had quite a few German prisoners under our supervision. They lived in a stockade near our airbase. Most of the prisoners under our care were young boys or older men. They worked in our dining hall and kept our quarters neat and clean. They had a great deal of freedom and were fed the same food we were served. None of them ever tried to run away or escape because, for the first time in several years, they were living like human beings and being well treated. One special prisoner we had was an older man, perhaps sixty years of age. He was never sent to the stockade in the evening as he had his own room in the basement of the Negresco Hotel. I never knew his name but all of us called him Minister. He could speak very good English and was always giving us lectures about how we would have to fight the Russians and how the Germans would help us fight them. He certainly knew a lot more about politics than we did because he was almost correct with his assessment in this matter. We allowed him to collect all of the cigarette butts which he stripped in order to salvage the tobacco. I'm sure he resold the salvaged tobacco on the black market and made quite a lot of money with his little enterprise. A carton of American cigarettes that cost us fifty cents would sell for as much as $200.00 on the black market in Germany and up to $40.00 a carton in France.

One evening a pal and I were walking down a narrow street near the Negresco Hotel when we noticed a gentleman dressed in evening clothes and wearing a top hat coming down the street in our direction. He had a large dog with him and the dog was scurrying back and forth in the street. Suddenly the dog would stop, raise a front paw and extend his tail straight out behind him. We watched the gentleman in the top hat walk up to the dog and with his cane (there was a pin in the end of the cane) stick the pin into a cigarette butt that he deposited in a sack slung over his shoulder. No doubt this gentleman had found a way to earn a living during those dark days. We thought he was quite dignified as he didn't have to bend over to pick up a cigarette butt. His dog reminded me of my dog, Pooch, as he was "shopping" for cigarettes for his master.

We had twelve or fifteen SS prisoners assigned to us in addition to the young boys and old men. They were arrogant, belligerent and surly and would try to spit on us if we got close to the stockade fence. We were never able to assign these men to work details so they just lounged around and enjoyed the food and other conveniences that were made available to them. This went on for some time until the day came when their leisure world came crashing down. A big, tough Polish boy by the name of Joe Griegel was transferred to our squadron. He had been in the infantry and had received a serious wound, so he was reclassified as unfit for combat. Our commanding officer immediately gave Joe the job of looking after the SS prisoners. You can imagine the shock these SS soldiers experienced when they met Joe. Joe literally took over their lives and their world was suddenly turned upside down. Joe organized work details for these SS prisoners and from that moment on he never gave them a chance to catch their breath. We all recall the total devastation Germany inflicted upon Poland and especially the city of Warsaw. Joe had lost many of his relatives during the German occupation of Poland, so suffice it to say that Joe had no love for the Germans, especially the SS troops. We concluded that the SS prisoners probably had a much easier time during their combat days than under the control of Joe Griegel.

Sometime after the surrender of Germany, we returned to England. That is where I was when Japan surrendered. We were in the process of forming new aircrews to go to the Pacific to join the battle against Japan. Needless to say, none of us were keen about this prospect, so when Japan capitulated we were ecstatic. There was a party in London that night that was something to remember. There was a huge bonfire at Trafalger Square, fireworks displays, dancing in the streets, booze and girls everywhere with unimaginable joy in everyone's heart and mind.

A few months after the war ended I was sent from England to Bremerhaven, Germany to be processed for my return to the United States. The very first sign I saw upon arriving in Bremerhaven read, "Remember boys, one drip, no ship"....the GI humor at work again. Once we had settled aboard our ship in Bremerhaven, I began to question why the military, in their infinite wisdom, would arrange for us to leave from Bremerhaven rather than from England. I eventually concluded the reasoning for this SNAFU processing. Perhaps this was a way for the U.S. Government to say "thanks" to us by awarding us the opportunity to play "tourist" for two or three weeks. In case some of you didn't know this bit of trivia, "SNAFU" means "Situation Normal, All Fouled Up". It should be noted the GI's assigned the fourth letter of SNAFU a different word that probably best described most problems all military personnel experienced.

While waiting for a ship to take me home, I met an old high school friend of mine in Bremerhaven. His name was John Abramo and he was from Grand Junction, Colorado. He and I stayed together from that moment on until we finally shook hands at the depot in Denver, Colorado and went our separate ways. John stood up for me as my best man when I married my wife. We remained good friends until John passed away in January of 2001.

My participation in the war was fairly insignificant compared to many of the other young men my age. I haven't had to deal with very many bad memories or experiences like so many others have had to do. Those memories that were distasteful to me I have long since tried to put to rest. However, many of the funny and humorous episodes are still fresh in my memory. You will forgive me if I share some of the interesting but somewhat off-color sayings all of us heard during our years in the service. Some of those humorous quips that we were exposed to are as follows:

"Drop your jocks and grab your socks, it's time to rise and shine."

"Stand on you tip-toes, turn your head and cough. I said turn your head, soldier, don't cough in my face." (Comment made while being checked for hernia).

"Fall in! Fall out! Milk it in! Milk it out! Sign here!" (Comment made during a short-arm inspection…a test to see if you had contracted VD).

"Hurry up to wait." (Standard procedure for everything we did).

"Fall out in your boots and rain coats. We're going to have a peter-parade." (Another comment made to alert us of an impending short-arm inspection).

"Never before have so many come so far for so little." (A version of Winston Churchill's famous speech). In his original speech, he was praising the British Spitfire pilots for their defense of Britain against the German Luftwaffe.

"She may look clean, BUT". (Slogan used to introduce VD films to the troops).

After being discharged from the service I returned to Glenwood Springs and took an entire week off before going to work at a Texaco service station. I really had no idea what I wanted to do, so I decided to give it a year before making any firm decisions. In the meantime, I married my high school sweetheart, Leta Huntley, on September 20, 1946. Sixty years later I am still married to the same sweet lady. I first knew Leta when I was in the second grade and she was in the first grade. I lived one block down the street from her house.

Before I knew it, I was pretty well settled down, making a decent living and enjoying my new life. I never did get around to going to college in spite of the fact I had several athletic scholarship offers as well as the GI Bill to fall back on. Our daughter, Teresa, was born on May 18, 1948 so at that point I gave up any idea that I would ever go to school. Instead I put my nose to the grindstone and tried to do the best I could for my family. I have always regretted not going to college as a better education would have made things a bit easier for me in later years. Our second child, Gary, was born on January 28, 1953 and by this time I was well established in my own business. I had acquired ownership of the Texaco Service Station and was a successful businessman in our little community.

In 1952 I sold the service station as I had made up my mind to try something different. As luck would have it, one of the Sales Representatives for the Caterpillar Dealer in Colorado was a regular customer at my service station. One day he asked me what I planned to do after I sold the service station. I half jokingly told him I would probably go to work for Caterpillar as I thought they needed a good man to represent them. About a week later this person, Ed Bayless, phoned me to say he was going to Denver to take care of some business at the Caterpillar Dealer's office. He suggested that I ride along with him and he would introduce me to the principals in the Denver office. We spent part of the following day at the Caterpillar facility in Denver and I was introduced to several of the management staff. I soon learned only college graduates with engineering backgrounds were considered for employment.   However, during my visit at their Denver office, I kept hearing over and over their main concern involved the used equipment inventory they had accumulated from taking trade-ins on new equipment. I concluded this subject was their "hot-button" so, just before leaving their office, I asked the Used Equipment Manager if he would be interested in making a financial arrangement with me if I could sell some of their used equipment. I'm sure he thought I was just making conversation so he readily agreed as a way of getting rid of me.

The day after Ed Bayless and I arrived back in Glenwood Springs I returned to Denver and visited the office of the Department of Commerce where I purchased a trade list of every importer of used equipment in Canada. The war had only recently ended and new Caterpillar equipment was still in short supply. Canada imposed a seventeen percent import duty on new equipment but the import duty on used equipment was only two percent. I immediately started writing letters to every importer of used equipment in Canada offering used equipment for sale. Within a few days I began to receive responses to my letters from firms who were interested in purchasing used Caterpillar equipment. Once again I re-visited the Caterpillar Dealer's office in Denver and presented them with the inquiries I had received from Canada. A few days later the Used Equipment Manager was on his way to Canada to visit these prospective buyers. The results were very positive as he received orders for more than half of the used equipment in the Denver Dealer's inventory and this represented several hundred thousand dollars in sales.

The day after the Used Equipment Manager returned to Denver he phoned me and asked if I could come to Denver for a job interview. I was hired on the spot and was informed I would be required to participate in a sales training program, which suited me perfectly. Three months later I was offered the job as in-house salesman at the Grand Junction, Colorado branch facility. I was very fortunate to have been promoted ahead of four other young men who had been in the program for some time. This was the beginning of a thirty-year love affair with Caterpillar Tractor Company.

I remained with the Caterpillar dealer in Denver until 1958, at which time I accepted a position with the Caterpillar dealer in Honolulu, Hawaii. My position was that of Sales Training Manager, and I held this position for one year. I was then sent to Guam in the Marianas Islands to establish a

339

Caterpillar branch operation there. During the two years we lived in Guam I was involved in other related activities. I established a Caterpillar agency in Naha, Okinawa and served as consultant to China Engineers while they were setting up a Caterpillar dealership in Hong Kong and the New Territories. I also installed a Caterpillar electrical generation plant on the island of Chi Chi Jima where the U.S. Navy maintained a small Loran Station.

After two years in Guam my family and I returned to Hawaii, and once again found myself involved in a number of special projects. I spent three months in Thailand working in consort with a group of major contractors. They were building several large air bases to accommodate the B-52 bombers for their impending bombing raids over Viet Nam. My job was to evaluate the equipment requirements and to write the specifications for all the equipment that would be necessary to build these projects. This was an enviable position for me because I wrote all the specifications around Caterpillar equipment. The results were quite satisfying to me and led to the sale of several million dollars of equipment sales for the Hawaii Caterpillar dealer.

My next interesting assignment took my family and me to Pago Pago, American Samoa. I was on loan from Caterpillar to the Samoan Government to head up a very ambitious development program. Samoa was, and still is, a U.S. possession under the administration and jurisdiction of the U.S. Department of Interior. The development plans called for the construction of an airport facility which included a modern terminal building, a 12,000 foot long runway that could accommodate 747 jet liners, several miles of new road construction, seventeen new school buildings and employee housing. I had 800 Samoans under my direction and this led to some very interesting but sometimes frustrating situations. The Samoans are a gentle and kindly race of people whom I soon learned to respect and admire. I also learned it

340

was imperative to earn their respect if one had any aspirations of accomplishing a specific job assignment. They weren't skilled construction workers but their willingness to learn was admirable, therefore I managed quite well. I realized they were skilled in areas where I was lacking, so I approached them with this thought firmly fixed in my mind. For example, a Samoan could climb up a coconut tree, dislodge six coconuts and have them all husked and open in fifteen minutes. Such a task would have taken me a day or more if, in fact, I could have managed this task at all.

Every day was a brand new experience that exposed an entirely new and different set of circumstances. Sometimes these problems were serious in nature but usually they were very funny and entertaining. The Samoans weren't always the ones who created these situations. All of the Americans working and living in Samoa were responsible for creating their own share of problems, including yours truly.

The next twenty-five years I spent with Caterpillar turned me into a modern Gulliver. Due to my involvement in foreign projects, my work gradually led me into specializing in unusual and unique assignments. My wife and I lived in thirteen countries for one year or longer and two of these countries we called home on two different occasions. I worked on special projects in dozens of countries. Some of our favorite places throughout the world are London, Paris, Melbourne and Sydney, Australia, Athens, New Zealand, Seoul, Korea, and Pago Pago, American Samoa, all of which we resided in one time or another. We even found Saudi Arabia interesting when we lived there for a year. During all of the years I worked for Caterpillar I never found it necessary to indulge myself with a hobby. My hobby was looking forward to going to work every day just to learn what was over the next hill. I believe that if I were to cut myself I might possibly bleed yellow, which is the color Caterpillar paints all of their equipment. I have often said that Jesus Christ and a band of Angels couldn't have found a job that suited me better than the one I enjoyed with Caterpillar for so many years. It was a special fraternity that rewarded me with the opportunity to form many lifelong friendships. I wish I could do it all over once again!

AMERICA FOR ME
Henry Van Dyke

Tis fine to see the Old World, and travel up and down
Among the famous places and cities of renown,
To admire the crumbly castles and the statues of the kings,
But now I think I've had enough of antiquated things.

So it's home again, and home again, America for me!
My heart is turning home again, and there I long to be,
In the land of youth and freedom beyond the ocean bars,
Where the air is full of sunlight and the flag is full of stars.

Oh, London is a man's town, there's power in the air,
And Paris is a woman's town, with flowers in her hair;
And it's sweet to dream of Venice, and it's great to study Rome,
But when it comes to living there is no place like home.

I like the German fir-woods, in green battalions drilled;
I like the gardens of Versailles with flashing fountains filled;
But, oh, to take your hand, my dear, and ramble for a day
In the friendly western woodland where Nature has her way!

I know that Europe's wonderful, yet something seems to lack;
The Past is too much with her, and the people looking back;
But the glory of the Present is to make the Future free,
We love our land for what she is and what she is to be.

Oh, it's home again, and home again, America for me!
I want a ship that's westward bound to plough the rolling sea,
To the blessed Land of Room Enough beyond the ocean bar,
Where the air is full of sunlight and the flag is full of stars.

WORLD WAR TWO MEMORIAL DEDICATION

By Hal Terrell

My wife and I attended the dedication of the long-awaited World War Two Memorial that took place on the National Mall in Washington D.C. on Saturday, May 29, 2004. It had been nearly sixty years after the war's end in 1945. The $175 million dollar memorial is a tribute to the sixteen million men and women who served during the war, as well as the millions who supported World War Two from the home front. It is also a tribute to the 400,000 plus young men and women who lost their lives during this conflict. The dedication of the Memorial came after years of speculation and concern that it would disrupt the view from the Lincoln Memorial to the Washington Monument.

The sun shone on my generation the day of the dedication. It was the largest gathering of World War Two veterans since the war ended in 1945. In spite of the objections of some, World War Two veterans and their families came by the tens of thousands for what will no doubt be the last hurrah for the four million veterans who are still alive today. Most of the remaining veterans are now in their late seventies and early eighties, but they were teens when the war started, and they put on their military uniforms to help save the world from Hitler and Hirohito.

World War Two was the most expensive armed conflict in history. It involved more than sixty countries and was fought on six continents. Sixty million lives were lost around the globe as a result of this war.

There were 216,000 women in uniform, and they represented two percent of Americans in uniform. By the time the war ended 654,000 black soldiers served in every branch of the military service, and more than 17,000 Japanese Americans served their country.

There is no doubt that the World War Two Memorial commemorates the largest, most important conflict in history. The Memorial sits directly between the Lincoln Memorial and the Washington Monument at the National Mall. The Memorial straddles the Mall at the east end of the Reflecting Pool between these two Memorials. The 7seventy-four acre site is anchored by a sunken plaza that features two arches representing the Atlantic and the Pacific Theaters. The fifty-six stone pillars represent the District of Columbia and each of the fifty states and territories. This national World War Two Memorial will serve to remind future generations of the significance of World War Two and the courage and determination of those who served in it.

I believe the World War Two Memorial has made more of an impression on me today because I was one of those lucky enough to survive to see it. I felt as if I was looking at the Memorial through the eyes of all the men I have known. Many of these men and women have already left this life.

World War Two shaped a world with its technological legacies, including radar, jet airplanes, ballistic missiles, computers, nuclear weapons and medical advancements. This was an era when national sacrifice was not an option. But now surviving members of my generation are facing our third 'near-death' experience. First came growing up during a depression. Next came combat, then old age. And yet I know that all of the remaining World War Two veterans can face death with equanimity, because of our life's experience. The World War Two Memorial is a comfort to me and other World War Two veterans as well.

The World War Two Memorial event had its share of sadness, including a moment of silence for the more than 400,000 U.S. service members killed in the war. But the day proved more celebratory than somber. The dedication program began as big bands played standards from the 1940s and impromptu dancing could be seen between the rows of men and women. These dancers who were strutting their stuff were in their late seventies and early eighties, but they could still put on a good show. The music brought back many memories and tears flowed freely as all of the World War Two veterans came together as one once again in numbers that will never be seen again. I am so sorry that the twelve million who have already left us were not be there to see the love and joy that completely dominated everyone who attended this affair. Repeatedly, emotions were evoked, often by little moments that stunned me. I was hugged and kissed by women and young ladies, approached by school children and young adults as well as older citizens. All of these people wanted to shake my hand or ask for my autograph and thank me for serving our country. Total strangers were spontaneously coming up to the veterans, offering a heartfelt thank you, taking our picture and heaping praise upon us. At times it was almost embarrassing to me as well as the other World War Two veterans, but it certainly put into perspective where we stand in our complicated society today.

Undoubtedly my day in the sun and on the grass at the National Mall represented the last gathering of a vanishing America. If you wanted to hear the greatest generation speak, if you had a question about fear, about death, about combat or home front sacrifice, you would have gotten to know my generation and what it stood for. I am confident that our succeeding generations can measure up just as my generation did.

The ceremonial opening of the National World War Two Memorial dedication was saturated in great oratory. Speakers had a lot to live up to but they came through like true champions. The speakers included President Bush, Senator Dole, Tom Hanks, Tom Brokaw and Rep. Mary Kaptur (D-Ohio). Other special guests included President H. W. Bush and President Bill Clinton. In the middle of President Bush's presentation of the World

War Two Memorial to the people of the United States his voice cracked and he struggled to hold back the tears. He honored his decorated father and all those who served. He said, "The dedication of our World War Two veterans saved our country, and thereby saved the liberty of mankind." President Bush went on to say, "Men whose step has slowed are thinking of the boys they knew when they were boys together. Women who watched trains leave and years pass can still see the handsome face of their young sweethearts. America will not forget them either."

Once again President Bush's voice cracked and his face looked strained as he told the Mall crowd, "World War Two veterans were the modest sons of a peaceful country, and millions of us are very proud to call them DAD. They gave the best years of their lives to the greatest mission their country has ever experienced." President Bush ended by asking every man and woman who saw and lived World War Two--every member of that generation—to please rise as you are able, and receive the thanks of our nation. Stepping back from the podium, President Bush led the applause for veterans who were stretched down the Mall farther then he could see. Some rose from wheelchairs, many with help. They were joined by tens of thousands who were watching via satellite.

The other speakers were just as eloquent as was President Bush, and their comments were just as emotional and moving. And yet their words seemed insufficient in the presence of so many members of the World War Two generation. It was a hallowed and humbling experience for me in such company. I felt very proud to be associated with such men..

President Bush ended his talk with the following words---"These were average men who lived during extraordinary times when times mattered most. An entire generation of Americans showed the finest qualities of our nation."

I would be chagrin not to mention the patriotism shown by the hundreds of love inspired volunteers who gave their time to make this event the success it was. Many young adults were lending a hand. School children from all across the nation had made beautiful boutonnieres for every World War Two veteran with the following message attached. "Dear veterans and World War Two generation, please accept this 'Star Spangled Tribute' boutonniere that I made after my teacher taught a very special lesson about the dignity, dedication and determination of the men and women of the World War Two generation. Thank you for protecting my LIFE, LIBERTY and HAPPINESS! You're awesome! God bless America."

I have no illusions that there will be those who will want to rain upon my parade. Nevertheless, I claim my God given right to be a staunch patriot and I would gladly defend my country once again if called upon to do so. Let me leave you with the following as food for thought. These resonant words are inscribed on the World War II memorial: "Our debt to the heroic men and valiant women in the service of our country can never be repaid. They have earned our undying gratitude. America will never forget their sacrifice."

President Harry Truman

"Today the guns are silent. A great victory has been won. The skies no longer rain death—the seas bear only commerce—men everywhere walk upright in the sunlight. The entire world is quietly at peace."

Gen. Douglas MacArthur

"You are about to embark on the greatest crusade toward which we have striven these many months. The eyes of the world are upon you. I have full confidence in your courage, devotion to duty and skill in battle. We will accept nothing less than full victory."

Gen. Dwight Eisenhower

"December 7, 1941, a date which will live in infamy. No matter how long it may take us to overcome this premeditated invasion, the American people in their righteous might will win through to absolute victory, so help us God."

President Franklin D. Roosevelt.

"For me attending the World War Two Memorial Dedication was an emotional and unforgettable experience."

REFLCTIONS
Author Unknown

You know, time has a way of moving quickly and catching you unaware of the passing years. It seems just yesterday that I was a young girl/boy, just married and embarking on my new life with my mate. And yet in a way, it seems like eons ago, and I wonder where all the years went. I know that I lived them all...

And I have glimpses of how it was back then and of all my hopes and dreams...But, here it is...the winter of my life and it catches me by surprise...How did I get here so fast? Where did the years go and where did my babies go? And where did my youth go?

I remember well...seeing older people through the years and thinking that those older people were years away from me and that winter was so far off I could not fathom it or imagine fully what it would be like...But, here it is...husband retired and he's really getting gray...he moves slower and I see an older man now. He's in much better shape than me...but, I see the great change...He is not the one I married who was dark and young and strong...but, like me, his age is beginning to show and we are now those older folks that we used to see and never thought we'd be.

Each day now, I find that just getting a shower is a real target for the day! And taking a nap is not a treat anymore...it's mandatory! If I don't take a nap on my own free will, I just fall asleep where I sit! And so, now I enter into this new season of my life unprepared for all the aches and pains and the loss of strength and ability to go and do things. But at least I know that though the winter has come I'm not sure how long it will last...I do know this, that when its over...it's over...I have regrets and there are things I wish I hadn't done...things I should have done...but indeed, there are many things I am happy to have done...Its all in a lifetime...

So, if you're not in your winter yet…let me remind you that it will be here faster than you think. So, whatever you would like to accomplish in your life please do it soon. Life goes by in a hurry so, do what you can today because you can never be sure whether this is your winter or not! You have no promise that you will see all the seasons of your life…so live for good today and say all the things that you want your loved ones to remember…

"Life is a gift to you. The way you live your life is your gift to those who come after. Make it a fantastic one and LIVE IT WELL!"

Isn't it strange that princes and kings

And clowns that caper in sawdust rings

And common folks like you and me

Are all builders of eternity.

To each is given a book of rules

A block of stone and a bag of tools

And each must shape ere time has flown

A stumbling block or a stepping stone.

I Hope this book will open your eyes and let the future in so you can begin to build your own memories.

EPILOGUE

The war against Japan and Germany had been a deadly and costly conflict. It changed the lives of millions of people worldwide and it took years to recover. Sixty-eight countries were involved at a cost of over 1.2 trillion dollars. Sixty million people lost their lives during WWII, and the United States spent three billion dollars for the reconstruction of Europe and Asia. Many of the men and women who were involved in this war are still alive but when they were young, "THEY SAVED THE WORLD".

Just prior to entering the war in December of 1941 there were 143 million people living in America. Our armed forces had 600,000 men and women in uniform when Congress passed the Selective Service Act. By the time the war ended, seventeen million men and 350,000 women had answered the call.

On the home front 19.5 million women had joined the war effort, building ships, planes, tanks, military vehicles, weapons and munitions. School children were called on to help harvest crops and young girls were learning basic first aid and basic nursing skills. Everyone collected paper, rubber and metal for reprocessing. Rationing of food, gas, tires, oil and luxury items were strictly regulated. Men and women in the service purchased war bonds with part of their meager income, as did their parents and the public as a whole. Even school children used some of their lunch money to buy war bond stamps. I am very proud of all the girls who were in my grade school and high school class for the part they played in winning the war against Germany and Japan.

This was the greatest effort ever seen in the annals of U.S. history. The WWII generation (1941 – 1945) saved the world from unspeakable evil and every single person of that era lent support to this effort. No other generation in history can make this claim. NONE! But, the cost to the American people was a staggering 340 billion dollars. The U.S. military suffered over one million casualties. A total of 105 thousand military personnel became prisoners of the Japanese and the Germans. There are still fifty thousand U.S. military personnel listed as missing to this day.

On December 7, 1941, there were 168 students attending high school in Glenwood Springs. Eighty-four of these students were young boys, sixteen, seventeen and eighteen years of age. By the time the war had ended, fourteen of these young men had lost their lives on some distant, far-flung shore. Another eighteen had received wounds in combat and many others suffered experiences that left them scarred for life, even though they would never discuss this subject with anyone.

During the landings at Omaha and Utah Beach in Normandy, France on June 6, 1944, 2,300 young men lost their lives during the first two hours. On this same day Glenwood Springs' population was approximately 2,300 men, women and children. The thought of every single person in Glenwood Springs being killed during a two-hour period is impossible to imagine, but when one puts this into prospective, that is what happened to the 2,300 young men during the invasion of Normandy on June 6, 1944. So, this begs the question, "WHO REALLY WINS IN A WAR?"

Samuel Ullman said, "Youth is not a time of life—it is a state of mind. It is not a matter of red cheeks, red lips and supple knees. It is a temper of the will; a quality of the imagination, a vigor of the emotions; it is a freshness of the deep springs of life." But, the thousands of young men who gave their lives for our country will never know that freshness of the deep spring of life. Years have wrinkled the skin of those WWII Veterans who survived the war, but our enthusiasm for life has not allowed our souls to wrinkles.

Worry, distrust, fear and despair are the things that break our spirits, not growing old. So, I say to all of my classmates, and other WWII Veterans, you are as young as your faith, as old as your doubts, as young as your self-confidence, as old as your fears, and as young as your hope.

In conclusion I would like to leave my readers with a final thought. "I loved growing up in Glenwood Springs. I lived through the Great Depression and I survived WWII, as did most of the men who have a chapter in this book. These experiences opened our eyes for the future and I sincerely hope my book will open my reader's eyes as well. I will love and remember with fondness my classmates and my WWII buddies until I forget to breathe." Life is not measured by the breath we take, but by the moments that take our breath!

A COMMON SOLDIER
Author Unknown

He was getting old and paunchy
And his hair was falling fast
And he sat around the Legion
Telling stories of the past.
Of a war that he had fought in
And the deeds that he had done,
In his exploits with his buddies
They were heroes every one.

Tho' sometimes to his neighbors,
His tales became a joke,
All his Legion buddies listened
For they knew whereof he spoke.
But we'll hear his tales no longer,
For old Bill has passed away,
And the world's a little poorer
For a soldier died today,

He'll not be mourned by many,
Just his children and his wife.
For he lived an ordinary
Quiet and uneventful life.
Held a job and raised a family,
Quietly going his own way;
And the world won't note his passing,
Though a soldier died today.

When politicians leave this earth
Their bodies lie in state,
While thousands note their passing
And proclaim they were great,
Papers tell their life stories from
The time they were young,
But the passing of a soldier
Goes unnoticed and unsung.

Is the greatest contribution
To the welfare of our land
A guy who breaks his promises
And cons his fellow man?
Or the ordinary fellow who
In times of war and strife
Goes off to serve his country
And offers up his life?

A politician's stipend and the
Style in which he lives
Are sometimes disproportionate
To the service that he gives
While the ordinary soldier
Who offers his all
Is paid off with a medal
And perhaps a pension small.

It's so easy to forget them,
For it was so long ago
That the "Old Bill's" of our country
Went to battle, but we know
It was not the politicians
With the compromise and ploys
Who won for us the freedom
That our country now enjoys.

Should you find yourself in danger
With your enemies at hand
Would you want a politician
With his ever shifting stand?
Or would you prefer a soldier
Who has sworn to defend
His home, his kin and country
And would fight until the end?

He was just a common soldier
And his ranks are growing thin
And his presence should remind us
We may need his like again
For when countries are in conflict
Then we find the soldier's part
Is to clean up troubles
That politicians start.

If we cannot do him honor
While he's here to hear the praise
Then at least let's give him homage
At the ending of his days.
Perhaps just a simple headline
In a paper that would say:
"Our country is in Mourning
For a soldier died today."

HOW TO REMEMBER ME
by Robert N. Test

"The day will come when my body will lie upon a white sheet neatly tucked under four corners of a mattress located in a hospital occupied with the living and the dying. At a certain moment a doctor will determine that my brain has ceased to function and, for all practical purposes, my life has stopped.

When that happens, do not attempt to instill artificial life into my body by the use of a machine. And don't call this my deathbed. Let it be called the Bed of Life, and let my body be taken from it to help others lead fuller lives.

Give my sight to the man who has never seen a sunrise, a baby's face or love in the eyes of a woman. Give my heart to a person whose own heart has caused nothing but endless days of pain. Give my blood to a teenager who was pulled from the wreckage of his car, so that he might live to see his grandchildren play. Give my kidneys to one who depends on a machine to exist. Take my bones, every nerve and muscle in my body and find a way to make a cripple walk.

Explore every corner of my brain. Take my cells if necessary, and let them grow so that, someday, a speechless boy will shout at the crack of a bat and a deaf girl will hear the sound of rain against her window. Burn what is left and scatter my ashes to the winds to help the flowers grow.

If you must bury something, let it be my faults, my weaknesses and all prejudice against my fellow man. Give my sins to the devil, and give my soul to God. If by chance you wish to remember me, do it with a kind deed or word to someone who needs you. If you do all I have asked, I will live forever". This will be my gift, as a WWII veteran, to my country, my WWII buddies, my family and my friends.

WHERE ARE THEY NOW

James "Bus" Abshire: Deceased
   U.S. Army-France, Germany. Awarded Silver Star, Wounded.

John Artaz: Fruita, Colorado.   Awarded Presidential Citation. Wounded
twice.
   U.S. Army Paratrooper, New Guinea, Philippines, Japan.

Jay Brutsche: Deceased Clifton, Colorado. Awarded Unit Citation.
   U.S. Navy Seabees, Pacific, Iwo Jima

Louis Columbo: Deceased
   U.S. Army Paratrooper, England, France, Holland, Belgium, Germany
   Awarded Presidential Citation & Bronze Star. Severely wounded at
Bastogne.

Leroy Comrie: Deceased
   U.S. Navy, Pacific. Participated in Bikini Atoll Project.

Lester Donegan: Deceased Guffy, Colorado
   Pacific, Philippines, Japan. Wounded. Awarded Asiatic-Pacific Medal.

Raymond Heisler: Deceased
   Handicapped. Did not serve in the military. Became a missionary in
Africa.

Wendell Hutchison: Whittier, California
   Merchant Marine Officer, Pacific, Atlantic. Awarded Asiatic, Pacific
Medal.

Charles Jackson: Albuquerque, New Mexico
   U.S. Navy, Pacific, Samar, PI, China. Awarded Asiatic, Pacific Medal.

William Jackson: Deceased
   U.S. Navy, Pacific, Guam. Served aboard floating dry dock. Awarded
Asiatic, Pacific Medal.

William McDonald: Deceased
   U.S. Marines, Peleliu, Okinawa, China, Korea. Awarded Unit Citation &
Bronze Star. Wounded twice.

Herbert Osburn: Deceased
U.S. 8th Army Air Force. Flew missions over France and Germany. Awarded European, African Campaign Medal.

Ralph Rakich: Windsor, Connecticut
U.S. Navy Submarine Service, Pacific. Served aboard submarine Rasher. Won several citations. Rasher sank 18 Japanese ships. Wounded. Awarded Asiatic, Pacific Campaign Medal.

.Alex Rule: Seward, Alaska
U.S. 8th Army Air Corps, England. Flew 25 missions over Germany, France, Belgium, Holland & Sweden. Awarded Presidential Citation, Distinguished Flying Cross, Air Medal, African, European Campaign Medal.

Rex Sidener: Grand Junction, Colorado
U.S. Marines, Pacific, Iwo Jima, Japan. Wounded. Awarded Asiatic, Pacific Campaign Medal.

Donald Sillivan: Bethlehem, Pennsylvania
U.S. Navy, Pacific, Atlantic. Navy gun crew. Lucky to survive the war. Awarded Asiatic, Pacific and Atlantic Campaign Medals.

Paul Simillion: Deceased
U.S. Navy Air-Gunner. Killed in training flight.

Robert Simillion: St. George, Utah
Pacific, China. Participated in invasion of Okinawa. Awarded Gold Life Saving Medal, Asiatic, Pacific Campaign Medal.

Earl Southard: Deceased
U.S. Army Paratroops, England. Jumped into France on D-Day. Was German Prisoner but escaped twice. Jumped again at Bastogne, Belgium. Awarded Prisoner of War Medal, European Campaign Medal.

Bobby Tate: Deceased
U.S. Army, England, France, Germany, Austria. Made invasion at Omaha Beach On D-day. Helped liberate German Death Camps. Awarded European Campaign Medal.

<u>Hal Terrell:</u> Parachute, Colorado

    U.S. 9th Army Air Corps, England, Italy, France, Germany.
Flew reconnaissance missions as crew member on medium bomber.
Awarded European, African Campaign Medal.

BIBLIOGRAPHY

BOOKS

Benamou, Jean-Pierre. Normandy 1944: An Illustrated Field-Guide June 7th to August 22nd 1944. Bayeux, France, Editions Heimdal, 1982.

Duncan, David Douglas. This Is War; a Photo-narrative in Three Parts. New York, Harper and Brothers Publication, 1950.

Flanagan, Lt. Gen., E. M. The Angels: History of the 11th Airborne Division. Novato, CA, Presidio Press, 1989.

Kimmett, Larry and Regis, Margaret. U.S. Submarines in WWII: An Illustrated History. Kingston, WA, Navigator Publishing, 1996.

Lodge, Major O. R. MC. The Recapture of Guam. Washington, D.C., US Government Printing Office, 1954.

Marling, Karal Ann and Wetenhall, John. Iwo Jima: Monuments, Memories and the American Hero. Cambridge, MA, Harvard University Press, 1991.

Rees, David, consultant ed. The Korean War: History and Tactics. New York, Crescent Books, 1984.

Sasgen, Pete T. Red Scorpion: The War Patrols of the USS Rasher. Annapolis, MD, U.S. Naval Institute Press, 1995.

Smith, Robert Ross. Triumph in the Philippines: The War In The Pacific, United States Army in WWII. Washington, D.C, Office of the Chief of Military History, Dept. of The Army, 1963.

Wheeler, Keith. The Road to Tokyo. Alexandria, VA, Time-Life Books (World War Two Series.), 1979.

Witt, Anita McCune. They Came From Missouri. Glenwood Springs, CO., Gran Farnum Printing, 1998.

POEMS

Cook, Roy J., comp. One Hundred and One Famous Poems. Chicago, Contemporary Books, Inc., 1958.

Felleman, Hazel, ed. The Best Loved Poems of the American People. Garden City, N.Y., Garden City Books. 1936.

Felleman, Hazel, ed. Poems That Live Forever. Garden City, N.Y., Doubleday & Co., 1965.

Kinnell, Galway. Selected Poems. Boston, MA, Houghton Mifflin Co., 1982.

Morris, Joseph and Adams, St. Clair, eds. The Book of Friendship Verse, N.Y., George Sully and Co., 1924.

MUSEUM

Frontier Historical Society. Garfield County High School Yampah, 1944. Glenwood Springs, CO. 1944.

Frontier Historical Society. The Glenwood Post. Glenwood Springs, CO., 1941-1946. Normandy American Cemetery and Memorial. "The American Battle Monuments Comm." Omaha Beach, Normandy, France.

INTERNET

The Airborne Historical Assoc. "History Lesson".
Alexander, Col., Joseph H., USMC (Ret.). "Sulfer Island Seized", World War II, Feb., 2000.

INTERVIEWS

A number of friends deserve my thanks for their assistance and help in writing this book. They are Brian Abshire, Norman Abshire, John Artaz, Tom Axelrod, John Bartlett, Jean-Pierre Benamou, Bill Bisard, Betty Tate Black, Henry Bosco, Jay Brutsche, Katie Columbo, Marge Abshire Cooper, Lester Donegan, William Eiswerth, Warren Gardner, Raymond Heisler, Wendell Hutchinson, Charles Jackson, William Jackson, Catherine Lucas, Rose Barone Marfitano, William McDonald, Norman Noe, Herb Osburn, Louis Pappas, Ralph Rakich, Perry Rodreick, Alex Rule, Helen Comrie Sidener, Rex Sidener, Donald Sillivan, Robert Simillion, Dr. George Smith and Emma Jammaron Vagneur.

ISBN 141201108-6